Betty Crocker

the 300 calorie cook book

300 tasty meals
for eating healthy every day

WILEY

Wiley Publishing, Inc.

General Mills

Editorial Director: Jeff Nowak

Publishing Manager: Christine Gray

Cookbook Manager: Lois Tlusty

Editor: Grace Wells

Recipe Development and Testing: Betty Crocker Kitchens

Photography:
General Mills Photography Studios and Image Library

Photographer: Chuck Nields

Food Stylists: Sue Brue and Barb Standal

Wiley Publishing, Inc.

Publisher: Natalie Chapman

Associate Publisher: Jessica Goodman

Executive Editor: Anne Ficklen

Editor: Adam Kowit

Production Editors: Amy Zarkos and Kristi Hart

Cover Design: Suzanne Sunwoo

Art Directior: Tai Blanche

Prop Stylist: Veronica Smith

Manufacturing Manager: Kevin Watt

Waterbury Publications, Inc.

Creative Director: Ken Carlson

Editorial Director: Lisa Kingsley

Associate Design Director: Doug Samuelson

Senior Designer: Chad Jewell

Associate Editor: Tricia Laning

Production Assistant: Mindy Samuelson

The Betty Crocker Kitchens seal guarantees success in your kitchen. Every recipe has been tested in America's Most Trusted Kitchens™ to meet our high standards of reliability, easy preparation and great taste.

FIND MORE GREAT IDEAS AT

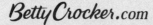

Published by Wiley Publishing, Inc., Hoboken, New Jersey

Published simultaneously in Canada

For general information on our other products and services or for technical support, please contact our Customer Care Department within the United States at (800) 762-2974, outside the United States at (317) 572-3993 or fax (317) 572-4002.

Wiley also publishes its books in a variety of electronic formats. Some content that appears in print may not be available in electronic books. For more information about Wiley products, visit our web site at www.wiley.com.

Library of Congress Cataloging-in-Publication Data is available upon request.

ISBN: 978-0-470-08059-7

Manufactured in the United States of America

10 9 8 7 6 5

why 300 calories?

Here's the scoop: It's about eating better, feeling great and fixing meals that are top notch. The fabulous recipes in this book will help you do all of that easily and, of course, deliciously!

The 300 Calorie Cookbook brings you delicious main dishes, all 300 calories or less per serving, that you can easily incorporate into your daily routine. They are wholesome, chock-full of flavor and totally satisfying. Nutrition and solid health credentials? Check! Variety and taste appeal? Check! The great main dishes here suit all your needs, no matter why you're counting calories. And when you have a dish that's 300 calories, you can add a range of healthy food choices to your daily diet—favorite flavors, fresh, seasonal produce and even healthy snacks.

With the incredible array of recipes in this book, eating healthier meals every day is a goal that's easy to attain. And, with all of the options for healthy eating that are available, it's really nice to have one great reference that you can turn to daily for delicious main dishes that your whole family will enjoy.

When you start with a tasty and good-for-you main dish, everything else falls into place. Sure, you can use these recipes as part of a healthy plan to lose weight, but you can also use them to maintain your weight or help your family eat better—because they taste great and are so satisfying. We know you'll find many ways to use these 300-calorie main dishes, so dig in!

Warmly,

Betty Crocker

contents

calories count

What Are Calories?

Calories are simply units measuring the energy value of food. You need a certain number of calories to keep your body functioning and provide energy. Eating more calories than you need, whether they come from carbohydrates, protein or fat, can result in weight gain. So to keep the number of calories in check, remember that, gram for gram, some foods are more concentrated sources of calories than others. Of course it can sometimes be difficult to know whether a food contains a lot of calories. That's where this book comes in! The 300 recipes contained here all offer up satisfying servings without a lot of calories.

With the wide variety of tasty, reduced-calorie foods available these days, it is easier than ever to control calorie intake. See the chart on pages 8–9 for the calorie counts of many common foods. Because fat contains more than twice the calories as protein or carbohydrates, start by focusing on cutting the fat content of foods you make, even by a little. Small changes in fat content will make a big difference in calorie content—and chances are, you won't even notice.

Your Daily Calorie Number

How many calories are right for you? Your individual daily intake of calories will depend on your body type and activity level. The key to leading a healthier lifestyle is to eat fewer calories or increase your activity level.

Here's an easy formula to help you estimate the amount of calories you need to maintain your current weight.

- **For a sedentary person (inactive most of the time), multiply current weight by 12.**

- **For a moderately active person (exercise a few times a week), multiply current weight by 14.**

- **For a very active person (participate regularly in heavy exercise), multiply current weight by 16 to 18.**

For example, for a sedentary woman who weighs 140 pounds: Multiply 140 by 12, and you get 1,680—the calories she needs per day to maintain her current weight. If weight loss is her goal, she would need to consume less than 1,680 calories per day.

5-Day Meal Plan

Eating healthy can be simple and tasty, as the recipes in this cookbook show, and you don't have to give up your favorite foods or feel deprived. Try to eat a variety of foods over the course of a week, and aim for moderation in portion sizes and quantity of food. And remember that it's important to balance the foods you eat with the amount of activity you get each day.

The 300-calories-or-less dishes in this book are a perfect fit for your daily healthy routine. Not only are they low in calories, but they're full of nutrients and delicious flavor, and they make it easy to stay on track. In addition, it's important to keep your metabolism going, boost your energy levels and keep you going throughout your busy day. Try to pack one or two mini low-calorie snacks to have at work or while you're on the go, so you're always prepared.

Here is a sample menu plan for 5 days—some simple examples of how to organize your daily meals and incorporate some of the recipes from this book. They include a variety of calorie totals, making it easy to personalize your day so you get the amount of calories that you need for your body type and lifestyle. Just remember: While eating low-calorie meals and snacks is important for maintaining a healthy weight, it's unsafe and unwise to drastically cut your daily calories.

Monday (Day 1)

BREAKFAST

1 cup oatmeal with ½ cup fat-free (skim) milk	195 calories
1 cup sliced fresh strawberries	50 calories
1 cup orange juice	100 calories

SNACK

1 medium apple	80 calories
1 blueberry muffin (2½ inch)	110 calories

LUNCH

Vegetarian Reuben Sandwiches (page 165)	230 calories
1 cup low-fat yogurt with ½ cup blueberries	195 calories
1 chocolate chip cookie (2⅓ inch)	50 calories

SNACK

1 cup popcorn popped with oil	70 calories

DINNER

Baked Chicken and Rice with Autumn Vegetables (page 88)	260 calories
Lettuce and tomato salad with 2 tablespoons reduced-fat ranch dressing	120 calories
Cornbread (2-inch square)	45 calories
1 brownie (2 × 1 inch)	110 calories

TOTAL MONDAY CALORIES	**1,615 CALORIES**

Tuesday (Day 2)

BREAKFAST

Garden Vegetable Frittata (page 137)	150 calories
Whole wheat English muffin	
with 2 tablespoons peanut butter	325 calories
1 cup grapefruit juice	80 calories

SNACK

1 medium banana	110 calories
¼ cup almonds	210 calories

LUNCH

New England clam chowder (1 cup)	90 calories
4 saltine crackers	60 calories

SNACK

1 cup carrot sticks	40 calories
½ cup vegetable juice cocktail	50 calories

DINNER

Herbed Salisbury Mushroom Steaks (page 22)	230 calories
1 medium baked potato	130 calories
1 cup broccoli spears with 1 tablespoon butter	140 calories
½ cup low-fat vanilla ice cream	110 calories

TOTAL TUESDAY CALORIES   **1,725 CALORIES**

Wednesday (Day 3)

BREAKFAST

½ medium cantaloupe	95 calories
1 bagel (3 inch) with 2 tablespoons	
cream cheese	255 calories
2 slices Canadian-style bacon	100 calories
1 cup milk	120 calories

SNACK

1 medium orange	60 calories
½ cup reduced-fat cottage cheese	100 calories

LUNCH

Tomato Basil Soup with Orzo (page 200)	160 calories
1 whole-grain hard roll	145 calories
½ cup grapes	55 calories

SNACK

½ medium avocado	140 calories
¼ cup cashews	195 calories

DINNER

Whole Wheat Fettuccine	
with Spring Vegetables (page 80)	300 calories
Fresh spinach salad with	
vinaigrette dressing (1 tablespoon olive oil)	150 calories
½ cup chocolate frozen yogurt	100 calories

TOTAL WEDNESDAY CALORIES   **1,975 CALORIES**

Thursday (Day 4)

BREAKFAST

2 pancakes (4 inch)	
with 2 tablespoons maple syrup	300 calories
1 slice lean ham	150 calories
½ cup fresh blueberries	40 calories

SNACK

2 slices Cheddar cheese	200 calories
6 whole wheat crackers	50 calories

LUNCH

Italian Chicken Noodle Soup (page 188)	170 calories
1 slice whole-grain bread	
with 1 tablespoon butter	175 calories
1 cup carrot and cucumber sticks	60 calories
½ cup low-fat chocolate milk	130 calories

SNACK

1 cup tomato juice	40 calories
1 cup pretzels	110 calories

DINNER

Roasted Tilapia with Vegetables (page 104)	290 calories
½ cup brown rice	110 calories
1 cup fresh raspberries with whipped topping	100 calories

TOTAL THURSDAY CALORIES   **1,925 CALORIES**

Friday (Day 5)

BREAKFAST

Mediterranean Eggs (page 323)	190 calories
½ cup pineapple pieces	40 calories
½ cup soymilk	50 calories

SNACK

1 granola bar	100 calories
½ cup apple juice	60 calories

LUNCH

Turkey wrap with whole wheat tortilla,	
tomatoes and 1 tablespoon mayonnaise	350 calories
1 medium pear	100 calories

SNACK

2 slices Swiss cheese	105 calories
½ cup cucumber slices	50 calories

DINNER

Garlic Shepherd's Pie (page 115)	290 calories
Mixed greens salad with	
2 tablespoons reduced-fat Italian dressing	120 calories
2 oatmeal raisin cookies (2¾ inch)	120 calories

TOTAL FRIDAY CALORIES   **1,575 CALORIES**

calorie chart

Use this handy, at-a-glance calorie chart to help you with your daily meal planning. It lists the average calorie counts for common foods used in meals or as snacks.

Food Item	Calories
Breads, Grains, Rice, Pasta and Beans	
Bread, 1 slice white	65
Bread, 1 slice whole wheat	110
Oatmeal, cooked, ½ cup	75
Pasta, cooked, ½ cup	100
Ready-to-eat cereal, 1 cup	120
Rice, white, cooked, ½ cup	105
Rice, brown, cooked, ½ cup	108
Vegetables	
Asparagus, cooked, ½ cup	25
Beets, cooked, ½ cup	35
Broccoli, cooked, ½ cup	20
Carrots, cooked, ½ cup	35
Cauliflower, cooked, ½ cup	14
Corn, canned or frozen, ½ cup	65
Green beans, cooked, ½ cup	35
Iceberg lettuce, fresh, 1 cup	10
Mixed veggies, frozen, cooked, ½ cup	50
Peas, cooked, ½ cup	60
Potato, baked, 1 medium	130
Spinach, uncooked, 1 cup	7
Tomato, uncooked, 1 medium	40
Fruit	
Apple, 1 medium	80
Banana, 1 medium	110
Blueberries, ½ cup	40
Cantaloupe, ½ medium	95
Grapefruit, ½ medium	40
Grapes, ½ cup	55
Orange, 1 medium	60
Orange juice, unsweetened, ¾ cup	75
Peach, 1 medium	40
Pear, 1 medium	100
Pineapple, ½ cup	40
Strawberries, ½ cup	25
Watermelon, ½ cup	24

Food Item	Calories
Meat	
Beef chuck pot roast, cooked, 3 ounces	147
Beef rib roast, cooked, 3 ounces	210
Beef round steak, cooked, 3 ounces	154
Beef sirloin, cooked, 3 ounces	155
Beef tenderloin, cooked, 3 ounces	175
Ground beef, lean (at least 80%), cooked, 3 ounces	260
Ground beef, extra-lean (at least 90%), cooked, 3 ounces	176
Veal loin chop, cooked, 3 ounces	140
Pork loin chop, cooked, 3 ounces	180
Pork tenderloin, cooked, 3 ounces	140
Ham, fully cooked, 3 ounces	150
Bacon, cooked, 4 slices	160
Canadian-style bacon, cooked, 2 pieces	89
Lamb loin chop, cooked, 3 ounces	175
Hot dog, without bun	140
Poultry	
Chicken breast, no skin, roasted, 3 ounces	150
Chicken breast, with skin, roasted, 3 ounces	190
Chicken thigh, no skin, roasted, 3 ounces	175
Chicken thigh, with skin, roasted, 3 ounces	215
Chicken drumstick, with skin, fried, 3 ounces	200
Chicken wings, with skin, fried, 3 ounces	300
Turkey breast, no skin, roasted, 3 ounces	145
Turkey breast, with skin, roasted, 3 ounces	160
Turkey dark meat, no skin, roasted, 3 ounces	160
Turkey dark meat, with skin, roasted, 3 ounces	180
Ground turkey breast, cooked, 3 ounces	160
Ground turkey dark meat, cooked, 3 ounces	200
Fish and Shellfish	
Crabmeat, canned, 3 ounces	85
Halibut, broiled, 3 ounces	100
Salmon, broiled, 3 ounces	135
Scallops, steamed, 3 ounces	100
Shrimp, steamed, 3 ounces	85
Shrimp, batter-dipped, fried, 3 ounces	300
Tuna, water-packed, 3 ounces	100

Food Item	Calories
Milk, Yogurt, Cheese, Cream and Eggs	
Milk, fat-free (skim), 1 cup	85
Milk, low-fat (1%), 1 cup	110
Milk, reduced-fat (2%), 1 cup	120
Milk, whole, 1 cup	150
Sour cream, 1 tablespoon	30
Yogurt, plain, fat-free, 1 cup	135
Yogurt, plain, low-fat, 1 cup	155
American cheese, 1½ ounces	173
Cheddar cheese, 1½ ounces	175
Cheddar cheese, reduced fat, 1½ ounces	135
Cheddar cheese, fat-free, 1½ ounces	68
Cheese spread, 2 ounces	120
Cottage cheese, ½ cup	90
Cream cheese, 1 ounce	100
Cream cheese, fat-free, 2 tablespoons	30
Mozzarella cheese, 1½ ounces	120
Mozzarella cheese, reduced-fat, 1½ ounces	105
Parmesan cheese, grated, 1½ ounces	140
Parmesan cheese, shredded, 1½ ounces	118
Egg, large whole	75
Egg, large white	17
Egg, large yolk	55
Egg product, fat-free, ¼ cup	30
Fats	
Butter, 1 tablespoon	100
Margarine, 1 tablespoon	100
Cooking spray	2
Vegetable oil, 1 tablespoon	120
Olive oil, 1 tablespoon	120
Mayonnaise, 1 tablespoon	100
Mayonnaise, fat-free, 1 tablespoon	11
Peanut butter, 1 tablespoon	95
Snacks	
Almonds, ¼ cup	210
Peanuts, ¼ cup	210
Popcorn, microwave light, 1 cup	20
Potato chips, 1 ounce	156
Pretzels, 1 ounce	110
Raisins, ¼ cup	109

Food Item	Calories
Sweets	
Jam or preserves, 1 tablespoon	50
Ice cream, vanilla, ½ cup	145
Sorbet, ½ cup	120
Frozen yogurt, regular, ½ cup	160
Frozen yogurt, low-fat, ½ cup	145
Frozen yogurt, fat-free, ½ cup	100
Sherbet, ½ cup	135
Chocolate bar, 1 ounce	145
Cola, 12 ounces	150

center of the plate

After a long day, there's nothing so satisfying as having a delicious, hearty piece of meat at the center of your plate. "Hearty" doesn't have to mean "calorie-filled," though, so you'll be able to have a side or two—and some dessert!

honey-glazed chicken breasts

Prep Time: 10 Minutes   Start to Finish: 1 Hour   Makes: 6 servings

6	boneless skinless chicken breasts (about 1¾ lb)	2	tablespoons lemon juice
½	cup orange juice	¼	teaspoon salt
½	cup honey		Grated orange peel, if desired

1. Heat oven to 375°F. Spray 13×9-inch pan with cooking spray. Place chicken in pan. In small bowl, mix remaining ingredients except orange peel; pour over chicken.

2. Cover with foil. Bake 20 minutes. Remove foil; turn chicken. Bake 20 to 30 minutes longer or until juice of chicken is clear when center of thickest part is cut (170°F). Sprinkle with orange peel.

1 Serving: Calories 260 (Calories from Fat 40); Total Fat 4.5g (Saturated Fat 1g; Trans Fat 0g); Cholesterol 80mg; Sodium 170mg; Total Carbohydrate 26g (Dietary Fiber 0g; Sugars 26g); Protein 29g   **% Daily Value:** Vitamin A 0%; Vitamin C 8%; Calcium 0%; Iron 6%   **Exchanges:** 1½ Other Carbohydrate, 4 Very Lean Meat, ½ Fat   **Carbohydrate Choices:** 2

serve with

Serve these sweetly glazed chicken breasts with steamed brown rice and a tossed green salad.

baked chicken
with fennel butter

Prep Time: 15 Minutes   Start to Finish: 1 Hour 15 Minutes   Makes: 6 servings

6	bone-in chicken breasts (about 3 lb)	1	tablespoon chopped fresh or
¼	cup butter or margarine, softened		1 teaspoon dried parsley flakes
4½	teaspoons chopped fresh or	½	teaspoon fennel seed
	1½ teaspoons dried basil leaves	⅛	teaspoon pepper

1. Heat oven to 375°F. Spray rack in shallow roasting pan with cooking spray.

2. Gently loosen skin from chicken with fingers. In small bowl, mix remaining ingredients. Spread butter mixture between chicken breast meat and skin; cover breast with skin. Place chicken, skin side up, on rack in pan.

3. Bake uncovered 50 to 60 minutes or until juice of chicken is clear when thickest part is cut to bone (170°F).

1 Serving: Calories 290 (Calories from Fat 150); Total Fat 17g (Saturated Fat 7g; Trans Fat 0g); Cholesterol 115mg; Sodium 130mg; Total Carbohydrate 0g (Dietary Fiber 0g; Sugars 0g); Protein 34g **% Daily Value:** Vitamin A 8%; Vitamin C 0%; Calcium 2%; Iron 6% **Exchanges:** 5 Lean Meat, ½ Fat **Carbohydrate Choices:** 0

health smart

Herbs and spices are great ways to add flavor without adding many calories. Other great seasoning ideas for this baked chicken dish would be to use fresh thyme, fresh tarragon or paprika.

270 calories

antipasto chicken

Prep Time: 10 Minutes   Start to Finish: 30 Minutes   Makes: 4 servings

1   tablespoon olive or vegetable oil
4   boneless skinless chicken breasts
       (about 1¼ lb)
1   teaspoon garlic-pepper blend
1   jar (6 oz) marinated artichoke hearts,
       undrained
1   small bell pepper (any color),
       chopped (½ cup)

2   medium tomatoes, chopped
       (1½ cups)
1   can (2¼ oz) sliced ripe olives, drained
1   tablespoon chopped fresh or
       1 teaspoon dried basil leaves
       Crumbled feta cheese, if desired

1. In 12-inch skillet, heat oil over medium heat. Sprinkle chicken with garlic-pepper blend. Cook in skillet about 8 minutes, turning once, until brown.

2. In medium bowl, mix remaining ingredients except cheese (if necessary, cut large artichoke pieces in half). Spoon mixture over chicken. Cook about 10 minutes longer or until juice of chicken is clear when center of thickest part is cut (170°F). Sprinkle with cheese.

1 Serving: Calories 270 (Calories from Fat 100); Total Fat 11g (Saturated Fat 2g; Trans Fat 0g); Cholesterol 85mg; Sodium 360mg; Total Carbohydrate 10g (Dietary Fiber 4g; Sugars 2g); Protein 33g   **% Daily Value:** Vitamin A 15%; Vitamin C 25%; Calcium 6%; Iron 15%   **Exchanges:** ½ Other Carbohydrate, 1 Vegetable, 4½ Very Lean Meat, 1½ Fat **Carbohydrate Choices:** ½

feta-topped chicken

Prep Time: 10 Minutes   Start to Finish: 25 Minutes   Makes: 4 servings

4 boneless skinless chicken breasts (about 1¼ lb)	¼ teaspoon seasoned pepper blend
2 tablespoons balsamic vinaigrette dressing	1 large plum (Roma) tomato, cut into 8 slices
1 teaspoon Italian seasoning	¼ cup crumbled feta cheese (1 oz)

1. Set oven control to broil. Spray rack of broiler pan with cooking spray. Brush both sides of chicken breasts with dressing. Sprinkle both sides with Italian seasoning and seasoned pepper blend.

2. Place chicken on rack in pan. Broil with tops 4 inches from heat about 10 minutes, turning once, until juice of chicken is clear when center of thickest part is cut (170°F).

3. Top each chicken breast with tomato and cheese. Broil 2 to 3 minutes longer or until cheese is lightly browned.

1 Serving: Calories 220 (Calories from Fat 80); Total Fat 8g (Saturated Fat 2.5g; Trans Fat 0g); Cholesterol 90mg; Sodium 260mg; Total Carbohydrate 3g (Dietary Fiber 0g; Sugars 3g); Protein 33g   **% Daily Value:** Vitamin A 10%; Vitamin C 4%; Calcium 6%; Iron 8%   **Exchanges:** 4½ Very Lean Meat, 1 Fat   **Carbohydrate Choices:** 0

try this

Feta cheese crumbles are available in a variety of flavors. Some have sun-dried tomatoes, basil or cracked pepper added. Any of these would be yummy in this recipe.

210 calories

orange- and ginger-glazed chicken

Prep Time: 25 Minutes   Start to Finish: 25 Minutes   Makes: 4 servings

4 boneless skinless chicken breasts (about 1¼ lb)	1 teaspoon finely chopped gingerroot or ½ teaspoon ground ginger
⅓ cup orange marmalade spreadable fruit	1 teaspoon Worcestershire sauce

1. Spray 10-inch skillet with cooking spray; heat over medium-high heat. Cook chicken in skillet about 5 minutes or until brown on bottom. Turn chicken. Stir in remaining ingredients; reduce heat to low.

2. Cover; simmer 10 to 15 minutes, stirring sauce occasionally, until sauce is thickened and juice of chicken is clear when center of thickest part is cut (170°F). Cut chicken into thin slices. Spoon sauce over chicken.

1 Serving: Calories 210 (Calories from Fat 35); Total Fat 4g (Saturated Fat 1g; Trans Fat 0g); Cholesterol 70mg; Sodium 85mg; Total Carbohydrate 19g (Dietary Fiber 0g; Sugars 13g); Protein 25g   **% Daily Value:** Vitamin A 0%; Vitamin C 2%; Calcium 0%; Iron 6%   **Exchanges:** 1 Other Carbohydrate, 3½ Very Lean Meat, ½ Fat   **Carbohydrate Choices:** 1

try this
It's easy to finely chop fresh gingerroot ahead of time and freeze to use as needed.

baked oregano chicken

Prep Time: 10 Minutes   Start to Finish: 35 Minutes   Makes: 4 servings

¼	cup dry bread crumbs	⅛	teaspoon pepper
2	tablespoons grated Parmesan cheese	¼	cup Dijon mustard
¼	teaspoon dried oregano leaves	4	boneless skinless chicken breasts
⅛	teaspoon garlic salt		(about 1¼ lb)

1. Heat oven to 425°F. Spray 15×10×1-inch pan with sides with cooking spray.

2. In small bowl, mix bread crumbs, cheese, oregano, garlic salt and pepper. Spread mustard on all sides of chicken breasts; coat with bread crumb mixture. Place in pan.

3. Bake uncovered about 25 minutes or until juice of chicken is clear when center of thickest part is cut (170°F).

1 Serving: Calories 180 (Calories from Fat 50); Total Fat 5g (Saturated Fat 1.5g; Trans Fat 0g); Cholesterol 75mg; Sodium 410mg; Total Carbohydrate 4g (Dietary Fiber 0g; Sugars 0g); Protein 28g   **% Daily Value:** Vitamin A 0%; Vitamin C 0%; Calcium 6%; Iron 8%   **Exchanges:** 4 Very Lean Meat, 1 Fat   **Carbohydrate Choices:** 0

serve with

Here's a great meal idea: Serve these breaded chicken breasts with broccoli spears and sliced fresh tomatoes.

thai chicken with basil

Prep Time: 20 Minutes   **Start to Finish:** 20 Minutes   **Makes:** 4 servings

4 boneless skinless chicken breasts (about 1¼ lb)	1 teaspoon sugar
2 tablespoons vegetable oil	¼ cup chopped fresh basil leaves
3 cloves garlic, finely chopped	1 tablespoon chopped fresh mint leaves
2 red or green jalapeño chiles, seeded, finely chopped	1 tablespoon chopped unsalted dry-roasted peanuts
1 tablespoon fish sauce	

1. Cut each chicken breast into 8 pieces; set aside.

2. In wok or 12-inch skillet, heat oil over medium-high heat. Cook garlic and chiles in oil, stirring constantly, until garlic is just golden.

3. Add chicken; cook 8 to 10 minutes, stirring frequently, or until chicken is no longer pink in center. Stir in fish sauce and sugar. Sprinkle with basil, mint and peanuts.

1 Serving: Calories 260 (Calories from Fat 120); Total Fat 13g (Saturated Fat 2.5g; Trans Fat 0g); Cholesterol 90mg; Sodium 430mg; Total Carbohydrate 4g (Dietary Fiber 1g; Sugars 2g); Protein 33g   **% Daily Value:** Vitamin A 8%; Vitamin C 10%; Calcium 4%; Iron 8%   **Exchanges:** 4½ Lean Meat   **Carbohydrate Choices:** 0

serve with

Serve this exotic chicken dish with basmati or jasmine rice and a crisp salad with Asian dressing, which adds extra flavor, color and nutrients to the meal.

blue cheese chicken tenders

Prep Time: 5 Minutes   Start to Finish: 20 Minutes   Makes: 4 servings

1 tablespoon vegetable oil	1 clove garlic, finely chopped
1 lb uncooked chicken breast tenders (not breaded)	⅓ cup blue cheese dressing
1 tablespoon lemon juice	Crumbled blue cheese, if desired
	Toasted walnuts, if desired*

1. In 10-inch skillet, heat oil over medium-high heat. Cook chicken, lemon juice and garlic in oil 8 to 10 minutes, stirring occasionally, until chicken is no longer pink in center.

2. Stir in dressing. Cook 2 to 4 minutes, stirring frequently, until hot. Sprinkle with blue cheese and walnuts.

*Note: To toast walnuts, heat oven to 350°F. Spread walnuts in ungreased shallow pan. Bake uncovered 6 to 10 minutes, stirring occasionally, until light brown. Or sprinkle in ungreased heavy skillet. Cook over medium heat 5 to 7 minutes, stirring frequently until walnuts begin to brown, then stirring constantly until light brown.

1 Serving: Calories 230 (Calories from Fat 130); Total Fat 14g (Saturated Fat 2g; Trans Fat 0g); Cholesterol 55mg; Sodium 300mg; Total Carbohydrate 2g (Dietary Fiber 0g; Sugars 0g); Protein 24g   **% Daily Value:** Vitamin A 0%; Vitamin C 0%; Calcium 0%; Iron 0%   **Exchanges:** 3 Medium-Fat Meat   **Carbohydrate Choices:** 0

italian chicken bracciole

photo on page C-2

Prep Time: 25 Minutes   Start to Finish: 1 Hour 40 Minutes   Makes: 6 servings

4	slices bacon, chopped	6	boneless skinless chicken thighs (about 1½ lb)
1	medium onion, chopped (½ cup)	1	tablespoon olive oil
1	clove garlic, chopped	1	tablespoon butter or margarine
¼	cup Italian-style dry bread crumbs	1	can (14.5 oz) diced tomatoes with Italian-style herbs, undrained
¼	cup grated Parmesan cheese	3	tablespoons tomato paste
2	tablespoons chopped fresh rosemary leaves		
1	egg		

1. Heat oven to 350°F. Spray 11×7-inch (2-quart) glass baking dish with cooking spray.

2. In 12-inch skillet, cook bacon over medium-high heat, stirring frequently, until crisp. Reduce heat to low. Add onion and garlic; cook 2 to 3 minutes, stirring occasionally, until soft. Remove from heat; stir in bread crumbs. Add cheese, rosemary and egg; mix well.

3. Unfold chicken thighs so inside faces up. Spoon about 2 tablespoons stuffing onto each thigh. Fold over and secure with toothpicks. In same skillet, heat oil and butter. Cook chicken in skillet 2 minutes on each side until brown. Place in baking dish. Mix tomatoes and tomato paste; pour over chicken.

4. Cover with foil. Bake 1 hour to 1 hour 15 minutes or until thermometer inserted in center of stuffing reads 165°F.

1 Serving: Calories 250 (Calories from Fat 130); Total Fat 14g (Saturated Fat 5g; Trans Fat 0g); Cholesterol 90mg; Sodium 500mg; Total Carbohydrate 9g (Dietary Fiber 1g; Sugars 4g); Protein 21g   **% Daily Value:** Vitamin A 8%; Vitamin C 8%; Calcium 10%; Iron 15%   **Exchanges:** ½ Other Carbohydrate, 3 Medium-Fat Meat   **Carbohydrate Choices:** ½

asian turkey with red onion salsa

Prep Time: 15 Minutes   Start to Finish: 2 Hours 50 Minutes   Makes: 6 servings

Turkey

1	tablespoon grated lemon peel
¼	cup lemon juice
2	tablespoons red wine vinegar
2	tablespoons reduced-sodium soy sauce
1	tablespoon olive or vegetable oil
1	clove garlic, finely chopped
1½	lb turkey breast tenderloins

Salsa

2	medium red onions, finely chopped (1½ cups)
1	medium tomato, finely chopped (¾ cup)
4	cloves garlic, finely chopped
4	medium green onions, chopped (¼ cup)
¼	cup lemon juice
2	tablespoons chopped fresh cilantro
2	tablespoons balsamic vinegar
1	tablespoon olive or vegetable oil
1	teaspoon reduced-sodium soy sauce
¼	teaspoon ground red pepper (cayenne)

1. In shallow glass or plastic dish or resealable food-storage plastic bag, mix lemon peel, lemon juice, vinegar, soy sauce, oil and garlic. Add turkey; turn to coat with marinade. Cover dish or seal bag. Refrigerate at least 2 hours but no longer than 4 hours, turning once.

2. Meanwhile, in glass or plastic bowl, mix salsa ingredients. Cover; refrigerate at least 2 hours.

3. Heat oven to 350°F. Spray 13×9-inch (3-quart) glass baking dish with cooking spray. Remove turkey from marinade; discard marinade. Place turkey in baking dish.

4. Bake uncovered about 35 minutes, brushing with drippings after 10 minutes, or until juice of turkey is clear when center of thickest part is cut (170°F). Serve with salsa.

1 Serving: Calories 230 (Calories from Fat 100); Total Fat 11g (Saturated Fat 2.5g; Trans Fat 0g); Cholesterol 65mg; Sodium 270mg; Total Carbohydrate 9g (Dietary Fiber 1g; Sugars 4g); Protein 25g   **% Daily Value:** Vitamin A 8%; Vitamin C 10%; Calcium 4%; Iron 8%   **Exchanges:** 1 Vegetable, 3½ Lean Meat   **Carbohydrate Choices:** ½

herbed salisbury-mushroom steaks

Prep Time: 25 Minutes   Start to Finish: 35 Minutes   Makes: 5 servings

1 package (8 oz) sliced fresh mushrooms (3 cups)	¼ cup fat-free (skim) milk
1 lb extra-lean (at least 90%) ground beef	¾ teaspoon dried thyme leaves
¼ cup unseasoned dry bread crumbs	3 tablespoons ketchup
¼ cup fat-free egg product	2 teaspoons vegetable oil
	1 jar (12 oz) fat-free beef gravy

1. Finely chop 1 cup of the mushrooms. In medium bowl, mix chopped mushrooms, beef, bread crumbs, egg product, milk, thyme and 1 tablespoon of the ketchup. Shape mixture into 5 oval patties, ½ inch thick.

2. In 12-inch nonstick skillet, heat oil over medium-high heat. Add patties; cook about 5 minutes, turning once, until brown.

3. Add remaining sliced mushrooms, remaining 2 tablespoons ketchup and the gravy. Heat to boiling; reduce heat to low. Cover and cook 5 to 10 minutes or until meat thermometer inserted in center of patties reads 160°F.

1 Serving: Calories 230 (Calories from Fat 80); Total Fat 9g (Saturated Fat 3g; Trans Fat 0g); Cholesterol 50mg; Sodium 630mg; Total Carbohydrate 13g (Dietary Fiber 0g; Sugars 4g); Protein 25g   **% Daily Value:** Vitamin A 6%; Vitamin C 2%; Calcium 4%; Iron 15%   **Exchanges:** 1 Starch, 3 Lean Meat   **Carbohydrate Choices:** 1

serve with
Round out this homey meal with a side of steamed green beans and a simple mixed-greens salad.

tex-mex meat loaf

Prep Time: 10 Minutes   **Start to Finish:** 1 Hour 10 Minutes   **Makes:** 6 servings

1½ lb extra-lean (at least 90%)
    ground beef
1   can (10 oz) diced tomatoes and green
    chiles, undrained
¼   cup fat-free egg product

¼   cup unseasoned dry bread crumbs
1   teaspoon salt-free garlic-herb blend
1   teaspoon chili powder
1   teaspoon ground cumin
    Chunky-style salsa, if desired

1. Heat oven to 375°F. In large bowl, mix all ingredients except salsa. Spoon mixture into ungreased 11×7-inch (2-quart) glass baking dish; pat into 9×5-inch loaf.

2. Bake uncovered about 1 hour or until meat thermometer inserted in center of loaf reads 160°F. Drain any liquid before slicing. Serve with salsa.

1 Serving: Calories 200 (Calories from Fat 70); Total Fat 8g (Saturated Fat 3g; Trans Fat 0g); Cholesterol 65mg; Sodium 190mg; Total Carbohydrate 6g (Dietary Fiber 0g; Sugars 1g); Protein 26g **% Daily Value:** Vitamin A 6%; Vitamin C 6%; Calcium 4%; Iron 15% **Exchanges:** ½ Other Carbohydrate, 3½ Lean Meat **Carbohydrate Choices:** ½

try this

For a spicier meat loaf, use the hot variety of diced tomatoes and green chiles instead of the regular, or add a pinch of ground red pepper to the meat mixture.

oriental pot roast

Prep Time: 15 Minutes   Start to Finish: 2 Hours 40 Minutes   Makes: 12 servings

1	boneless beef arm or chuck roast (3 lb)	1	clove garlic, crushed
1	large onion, sliced	2	medium stalks celery, sliced (1 cup)
1	can (15.25 oz) pineapple chunks in juice, drained, juice reserved	1	package (10 oz) frozen spinach leaves, thawed, drained
3	tablespoons reduced-sodium soy sauce	1	can (4 oz) mushroom pieces and stems, drained
1	teaspoon ground ginger		

1. Trim excess fat from beef. Heat nonstick Dutch oven over medium heat. Cook beef in Dutch oven until brown on all sides; drain. Place onion on beef.

2. In small bowl, mix reserved pineapple juice, the soy sauce, ginger and garlic; pour over beef. Heat to boiling; reduce heat. Cover; simmer about 2 hours or until meat is tender.

3. Add celery. Cover; simmer 20 minutes. Add pineapple, spinach and mushrooms. Cover; simmer 5 minutes longer. Remove beef, pineapple and vegetables. Skim any fat from broth. Serve broth with beef, pineapple and vegetables.

1 Serving: Calories 140 (Calories from Fat 40); Total Fat 4.5g (Saturated Fat 1.5g; Trans Fat 0g); Cholesterol 30mg; Sodium 220mg; Total Carbohydrate 9g (Dietary Fiber 1g; Sugars 6g); Protein 16g   **% Daily Value:** Vitamin A 40%; Vitamin C 4%; Calcium 4%; Iron 10%   **Exchanges:** ½ Other Carbohydrate, 2 Lean Meat   **Carbohydrate Choices:** ½

beef tenderloin with
pear-cranberry chutney

photo on page C-2

Prep Time: 35 Minutes   Start to Finish: 35 Minutes   Makes: 4 servings

½ large red onion, thinly sliced	½ cup fresh or frozen cranberries
2 cloves garlic, finely chopped	2 tablespoons packed brown sugar
2 tablespoons dry red wine or grape juice	½ teaspoon pumpkin pie spice
2 firm ripe pears, peeled, diced	4 beef tenderloin steaks, about 1 inch thick (4 oz each)

1. Heat 12-inch nonstick skillet over medium-high heat. Cook onion, garlic and wine in skillet about 5 minutes, stirring frequently, until onion is tender but not brown.

2. Stir in pears, cranberries, brown sugar and pumpkin pie spice; reduce heat. Simmer uncovered about 10 minutes, stirring frequently, until cranberries burst. Place chutney in small bowl; set aside.

3. In same skillet, cook beef over medium heat about 8 minutes for medium doneness (160°F), turning once. Serve with chutney.

1 Serving: Calories 260 (Calories from Fat 80); Total Fat 8g (Saturated Fat 3g; Trans Fat 0g); Cholesterol 65mg; Sodium 60mg; Total Carbohydrate 23g (Dietary Fiber 4g; Sugars 17g); Protein 25g **% Daily Value:** Vitamin A 2%; Vitamin C 6%; Calcium 4%; Iron 15% **Exchanges:** 1 Fruit, ½ Other Carbohydrate, 3½ Lean Meat **Carbohydrate Choices:** 1½

health smart

By selecting small portions of lean red meat cuts (round tip, eye of round, top round, top loin, tenderloin or sirloin), you can enjoy red meat as part of a healthy diet.

beef with spiced pepper sauce

Prep Time: 30 Minutes   Start to Finish: 30 Minutes   Makes: 4 servings

1   lb boneless beef top sirloin steak, about ¾ inch thick

3   tablespoons ketchup

3   tablespoons water

¾   teaspoon soy sauce

½   medium bell pepper (any color), cut into thin strips

1   small onion, thinly sliced
     Coarsely ground pepper

1. Trim excess fat from beef. Place beef between pieces of plastic wrap or waxed paper; pound with flat side of meat mallet or rolling pin to tenderize. Cut into 4 serving pieces.

2. In small bowl, beat ketchup, water and soy sauce with wire whisk or fork until blended; set aside.

3. Spray 10-inch skillet with cooking spray; heat over medium-high heat. Cook beef in skillet 3 minutes, turning once. Add bell pepper and onion. Stir in ketchup mixture; reduce heat to low. Cover; simmer 12 minutes or just until tender. Remove beef from skillet; keep warm.

4. Stir ground pepper into sauce in skillet; heat to boiling. Boil 2 minutes, stirring frequently, until sauce is slightly thickened. Serve over beef.

1 Serving: Calories 150 (Calories from Fat 30); Total Fat 3.5g (Saturated Fat 1g; Trans Fat 0g); Cholesterol 60mg; Sodium 230mg; Total Carbohydrate 6g (Dietary Fiber 0g; Sugars 4g); Protein 23g   **% Daily Value:** Vitamin A 6%; Vitamin C 15%; Calcium 0%; Iron 15%   **Exchanges:** ½ Other Carbohydrate, 3 Very Lean Meat, ½ Fat   **Carbohydrate Choices:** ½

honey-mint lamb chops

photo on page C-3

Prep Time: 25 Minutes   Start to Finish: 25 Minutes   Makes: 4 servings

8 lamb rib or loin chops, about 1 inch thick (about 2 lb)	1 teaspoon chopped fresh or ¼ teaspoon dried mint leaves
2 tablespoons dry white wine or apple juice	¼ teaspoon salt
2 tablespoons honey	⅛ teaspoon pepper

1. Set oven control to broil. Spray broiler pan rack with cooking spray.

2. Remove excess fat from lamb. In small bowl, mix remaining ingredients.

3. Place lamb on rack in pan. Broil with tops 2 to 3 inches from heat 12 to 14 minutes, brushing with honey mixture and turning after 6 minutes, for medium doneness (160°F). Discard any remaining honey mixture.

1 Serving: Calories 210 (Calories from Fat 90); Total Fat 10g (Saturated Fat 4g; Trans Fat 1g); Cholesterol 65mg; Sodium 210mg; Total Carbohydrate 9g (Dietary Fiber 0g; Sugars 9g); Protein 20g   **% Daily Value:** Vitamin A 0%; Vitamin C 0%; Calcium 0%; Iron 8%   **Exchanges:** ½ Other Carbohydrate, 3 Lean Meat   **Carbohydrate Choices:** ½

try this

The honey and mint combination is great with lamb, but thyme and honey is a great combo, too. Just use 1 teaspoon chopped fresh or ¼ teaspoon dried thyme leaves instead of the mint.

mustard lamb chops

Prep Time: 25 Minutes   **Start to Finish:** 25 Minutes   **Makes:** 6 servings

6 lamb sirloin or shoulder chops, about ¾ inch thick (about 2 lb)	2 tablespoons Dijon mustard
1 tablespoon chopped fresh or 1 teaspoon dried thyme leaves	¼ teaspoon salt

1. Set oven control to broil. Spray rack of broiler pan with cooking spray.

2. Remove excess fat from lamb. In small bowl, mix remaining ingredients. Brush half of mustard mixture evenly over lamb.

3. Place lamb on rack in pan. Broil with tops 3 to 4 inches from heat about 4 minutes or until brown. Turn lamb; brush with remaining mustard mixture. Broil 5 to 7 minutes longer for medium doneness (160°F).

1 Serving: Calories 140 (Calories from Fat 60); Total Fat 7g (Saturated Fat 2.5g; Trans Fat 0g); Cholesterol 65mg; Sodium 270mg; Total Carbohydrate 0g (Dietary Fiber 0g; Sugars 0g); Protein 20g   **% Daily Value:** Vitamin A 0%; Vitamin C 0%; Calcium 0%; Iron 10%   **Exchanges:** 3 Very Lean Meat, 1 Fat   **Carbohydrate Choices:** 0

plum-mustard
pork chops

Prep Time: 15 Minutes   Start to Finish: 15 Minutes   Makes: 4 servings

4	boneless pork loin chops, ½ inch thick (5 oz each)	¼	cup Chinese plum sauce or apricot jam
¼	teaspoon salt	4	teaspoons yellow mustard
¼	teaspoon pepper		

1. Heat 10-inch nonstick skillet over medium-high heat. Sprinkle pork chops with salt and pepper. Cook pork in skillet 5 to 6 minutes, turning after 3 minutes, until no longer pink in center.

2. Meanwhile, in small bowl, mix plum sauce and mustard. Serve with pork.

1 Serving: Calories 210 (Calories from Fat 70); Total Fat 8g (Saturated Fat 3g; Trans Fat 0g); Cholesterol 65mg; Sodium 400mg; Total Carbohydrate 11g (Dietary Fiber 0g; Sugars 7g); Protein 23g **% Daily Value:** Vitamin A 0%; Vitamin C 2%; Calcium 0%; Iron 6% **Exchanges:** ½ Other Carbohydrate, 3½ Lean Meat **Carbohydrate Choices:** 1

serve with
Complement the sweet-tangy pork chops with small baked sweet potatoes and a tossed baby spinach salad.

270 calories

cajun smothered pork chops

Prep Time: 15 Minutes   Start to Finish: 15 Minutes   Makes: 4 servings

4	bone-in pork loin chops, ½ inch thick (about 1¾ lb)	½	medium onion, sliced
2	teaspoons salt-free extra-spicy seasoning blend	1	jalapeño chile, seeded, chopped
2	teaspoons canola oil	1	can (14.5 oz) organic diced tomatoes, undrained

1. Sprinkle both sides of pork chops with seasoning blend. In 12-inch nonstick skillet, heat oil over medium-high heat. Add onion and jalapeño; cook about 2 minutes, stirring occasionally, until slightly tender. Push mixture to one side of skillet.

2. Add pork to other side of skillet. Cook about 3 minutes, turning once, until brown. Add tomatoes. Heat to boiling; reduce heat. Cover; cook 4 to 8 minutes or until pork is no longer pink in center.

1 Serving: Calories 270 (Calories from Fat 120); Total Fat 13g (Saturated Fat 4g; Trans Fat 0g); Cholesterol 90mg; Sodium 190mg; Total Carbohydrate 6g (Dietary Fiber 1g; Sugars 3g); Protein 32g **% Daily Value:** Vitamin A 4%; Vitamin C 10%; Calcium 4%; Iron 10% **Exchanges:** ½ Starch, 4 Lean Meat **Carbohydrate Choices:** ½

serve with

Add a side of black beans and rice and sliced cucumbers. Look for convenient black beans–and-rice side dishes in the rice section of your supermarket.

240 calories

caribbean pork roast

Prep Time: 20 Minutes   Start to Finish: 6 Hours   Makes: 8 servings

1 boneless pork center loin roast (2 to 2½ lb)	1 medium bell pepper (any color), cut into 8 pieces
1 cup orange juice	1 medium onion, quartered
½ cup lime juice	4 cloves garlic, finely chopped
1½ teaspoons ground cumin	Salt and pepper, if desired
1½ teaspoons red pepper sauce	1½ teaspoons sugar
¾ teaspoon ground allspice	½ teaspoon salt

1. Trim excess fat from pork. Pierce pork deeply in several places with meat fork or skewer; place in resealable food-storage plastic bag.

2. In blender or food processor, place remaining ingredients except salt and pepper, sugar and ½ teaspoon salt. Cover and blend on medium speed until smooth. Pour blended mixture over pork. Seal bag; place in dish. Refrigerate, turning bag occasionally, at least 4 hours but no longer than 24 hours.

3. Heat oven to 325°F. Remove pork from marinade; refrigerate marinade. Sprinkle pork with salt and pepper; place on rack in shallow roasting pan. Bake uncovered 1 hour to 1 hour 30 minutes or until meat thermometer inserted into center of pork reads 155°F. Remove from heat; cover with foil and let stand 10 minutes until thermometer reads 160°F.

4. Meanwhile, in 1½-quart saucepan, mix marinade, sugar and ½ teaspoon salt. Heat to boiling; reduce heat. Simmer uncovered about 5 minutes, stirring occasionally, until mixture is slightly thickened. Slice pork; serve with sauce.

1 Serving: Calories 240 (Calories from Fat 90); Total Fat 10g (Saturated Fat 3.5g; Trans Fat 0g); Cholesterol 80mg; Sodium 210mg; Total Carbohydrate 8g (Dietary Fiber 0g; Sugars 6g); Protein 29g **% Daily Value:** Vitamin A 2%; Vitamin C 25%; Calcium 2%; Iron 8% **Exchanges:** ½ Other Carbohydrate, 4 Lean Meat **Carbohydrate Choices:** ½

caramelized pork slices

Prep Time: 20 Minutes   Start to Finish: 20 Minutes   Makes: 4 servings

1	lb pork tenderloin, cut into ½-inch slices	1	tablespoon orange juice
2	cloves garlic, finely chopped	1	tablespoon molasses
2	tablespoons packed brown sugar	½	teaspoon salt
		¼	teaspoon pepper

1. Spray 10-inch skillet with cooking spray; heat over medium-high heat. Cook pork and garlic in skillet 6 to 8 minutes, turning occasionally, until pork is no longer pink in center. Drain if necessary.

2. Stir in remaining ingredients; cook until mixture thickens and coats pork.

1 Serving: Calories 190 (Calories from Fat 40); Total Fat 4.5g (Saturated Fat 1.5g; Trans Fat 0g); Cholesterol 70mg; Sodium 350mg; Total Carbohydrate 12g (Dietary Fiber 0g; Sugars 10g); Protein 26g   **% Daily Value:** Vitamin A 0%; Vitamin C 0%; Calcium 2%; Iron 10%   **Exchanges:** 1 Other Carbohydrate, 3½ Very Lean Meat, ½ Fat   **Carbohydrate Choices:** 1

portion control is important

It's important to learn to recognize what a sensible portion size looks like—and it's probably smaller than you think!

- Take time to measure your portions, and soon you'll be able to estimate them correctly.
- For favorite utensils, fill each with water, then pour into a measuring cup to determine how much each one holds.
- Remember what a portion looks like in a particular bowl or plate— say, a ½-cup serving of cereal in a bowl—then use that bowl every time you eat that cereal.

italian roasted pork tenderloin

Prep Time: 10 Minutes   Start to Finish: 45 Minutes   Makes: 6 servings

1	teaspoon olive oil	¼	teaspoon pepper
½	teaspoon salt	1	clove garlic, finely chopped
½	teaspoon fennel seed, crushed	2	pork tenderloins (about ¾ lb each)

1. Heat oven to 375°F. Spray rack of roasting pan with cooking spray. In small bowl, mash oil and seasonings with spoon into a paste. Rub paste over pork.

2. Place pork on rack in shallow roasting pan. Roast 25 to 35 minutes or until pork has slight blush of pink in center and meat thermometer inserted in center reads 160°F.

1 Serving: Calories 150 (Calories from Fat 45); Total Fat 5g (Saturated Fat 1.5g; Trans Fat 0g); Cholesterol 70mg; Sodium 250mg; Total Carbohydrate 0g (Dietary Fiber 0g; Sugars 0g); Protein 26g   **% Daily Value:** Vitamin A 0%; Vitamin C 0%; Calcium 0%; Iron 8%   **Exchanges:** 3½ Very Lean Meat, ½ Fat   **Carbohydrate Choices:** 0

try this

Pork tenderloin is a wonderful lean cut of meat that is readily available and easy to cook. Just be sure to cook as directed and don't overcook so that it stays tender and juicy. Check the temperature at the minimum roasting time.

peppered pork in mushroom sauce
photo on page C-2

Prep Time: 30 Minutes   Start to Finish: 30 Minutes   Makes: 4 servings

1 lb pork tenderloin	2 tablespoons all-purpose flour
1 teaspoon seasoned pepper blend	2 tablespoons balsamic vinegar
¼ teaspoon salt	2 teaspoons dried rosemary leaves, crushed
2 teaspoons olive or canola oil	
1 cup chicken broth with 33% less sodium	1 package (8 oz) fresh whole mushrooms

1. Cut pork into 4 equal pieces. Between pieces of plastic wrap or waxed paper, flatten pork pieces with flat side of meat mallet to 4×3½-inch pieces, less than ½ inch thick.

2. Sprinkle both sides of pork pieces with seasoned pepper blend and salt; press seasonings into meat. In 12-inch nonstick skillet, heat oil over medium-high heat. Add pork; cook about 5 minutes, turning once, until brown.

3. In small bowl, mix broth and flour until smooth. Add broth mixture and remaining ingredients to skillet. Heat to boiling; reduce heat. Cover; cook 8 to 10 minutes, stirring occasionally, until pork is no longer pink in center and mushrooms are tender.

1 Serving: Calories 200 (Calories from Fat 60); Total Fat 7g (Saturated Fat 2g; Trans Fat 0g); Cholesterol 70mg; Sodium 420mg; Total Carbohydrate 7g (Dietary Fiber 1g; Sugars 1g); Protein 28g   **% Daily Value:** Vitamin A 0%; Vitamin C 0%; Calcium 2%; Iron 15%   **Exchanges:** 1 Vegetable, 3½ Very Lean Meat, 1 Fat   **Carbohydrate Choices:** ½

pork medallions with hot pineapple glaze

Prep Time: 15 Minutes   **Start to Finish:** 15 Minutes   **Makes:** 4 servings

1	lb pork tenderloin, cut into ¼-inch slices	2	teaspoons Worcestershire sauce
¼	teaspoon salt	2	teaspoons cider vinegar
⅓	cup pineapple or orange marmalade spreadable fruit	½	teaspoon grated gingerroot
		¼	teaspoon crushed red pepper flakes, if desired

1. Sprinkle both sides of pork with salt. Heat 12-inch nonstick skillet over medium-high heat. Cook pork in skillet 5 to 6 minutes, turning once, until no longer pink in center. Remove pork from skillet; keep warm.

2. Mix remaining ingredients in skillet; heat to boiling. Boil and stir 1 minute. Serve sauce over pork.

1 Serving: Calories 220 (Calories from Fat 40); Total Fat 4.5g (Saturated Fat 1.5g; Trans Fat 0g); Cholesterol 70mg; Sodium 230mg; Total Carbohydrate 19g (Dietary Fiber 0g; Sugars 13g); Protein 26g   **% Daily Value:** Vitamin A 0%; Vitamin C 2%; Calcium 0%; Iron 10%   **Exchanges:** 1 Other Carbohydrate, 3½ Very Lean Meat, ½ Fat   **Carbohydrate Choices:** 1

pork tenderloin with rosemary

Prep Time: 5 Minutes   Start to Finish: 35 Minutes   Makes: 3 servings

1 clove garlic, peeled	1½ teaspoons finely chopped or
¼ teaspoon salt	½ teaspoon dried rosemary leaves,
⅛ teaspoon pepper	crushed
1 pork tenderloin (about ¾ lb)	

1. Heat oven to 425°F. Spray an 8-inch square or 11×7-inch pan with cooking spray.

2. Crush garlic in a garlic press. Sprinkle salt and pepper over all sides of pork. Rub garlic and rosemary on all sides of pork. Place in pan.

3. Bake uncovered 20 to 30 minutes or until pork has slight blush of pink in center and a meat thermometer inserted in center reads 160°F. Cut pork crosswise into thin slices.

1 Serving: Calories 150 (Calories from Fat 45); Total Fat 5g (Saturated Fat 1.5g; Trans Fat 0g); Cholesterol 70mg; Sodium 250mg; Total Carbohydrate 0g (Dietary Fiber 0g; Sugars 0g); Protein 26g **% Daily Value:** Vitamin A 0%; Vitamin C 0%; Calcium 0%; Iron 8% **Exchanges:** 3½ Very Lean Meat, ½ Fat **Carbohydrate Choices:** 0

tuna with three-herb pesto

Prep Time: 20 Minutes   Start to Finish: 20 Minutes   Makes: 4 servings

4	tuna, swordfish or other firm fish steaks, ¾ inch thick (4 oz each)	¼	cup loosely packed fresh basil leaves
3	teaspoons olive or vegetable oil	4	medium green onions, sliced (¼ cup)
½	teaspoon salt	1	clove garlic, cut in half
1	cup loosely packed fresh cilantro leaves	2	tablespoons lime juice
½	cup loosely packed fresh Italian (flat-leaf) parsley leaves	¼	cup chicken broth with 33% less sodium
		1	tablespoon grated Parmesan cheese

1. Set oven control to broil. Brush both sides of tuna steaks with 1 teaspoon of the oil. Place on rack in broiler pan. Broil with tops 4 inches from heat 8 to 10 minutes, turning once and sprinkling with ¼ teaspoon of the salt, until fish flakes easily with fork and is slightly pink in center.

2. Meanwhile, in food processor bowl with metal blade, place cilantro, parsley, basil, onions, garlic, lime juice and the remaining 2 teaspoons oil and ¼ teaspoon salt. Cover and process about 10 seconds or until finely chopped. With processor running, slowly pour in broth and continue processing until almost smooth. Stir in cheese. Serve 3 tablespoons pesto with each tuna steak.

1 Serving: Calories 210 (Calories from Fat 90); Total Fat 10g (Saturated Fat 2g; Trans Fat 0g); Cholesterol 45mg; Sodium 410mg; Total Carbohydrate 3g (Dietary Fiber 0g; Sugars 0g); Protein 28g   **% Daily Value:** Vitamin A 25%; Vitamin C 15%; Calcium 6%; Iron 10%   **Exchanges:** 4 Lean Meat   **Carbohydrate Choices:** 0

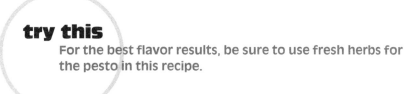

try this
For the best flavor results, be sure to use fresh herbs for the pesto in this recipe.

orange and dill pan-seared tuna

Prep Time: 20 Minutes   Start to Finish: 20 Minutes   Makes: 4 servings

4 tuna, swordfish or other firm fish steaks, ¾ inch thick (4 oz each)	1 tablespoon chopped fresh or ¼ teaspoon dried dill weed
½ teaspoon peppered seasoned salt	1 tablespoon butter or margarine
1 small red onion, thinly sliced (½ cup)	1 teaspoon grated orange peel, if desired
¾ cup orange juice	

1. Heat 10-inch nonstick skillet over medium-high heat. Sprinkle both sides of fish with peppered seasoned salt. Add fish to skillet; reduce heat to medium-low. Cover; cook 6 to 8 minutes, turning once, until fish flakes easily with fork (tuna may still be slightly pink in center). Remove fish from skillet; keep warm.

2. Add onion to skillet. Cook over medium-high heat 2 minutes, stirring occasionally. Stir in orange juice; cook 2 minutes longer. Stir in dill weed, butter and orange peel. Cook 1 to 2 minutes or until slightly thickened. Serve sauce over fish.

1 Serving: Calories 190 (Calories from Fat 80); Total Fat 9g (Saturated Fat 3g; Trans Fat 0g); Cholesterol 75mg; Sodium 250mg; Total Carbohydrate 7g (Dietary Fiber 0g; Sugars 6g); Protein 22g   **% Daily Value:** Vitamin A 6%; Vitamin C 20%; Calcium 2%; Iron 4%   **Exchanges:** ½ Other Carbohydrate, 3 Very Lean Meat, 1½ Fat   **Carbohydrate Choices:** ½

citrus salmon

Prep Time: 15 Minutes   Start to Finish: 40 Minutes   Makes: 8 servings

1 salmon or other medium-firm fish fillet (3 lb)	¼ cup grated lemon peel
½ teaspoon salt	½ cup orange juice
¼ cup finely chopped fresh parsley	2 tablespoons white balsamic vinegar
¼ cup finely chopped fresh tarragon leaves	1 tablespoon olive or vegetable oil

1. Heat oven to 375°F. Spray 13×9-inch (3-quart) glass baking dish with cooking spray.

2. Pat salmon dry with paper towel. Place salmon, skin side down, in baking dish. Sprinkle with salt.

3. In small bowl, mix parsley, tarragon and lemon peel. Press mixture evenly on salmon. In same bowl, mix orange juice, vinegar and oil; set aside.

4. Bake uncovered 10 minutes. Pour juice mixture over salmon; bake 10 to 15 minutes longer or until fish flakes easily with fork. Serve salmon with orange sauce from pan.

1 Serving: Calories 230 (Calories from Fat 90); Total Fat 10g (Saturated Fat 2.5g; Trans Fat 0g); Cholesterol 95mg; Sodium 240mg; Total Carbohydrate 3g (Dietary Fiber 0g; Sugars 2g); Protein 31g   **% Daily Value:** Vitamin A 15%; Vitamin C 15%; Calcium 4%; Iron 8%   **Exchanges:** 4 Lean Meat   **Carbohydrate Choices:** 0

wise food choices

Don't eliminate meats from your diet, but try to choose cuts that have more of the "good stuff" and less of the "not-so-good stuff." Here are some tips to get you started.

- Look for lean beef cuts such as round steak, sirloin tip, tenderloin and extra-lean ground beef. Tenderloin, loin chops, center cut ham and Canadian bacon are leaner cuts of pork.
- Chicken or turkey breast meat has fewer calories than dark meat. Half the calories are in the skin, so purchase skinless poultry or remove the skin before eating.
- You might want to try something new like bison, venison, ostrich, rabbit and pheasant—they're all lean choices.
- Fish and shellfish tend to contain less fat than meat and poultry.

broiled salmon with orange-mustard glaze

Prep Time: 5 Minutes   Start to Finish: 20 Minutes   Makes: 4 servings

1 lb salmon or other medium-firm fish fillets	2 teaspoons mustard seed
2 tablespoons orange marmalade	¼ teaspoon salt
	⅛ teaspoon red pepper sauce

1. Set oven control to broil. Spray broiler pan rack with cooking spray. Place salmon, skin side down, on rack in broiler pan. Broil with tops 4 inches from heat 10 to 15 minutes or until fish flakes easily with fork.

2. Meanwhile, in small bowl, mix remaining ingredients. Spread on salmon during last 5 minutes of broiling.

1 Serving: Calories 190 (Calories from Fat 60); Total Fat 7g (Saturated Fat 2g; Trans Fat 0g); Cholesterol 75mg; Sodium 220mg; Total Carbohydrate 7g (Dietary Fiber 0g; Sugars 5g); Protein 25g   **% Daily Value:** Vitamin A 2%; Vitamin C 2%; Calcium 2%; Iron 6%   **Exchanges:** ½ Other Carbohydrate, 3½ Lean Meat   **Carbohydrate Choices:** ½

health smart

Not only is salmon delicious, but it contains omega-3 fatty acids that may be helpful in many ways, including possibly reducing the risk of heart disease.

snapper with sautéed tomato pepper sauce

Prep Time: 20 Minutes   Start to Finish: 20 Minutes   Makes: 4 servings

1 lb red snapper, cod or other medium-firm fish fillets (about 1 inch thick)	1 small onion, sliced
½ teaspoon salt	2 tablespoons finely chopped fresh cilantro or parsley
1 large tomato, chopped (1 cup)	¼ cup dry white wine or chicken broth
1 small bell pepper (any color), chopped (½ cup)	Additional chopped fresh cilantro or parsley, if desired

1. If fish fillets are large, cut into 4 serving pieces; sprinkle with ¼ teaspoon of the salt. Spray 10-inch skillet with cooking spray; heat over medium heat. Arrange fish in single layer in skillet. Cook uncovered 4 to 6 minutes, turning once, until fish flakes easily with fork. Remove fish; keep warm.

2. In same skillet, cook tomato, bell pepper, onion and cilantro over medium heat 3 to 5 minutes, stirring frequently, until bell pepper and onion are crisp-tender. Stir in wine and remaining ¼ teaspoon salt; cook about 1 minute or until hot. Spoon tomato mixture over fish. Sprinkle with cilantro.

1 Serving: Calories 140 (Calories from Fat 20); Total Fat 2g (Saturated Fat 0.5g; Trans Fat 0g); Cholesterol 60mg; Sodium 900mg; Total Carbohydrate 5g (Dietary Fiber 1g; Sugars 2g); Protein 24g   **% Daily Value:** Vitamin A 10%; Vitamin C 20%; Calcium 4%; Iron 4%   **Exchanges:** ½ Other Carbohydrate, 3½ Very Lean Meat   **Carbohydrate Choices:** ½

cajun oven-fried trout

Prep Time: 10 Minutes   Start to Finish: 20 Minutes   Makes: 4 servings

1 lb trout or other medium-firm fish fillets, about ¾ inch thick	⅓ cup unseasoned dry bread crumbs
¼ cup buttermilk or fat-free (skim) milk	1 teaspoon Cajun or Creole seasoning
1 egg white, slightly beaten	Butter-flavored cooking spray
⅓ cup yellow cornmeal	Lemon wedges, if desired

1. Move oven rack to position slightly above middle of oven. Heat oven to 500°F. Remove and discard skin from fish. Cut fish into 2×1½-inch pieces.

2. In small bowl, mix buttermilk and egg white with fork. In another small bowl, mix cornmeal, bread crumbs and Cajun seasoning. Dip fish into buttermilk mixture, then coat with cornmeal mixture. Place in ungreased 13×9-inch pan. Lightly spray cooking spray on fish.

3. Bake about 10 minutes or until fish flakes easily with fork. Serve with lemon wedges.

1 Serving: Calories 250 (Calories from Fat 80); Total Fat 9g (Saturated Fat 1.5g; Trans Fat 0g); Cholesterol 65mg; Sodium 290mg; Total Carbohydrate 16g (Dietary Fiber 0g; Sugars 1g); Protein 27g **% Daily Value:** Vitamin A 0%; Vitamin C 0%; Calcium 8%; Iron 15% **Exchanges:** 1 Starch, 3 Very Lean Meat, 1½ Fat **Carbohydrate Choices:** 1

health smart

Trout is a source of vitamin B12, which is helpful for keeping our cells working well and for other important functions.

graham-crusted tilapia

Prep Time: 15 Minutes   Start to Finish: 25 Minutes   Makes: 4 servings

1	lb tilapia, cod, haddock or other medium-firm fish fillets, about ¾ inch thick	¼	teaspoon salt
½	cup graham cracker crumbs (about 8 squares)	⅛	teaspoon pepper
1	teaspoon grated lemon peel	¼	cup fat-free (skim) milk
		2	tablespoons canola oil
		2	tablespoons chopped toasted pecans*

1. Move oven rack to position slightly above middle of oven. Heat oven to 500°F.

2. Cut fish fillets crosswise into 2-inch-wide pieces. In shallow dish, mix cracker crumbs, lemon peel, salt and pepper. Place milk in another shallow dish.

3. Dip fish into milk, then coat with cracker mixture. Place in ungreased 13×9-inch pan. Drizzle oil over fish; sprinkle with pecans.

4. Bake about 10 minutes or until fish flakes easily with fork.

***Note:** To toast pecans, heat oven to 350°F. Spread pecans in ungreased shallow pan. Bake uncovered 6 to 10 minutes, stirring occasionally, until light brown. Or sprinkle in ungreased heavy skillet. Cook over medium heat 5 to 7 minutes, stirring frequently until pecans begin to brown, then stirring constantly until light brown.

1 Serving: Calories 230 (Calories from Fat 100); Total Fat 12g (Saturated Fat 1.5g; Trans Fat 0g); Cholesterol 60mg; Sodium 300mg; Total Carbohydrate 9g (Dietary Fiber 0g; Sugars 5g); Protein 23g **% Daily Value:** Vitamin A 0%; Vitamin C 0%; Calcium 4%; Iron 4% **Exchanges:** ½ Starch, 3 Lean Meat, ½ Fat **Carbohydrate Choices:** ½

180 calories

mediterranean sole with ratatouille

Prep Time: 20 Minutes   Start to Finish: 30 Minutes   Makes: 4 servings

1 medium bell pepper (any color), chopped (1 cup)	1 can (14.5 oz) organic diced tomatoes with garlic and onion, undrained
1 medium onion, cut into 8 wedges, separated	4 teaspoons chopped fresh or 2 teaspoons dried oregano leaves
1 small bulb fennel, thinly sliced	¾ lb sole, orange roughy or other delicate- to medium-firm fish fillets (about ¼ inch thick)
1 small eggplant (1 lb), peeled, cut into ½-inch cubes	Feta cheese, if desired

1. Spray 12-inch skillet with cooking spray; heat over medium heat. Add bell pepper, onion and fennel; cook about 5 minutes, stirring frequently, until vegetables are crisp-tender.

2. Stir in eggplant, tomatoes and 2 teaspoons of the oregano; reduce heat to medium-low. Cover; cook 15 minutes, stirring frequently.

3. Cut fish fillets into 4 serving pieces. Roll up each piece, beginning at narrow end, and secure with toothpicks; sprinkle with remaining 2 teaspoons oregano. Place fish rolls, seam side down, in eggplant mixture. Cover; cook about 8 minutes or until fish flakes easily with fork.

4. Using slotted spoon, remove fish to serving platter. Remove toothpicks. Serve eggplant mixture with fish. Sprinkle with cheese.

1 Serving: Calories 180 (Calories from Fat 15); Total Fat 1.5g (Saturated Fat 0g; Trans Fat 0g); Cholesterol 40mg; Sodium 390mg; Total Carbohydrate 24g (Dietary Fiber 6g; Sugars 12g); Protein 17g **% Daily Value:** Vitamin A 25%; Vitamin C 60%; Calcium 8%; Iron 10% **Exchanges:** 1 Other Carbohydrate, 2 Vegetable, 2 Very Lean Meat **Carbohydrate Choices:** 1½

spinach-filled fish rolls

Prep Time: 10 Minutes   Start to Finish: 30 Minutes   Makes: 4 servings

1 lb sole, orange roughy or other delicate- to medium-firm fish fillets	⅓ cup fat-free mayonnaise or salad dressing
1½ cups firmly packed fresh spinach leaves	½ teaspoon Dijon mustard
¼ teaspoon garlic salt	¼ cup garlic-flavored croutons, crushed Lemon wedges, if desired

1. Heat oven to 400°F. Spray 8-inch square (2-quart) glass baking dish with cooking spray.

2. If fish fillets are large, cut fillets into 4 serving pieces. Place spinach on fish; sprinkle with garlic salt. Roll up each fillet, beginning at narrow end. Place rolls, with points underneath, in baking dish. In small bowl, mix mayonnaise and mustard; spoon onto each fish roll. Sprinkle with crushed croutons.

3. Bake uncovered 15 to 20 minutes or until fish flakes easily with fork. Serve with lemon wedges.

1 Serving: Calories 120 (Calories from Fat 20); Total Fat 2.5g (Saturated Fat 1g; Trans Fat 0g); Cholesterol 55mg; Sodium 360mg; Total Carbohydrate 5g (Dietary Fiber 0g; Sugars 2g); Protein 20g   **% Daily Value:** Vitamin A 20%; Vitamin C 2%; Calcium 2%; Iron 4%   **Exchanges:** 1 Vegetable, 2½ Very Lean Meat   **Carbohydrate Choices:** 0

health smart

Lean white fish like the sole in this recipe is a great choice if you are trying to replace some of the meat in your diet with fish. Other great choices are halibut, orange roughy, flounder and cod. With a subtle yet distinct flavor, these fish lend themselves to countless menu options and are fairly low in fat and calories.

220 calories

shrimp and scallops in wine sauce

Prep Time: 20 Minutes   Start to Finish: 20 Minutes   Makes: 4 servings

2 tablespoons olive or vegetable oil	1 lb uncooked deveined peeled medium shrimp, thawed if frozen, tail shells removed
1 clove garlic, finely chopped	
2 medium green onions, sliced (2 tablespoons)	1 lb sea scallops, cut in half
2 medium carrots, thinly sliced (1 cup)	½ cup dry white wine or chicken broth
1 tablespoon chopped fresh or 1 teaspoon parsley flakes	1 tablespoon lemon juice
	¼ to ½ teaspoon crushed red pepper flakes

1. In 12-inch nonstick skillet, heat oil over medium heat. Cook garlic, onions, carrots and parsley in oil about 5 minutes, stirring occasionally, until carrots are crisp-tender.

2. Stir in remaining ingredients. Cook 4 to 5 minutes, stirring frequently, until shrimp are pink and scallops are white and opaque.

1 Serving: Calories 220 (Calories from Fat 80); Total Fat 9g (Saturated Fat 1.5g; Trans Fat 0g); Cholesterol 190mg; Sodium 490mg; Total Carbohydrate 4g (Dietary Fiber 1g; Sugars 2g); Protein 31g   **% Daily Value:** Vitamin A 110%; Vitamin C 6%; Calcium 10%; Iron 25%   **Exchanges:** 4 Lean Meat   **Carbohydrate Choices:** 0

corn 'n crab cakes

Prep Time: 20 Minutes   Start to Finish: 1 Hour   Makes: 4 servings

½ cup frozen whole kernel corn, thawed	2 cans (6 oz each) white crabmeat, drained, cartilage removed
4 medium green onions, chopped (¼ cup)	1 egg or 2 egg whites
⅓ cup fat-free mayonnaise or salad dressing	2 tablespoons water
1 tablespoon 40%-less-sodium taco seasoning mix	½ cup unseasoned dry bread crumbs
	3 tablespoons chunky-style salsa

1. Line cookie sheet with waxed paper. In medium bowl, mix corn, onions, mayonnaise, taco seasoning mix and crabmeat. Shape into 8 patties, using slightly less than ¼ cup for each. Place on cookie sheet; freeze 15 minutes.

2. Heat oven to 450°F. Spray another cookie sheet with cooking spray. In shallow bowl, beat egg and water with wire whisk or fork until blended. Place bread crumbs in another shallow bowl.

3. Dip each patty into egg mixture, coating both sides, then coat with bread crumbs. Place on sprayed cookie sheet. Bake 15 minutes; turn patties. Bake about 10 minutes longer or until golden brown. Serve with salsa.

1 Serving: Calories 180 (Calories from Fat 35); Total Fat 3.5g (Saturated Fat 1g; Trans Fat 0g); Cholesterol 120mg; Sodium 690mg; Total Carbohydrate 19g (Dietary Fiber 2g; Sugars 4g); Protein 19g   **% Daily Value:** Vitamin A 6%; Vitamin C 4%; Calcium 10%; Iron 10%   **Exchanges:** 1 Starch, 2½ Very Lean Meat, ½ Fat   **Carbohydrate Choices:** 1

try this

Use a fork or small spatula to turn the patties when coating them with the egg mixture and bread crumbs.

savory
skillet
meals

There are so many reasons to love skillet meals—they're simple, tasty and satisfying. With the delicious options in this chapter, you can add one more reason to the list: They're healthy.

summer garden chicken stir-fry

photo on page C-2

Prep Time: 30 Minutes   Start to Finish: 30 Minutes   Makes: 4 servings

1	lb boneless skinless chicken breasts, cut into 1-inch pieces	3	tablespoons reduced-sodium soy sauce
2	cloves garlic, finely chopped	2	to 3 teaspoons sugar
2	teaspoons finely chopped gingerroot	2	cups fresh broccoli florets
1	medium onion, cut into thin wedges	1	cup sliced fresh mushrooms (3 oz)
1	cup ready-to-eat baby-cut carrots, cut lengthwise in half	½	cup chopped bell pepper (any color)
1	cup fat-free chicken broth	2	teaspoons cornstarch
			Hot cooked brown rice, if desired

1. Heat 12-inch nonstick skillet over medium-high heat. Add chicken, garlic and gingerroot; cook and stir 2 to 3 minutes or until chicken is brown.

2. Stir in onion, carrots, ¾ cup of the broth, the soy sauce and sugar. Cover and cook over medium heat 5 minutes, stirring occasionally.

3. Stir in broccoli, mushrooms and bell pepper. Cover and cook about 5 minutes, stirring occasionally, until chicken is no longer pink in center and vegetables are crisp-tender.

4. In small bowl, mix cornstarch and remaining ¼ cup broth; stir into chicken mixture. Cook, stirring frequently, until sauce is thickened. Serve over rice.

1 Serving: Calories 200 (Calories from Fat 35); Total Fat 4g (Saturated Fat 1g; Trans Fat 0g); Cholesterol 70mg; Sodium 610mg; Total Carbohydrate 15g (Dietary Fiber 4g; Sugars 8g); Protein 28g   **% Daily Value:** Vitamin A 150%; Vitamin C 70%; Calcium 6%; Iron 10%   **Exchanges:** ½ Starch, 1 Vegetable, 3½ Very Lean Meat, ½ Fat   **Carbohydrate Choices:** 1

try this

Look for jars of minced or chopped garlic in water in the produce section. Check the jar to see how much equals 2 cloves of garlic, since amounts can differ. The fresh flavor and convenience can't be beat.

coconut curry chicken

Prep Time: 15 Minutes   Start to Finish: 25 Minutes   Makes: 4 servings

1   tablespoon curry powder
¾   lb boneless skinless chicken breasts
1   teaspoon vegetable oil
1   small onion, cut into 2×¼-inch strips
1   small zucchini, cut into ¼-inch slices
1   medium bell pepper (any color), cut
      into ¾-inch squares

⅓   cup light unsweetened coconut milk
1   tablespoon brown bean sauce
1   teaspoon grated gingerroot
½   teaspoon salt
2   tablespoons shredded coconut,
      toasted*

1. Rub curry powder on chicken. Cut chicken into ¾-inch pieces. Let stand 10 minutes.

2. Spray wok or 12-inch skillet with cooking spray; heat over medium-high heat until cooking spray starts to bubble. Add chicken; stir-fry 2 minutes. Move chicken to side of wok.

3. Add oil to center of wok. Add onion, zucchini and bell pepper; stir-fry 2 minutes. Add coconut milk, bean sauce, gingerroot and salt; cook and stir until sauce coats vegetables and chicken and is heated through. Sprinkle with toasted coconut.

*Note: To toast coconut, sprinkle in ungreased heavy skillet. Cook over medium-low heat 6 to 14 minutes, stirring frequently until browning begins, then stiring constantly until golden brown.

1 Serving: Calories 170 (Calories from Fat 60); Total Fat 6g (Saturated Fat 3g; Trans Fat 0g); Cholesterol 55mg; Sodium 400mg; Total Carbohydrate 8g (Dietary Fiber 2g; Sugars 4g); Protein 20g   **% Daily Value:** Vitamin A 4%; Vitamin C 25%; Calcium 2%; Iron 8%   **Exchanges:** 1 Vegetable, 2½ Lean Meat   **Carbohydrate Choices:** ½

health smart

Toasted coconut adds an exotic tropical flavor but does contain a fair amount of fat. This recipe uses just a small amount of toasted coconut along with reduced-fat coconut milk, so you can enjoy the flavor without excess fat and calories.

spinach and chicken skillet

Prep Time: 25 Minutes   **Start to Finish:** 25 Minutes   **Makes:** 6 servings

6 boneless skinless chicken breasts (about 1¾ lb)	1 bag (10 oz) fresh spinach, stems removed, chopped
1 cup fat-free (skim) milk	¼ teaspoon salt
½ cup fat-free chicken broth	¼ teaspoon pepper
1 medium onion, chopped (½ cup)	¼ teaspoon ground nutmeg Additional pepper, if desired

1. Heat 12-inch nonstick skillet over medium heat. Cook chicken in skillet 2 minutes on each side; reduce heat to medium-low. Stir in milk, broth and onion. Cook about 5 minutes, turning chicken occasionally, until onion is tender.

2. Stir in spinach. Cook 3 to 4 minutes, stirring occasionally, until spinach is completely wilted and juice of chicken is clear when center of thickest part is cut (170°F). Remove chicken from skillet; keep warm.

3. Increase heat to medium. Cook spinach mixture about 3 minutes or until liquid has almost evaporated. Stir in salt, pepper and nutmeg. Serve chicken on spinach. Sprinkle with additional pepper.

1 Serving: Calories 190 (Calories from Fat 40); Total Fat 4.5g (Saturated Fat 1.5g; Trans Fat 0g); Cholesterol 80mg; Sodium 260mg; Total Carbohydrate 5g (Dietary Fiber 1g; Sugars 3g); Protein 32g   **% Daily Value:** Vitamin A 90%; Vitamin C 10%; Calcium 10%; Iron 15%   **Exchanges:** 1 Vegetable, 4½ Very Lean Meat, ½ Fat   **Carbohydrate Choices:** ½

health smart

Milk is an excellent source of calcium and vitamin D, great nutrients for healthy bones and teeth as well as possible prevention of osteoporosis.

240 calories

savory chicken and rice

Prep Time: 35 Minutes   Start to Finish: 35 Minutes   Makes: 4 servings

1	lb boneless skinless chicken breasts, cut into 1-inch pieces
1½	cups sliced fresh mushrooms (4 oz)
1	cup ready-to-eat baby-cut carrots
1⅔	cups water
1	package (4.3 oz) long grain and wild rice mix with herbs

1. Heat 10-inch nonstick skillet over medium heat. Cook chicken in skillet about 5 minutes, stirring occasionally, until no longer pink in center. Stir in remaining ingredients including seasonings from rice mix.

2. Heat to boiling; reduce heat to low. Cover and simmer 15 minutes, stirring occasionally. Uncover and simmer about 3 minutes longer, stirring occasionally, until carrots are tender and liquid is absorbed.

1 Serving: Calories 240 (Calories from Fat 35); Total Fat 4g (Saturated Fat 1g; Trans Fat 0g); Cholesterol 70mg; Sodium 360mg; Total Carbohydrate 25g (Dietary Fiber 2g; Sugars 2g); Protein 28g   **% Daily Value:** Vitamin A 120%; Vitamin C 2%; Calcium 4%; Iron 10%   **Exchanges:** 1½ Starch, 3½ Very Lean Meat   **Carbohydrate Choices:** 1½

health smart
Carrots are a tasty low-fat, low-calorie source of fiber and vitamin A.

moroccan skillet chicken

photo on page C-4

Prep Time: 10 Minutes   Start to Finish: 30 Minutes   Makes: 4 servings

1	tablespoon olive or vegetable oil	3	small zucchini, cut into ½-inch slices (2 cups)
4	boneless skinless chicken breasts (1 lb)	1	medium bell pepper (any color), sliced
1	teaspoon salt	1½	teaspoons ground cumin
1	can (14.5 oz) diced tomatoes, drained	½	teaspoon ground cinnamon
1	can (2.25 oz) sliced ripe olives, drained	1	teaspoon grated lemon peel

1. In 12-inch nonstick skillet, heat oil over medium-high heat. Sprinkle chicken with ½ teaspoon of the salt; add to skillet. Cook about 5 minutes, turning once, until brown.

2. In medium bowl, mix tomatoes, olives, zucchini, bell pepper, cumin, cinnamon and remaining ½ teaspoon salt; pour over chicken in skillet.

3. Heat to boiling; reduce heat. Cover; simmer 15 to 20 minutes or until juice of chicken is clear when center of thickest part is cut (170°F). Sprinkle with lemon peel.

1 Serving: Calories 250 (Calories from Fat 90); Total Fat 10g (Saturated Fat 2g; Trans Fat 0g); Cholesterol 85mg; Sodium 940mg; Total Carbohydrate 10g (Dietary Fiber 3g; Sugars 5g); Protein 32g   **% Daily Value:** Vitamin A 20%; Vitamin C 60%; Calcium 8%; Iron 15%   **Exchanges:** 2 Vegetable, 4 Very Lean Meat, 1½ Fat   **Carbohydrate Choices:** ½

serve with
Team this savory chicken dish with whole wheat couscous tossed with raisins and toasted slivered almonds.

home-style chicken dinner

Prep Time: 35 Minutes   Start to Finish: 35 Minutes   Makes: 4 servings

1	tablespoon olive or vegetable oil	1	jar (12 oz) home-style chicken gravy
1	teaspoon finely chopped garlic	1	bag (1 lb) frozen broccoli florets, cauliflower and carrots (or other combination)
4	boneless skinless chicken breasts (about 1¼ lb)		
¼	teaspoon salt	½	cup halved grape or cherry tomatoes
¼	teaspoon pepper		

1. In 12-inch skillet, heat oil over medium heat. Add garlic; cook 1 to 2 minutes, stirring frequently. Sprinkle chicken with salt and pepper; add to skillet. Cook 15 to 20 minutes, turning once, until juice of chicken is clear when center of thickest part is cut (170°F). Remove chicken from skillet; cover to keep warm.

2. In same skillet, mix gravy, frozen vegetables and the tomatoes. Cover; cook 6 to 8 minutes, stirring occasionally, until vegetables are crisp-tender.

3. Return chicken to skillet. Cover; simmer about 2 minutes or until chicken is thoroughly heated.

1 Serving: Calories 300 (Calories from Fat 120); Total Fat 13g (Saturated Fat 3g; Trans Fat 0g); Cholesterol 85mg; Sodium 740mg; Total Carbohydrate 12g (Dietary Fiber 4g; Sugars 3g); Protein 36g   **% Daily Value:** Vitamin A 70%; Vitamin C 35%; Calcium 6%; Iron 10%   **Exchanges:** ½ Starch, 1 Vegetable, 4½ Very Lean Meat, 2 Fat   **Carbohydrate Choices:** 1

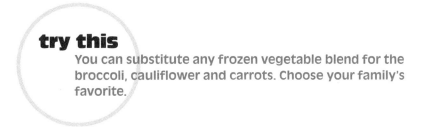

try this
You can substitute any frozen vegetable blend for the broccoli, cauliflower and carrots. Choose your family's favorite.

chicken with thyme and mixed vegetables

Prep Time: 30 Minutes   Start to Finish: 30 Minutes   Makes: 4 servings

2	teaspoons chopped fresh or ½ teaspoon dried thyme leaves	1	tablespoon butter or margarine
½	teaspoon salt	1	tablespoon olive or vegetable oil
⅛	teaspoon pepper	1	teaspoon finely chopped garlic
4	boneless skinless chicken breasts (about 1¼ lb)	1	bag (1 lb) frozen broccoli florets, cauliflower and carrots (or other combination)

1. In small bowl, mix thyme, salt and pepper; sprinkle over chicken and set aside.

2. In 12-inch skillet, heat butter and oil over medium heat. Add garlic; cook 1 to 2 minutes, stirring frequently. Add chicken; cook uncovered 8 to 12 minutes, turning once, until light golden brown.

3. Stir in frozen vegetables. Cover; cook 6 to 8 minutes, stirring occasionally, until vegetables are hot and crisp-tender, and juice of chicken is clear when center of thickest part is cut (170°F).

1 Serving: Calories 260 (Calories from Fat 100); Total Fat 11g (Saturated Fat 3.5g; Trans Fat 0g); Cholesterol 95mg; Sodium 420mg; Total Carbohydrate 6g (Dietary Fiber 3g; Sugars 2g); Protein 34g   **% Daily Value:** Vitamin A 50%; Vitamin C 30%; Calcium 4%; Iron 10%   **Exchanges:** 1 Vegetable, 4 Lean Meat   **Carbohydrate Choices:** ½

try this

Try using 4 cups cut-up assorted fresh vegetables, such as carrots, bell peppers, onions, broccoli and yellow summer squash, or whatever you have on hand, instead of the frozen vegetables.

260 calories

chicken with mushrooms and carrots

Prep Time: 30 Minutes   Start to Finish: 30 Minutes   Makes: 4 servings

4 slices bacon, chopped	1 tablespoon cornstarch
4 boneless skinless chicken breasts (about 1¼ lb)	2 teaspoons chopped fresh or ½ teaspoon dried thyme leaves
¼ teaspoon pepper	¼ teaspoon salt
2 cups ready-to-eat baby-cut carrots	4 oz small fresh mushrooms, cut in half (about 1⅓ cups)
1 cup chicken broth	
¼ cup dry white wine or chicken broth	

1. In 12-inch nonstick skillet, cook bacon over medium heat 6 to 8 minutes, stirring occasionally, until crisp. Remove bacon to paper towel to drain.

2. Add chicken to bacon drippings in skillet; sprinkle with pepper. Cook over medium heat 4 to 5 minutes, turning once, until well browned. Add carrots and ¼ cup of the broth. Cover; cook 7 to 9 minutes or until carrots are crisp-tender and juice of chicken is clear when center of thickest part is cut (170°F).

3. In small bowl, place remaining ¾ cup broth. Add wine, cornstarch, thyme and salt; mix well. Add broth mixture and mushrooms to skillet. Cook 3 to 5 minutes, stirring once or twice, until bubbly. Cover; cook about 3 minutes longer or until mushrooms are tender. Sprinkle with bacon.

1 Serving: Calories 260 (Calories from Fat 80); Total Fat 8g (Saturated Fat 2.5g; Trans Fat 0g); Cholesterol 95mg; Sodium 710mg; Total Carbohydrate 9g (Dietary Fiber 2g; Sugars 3g); Protein 37g   **% Daily Value:** Vitamin A 150%; Vitamin C 4%; Calcium 4%; Iron 10%   **Exchanges:** ½ Other Carbohydrate, 1 Vegetable, 5 Very Lean Meat, 1 Fat **Carbohydrate Choices:** ½

chicken and ravioli carbonara

Prep Time: 25 Minutes   Start to Finish: 25 Minutes   Makes: 4 servings

2 tablespoons fat-free Italian dressing	½ cup fat-free half-and-half
¾ lb boneless skinless chicken breasts, cut into ½-inch strips	3 slices bacon, crisply cooked, crumbled
¾ cup chicken broth	Shredded Parmesan cheese, if desired
1 package (9 oz) refrigerated cheese-filled ravioli	Chopped fresh parsley, if desired

1. In 10-inch skillet, heat dressing over high heat. Cook chicken in dressing 2 to 4 minutes, turning occasionally, until brown.

2. Add broth and ravioli to skillet. Heat to boiling; reduce heat to medium. Cook uncovered about 4 minutes or until ravioli are tender and almost all broth has evaporated.

3. Stir in half-and-half; reduce heat. Simmer uncovered 3 to 5 minutes or until chicken is no longer pink in center, and sauce is hot and desired consistency (cook longer for a thicker sauce). Sprinkle with bacon, cheese and parsley.

1 Serving: Calories 280 (Calories from Fat 100); Total Fat 11g (Saturated Fat 4.5g; Trans Fat 0g); Cholesterol 125mg; Sodium 1010mg; Total Carbohydrate 14g (Dietary Fiber 0g; Sugars 3g); Protein 30g   **% Daily Value:** Vitamin A 4%; Vitamin C 0%; Calcium 15%; Iron 10%   **Exchanges:** 1 Starch, 4 Lean Meat   **Carbohydrate Choices:** 1

try this

For a splash of vibrant color and some extra vitamins A and C, cut one red or orange bell pepper into ¼-inch strips and add to the skillet with the broth and ravioli.

creamy chicken-
noodle skillet

Prep Time: 15 Minutes   Start to Finish: 25 Minutes   Makes: 4 servings

1   tablespoon canola oil
1   lb boneless skinless chicken breasts,
       cut into 1-inch pieces
1   medium onion, chopped (½ cup)
1   cup ready-to-eat baby-cut carrots,
       cut lengthwise in half

1   cup frozen broccoli cuts
1   cup uncooked egg noodles (2 oz)
1   can (14 oz) chicken broth
1   can (10¾ oz) condensed 98% fat-free
       cream of chicken soup with 45% less
       sodium

1. In 12-inch nonstick skillet, heat oil over medium-high heat. Cook chicken and onion in oil 6 to 8 minutes, stirring frequently, until chicken is brown and onion is just tender.

2. Stir in remaining ingredients. Heat to boiling; reduce heat. Cover; simmer 10 minutes. Uncover; simmer 5 to 8 minutes longer, stirring occasionally, until noodles are tender.

1 Serving: Calories 300 (Calories from Fat 90); Total Fat 10g (Saturated Fat 2g; Trans Fat 0g); Cholesterol 80mg; Sodium 800mg; Total Carbohydrate 23g (Dietary Fiber 3g; Sugars 3g); Protein 32g   **% Daily Value:** Vitamin A 120%; Vitamin C 20%; Calcium 6%; Iron 15%   **Exchanges:** 1½ Starch, 4 Very Lean Meat, 1 Fat   **Carbohydrate Choices:** 1½

10 essential items for a healthy pantry

What can you keep on hand for healthy eating when you don't have much time to cook? Try stocking your pantry with these:

1. Canned beans: pinto, black, chickpeas, soybeans
2. Canned water-packed fruits
3. Canned water-packed tuna
4. Canola oil or olive oil
5. Dried fruits: cranberries, raisins, apricots, bananas
6. Peanut butter
7. Ready-to-eat baby-cut carrots
8. Ready-to-eat whole-grain cereals
9. Whole grains: quick-cooking whole wheat couscous, whole wheat pasta, brown rice, barley, bulgur wheat, old-fashioned oatmeal
10. Yogurt

cheesy chicken skillet dinner

Prep Time: 20 Minutes   Start to Finish: 20 Minutes   Makes: 6 servings

1	teaspoon canola or vegetable oil	1	medium zucchini, cut into ⅛-inch slices (2 cups)
1¼	lb boneless skinless chicken breasts, cut into ¾-inch pieces	2	tablespoons soy sauce
2	large carrots, cut into ⅛-inch slices (2 cups)	8	medium green onions, sliced (½ cup)
		2	cups shredded reduced-fat sharp Cheddar cheese (8 oz)

1. In 12-inch nonstick skillet, heat oil over medium-high heat. Add chicken; cook 4 to 5 minutes, stirring frequently, or until no longer pink in center. Remove from skillet.

2. Add carrots and zucchini to skillet; cook 4 to 5 minutes, stirring frequently, or until crisp-tender. Add chicken and soy sauce; toss until chicken and vegetables are coated with soy sauce.

3. Sprinkle with onions and cheese. Cover; let stand until cheese is melted.

1 Serving: Calories 210 (Calories from Fat 60); Total Fat 7g (Saturated Fat 2.5g; Trans Fat 0g); Cholesterol 65mg; Sodium 730mg; Total Carbohydrate 6g (Dietary Fiber 1g; Sugars 3g); Protein 31g   **% Daily Value:** Vitamin A 90%; Vitamin C 8%; Calcium 30%; Iron 8%   **Exchanges:** ½ Other Carbohydrate, 3½ Lean Meat   **Carbohydrate Choices:** ½

serve with
Pair this cheesy dish with a side of whole wheat pasta or brown rice and a lettuce salad.

260 calories

turkey-mac skillet

Prep Time: 25 Minutes   Start to Finish: 25 Minutes   Makes: 6 servings

2	teaspoons canola oil	½	teaspoon salt
1¼	lb ground turkey breast		Dash pepper
1	cup uncooked wagon wheel pasta (2 oz)	2	medium stalks celery, thinly sliced (1 cup)
½	cup chunky-style salsa	1	medium tomato, chopped (¾ cup)
1	cup water	2	cans (8 oz each) tomato sauce

1. In 12-inch skillet, heat oil over medium-high heat. Cook turkey in oil 5 to 7 minutes, stirring occasionally, until no longer pink; drain.

2. Stir in remaining ingredients. Heat to boiling; reduce heat to low. Cover and simmer 8 to 10 minutes or until pasta is tender.

1 Serving: Calories 260 (Calories from Fat 70); Total Fat 7g (Saturated Fat 1.5g; Trans Fat 0g); Cholesterol 65mg; Sodium 830mg; Total Carbohydrate 25g (Dietary Fiber 3g; Sugars 4g); Protein 25g   **% Daily Value:** Vitamin A 20%; Vitamin C 15%; Calcium 4%; Iron 15%   **Exchanges:** 1½ Starch, 1 Vegetable, 2½ Lean Meat   **Carbohydrate Choices:** 1½

health smart

To increase the vitamin, mineral and fiber content in this recipe, choose whole wheat or multigrain pasta and stir in some cooked kidney, pinto or black beans in step 2.

smoked turkey and couscous

Prep Time: 15 Minutes   Start to Finish: 25 Minutes   Makes: 4 servings

1 can (14 oz) chicken broth	1½ teaspoons chopped fresh or
2 cups fresh broccoli florets	½ teaspoon dried tarragon leaves
1 cup cut-up smoked turkey	½ cup uncooked couscous
	½ cup shredded Cheddar cheese (2 oz)

1. In 10-inch skillet, heat broth to boiling. Stir in broccoli, turkey and tarragon. Cover; cook 3 to 4 minutes or until broccoli is crisp-tender.

2. Stir couscous into turkey mixture; remove from heat. Cover; let stand about 5 minutes or until liquid is absorbed.

3. Fluff couscous mixture with fork. Sprinkle with cheese. Cover; let stand 3 to 5 minutes or until cheese is melted.

1 Serving: Calories 210 (Calories from Fat 60); Total Fat 7g (Saturated Fat 3.5g; Trans Fat 0g); Cholesterol 30mg; Sodium 940mg; Total Carbohydrate 21g (Dietary Fiber 2g; Sugars 2g); Protein 15g   **% Daily Value:** Vitamin A 8%; Vitamin C 35%; Calcium 10%; Iron 6%   **Exchanges:** 1 Starch, 1 Vegetable, 1½ Medium-Fat Meat   **Carbohydrate Choices:** 1½

teriyaki beef stir-fry

Prep Time: 30 Minutes   Start to Finish: 30 Minutes   Makes: 6 servings

1   lb extra-lean (at least 90%)
       ground beef
2   teaspoons soy sauce
1   teaspoon finely chopped gingerroot
¼   cup sliced green onions (4 medium)
1   clove garlic, finely chopped
1   small bell pepper (any color), thinly
       sliced

½   large red onion, thinly sliced
2   stalks bok choy, cut into 1-inch slices
       (1 cup)
1   cup teriyaki marinade (from 12-oz
       bottle)
1   package (8 oz) Chinese noodles or
       spaghetti

1. In large bowl, mix beef, soy sauce, ½ teaspoon of the gingerroot, the green onions and garlic.

2. Into 10-inch skillet, spoon beef mixture by rounded tablespoonfuls. Cook over medium-high heat about 6 minutes, turning occasionally with spatula, until beef is no longer pink in center. Remove beef from skillet; keep warm. Drain drippings, reserving 1 tablespoon.

3. In same skillet, cook remaining ½ teaspoon gingerroot in drippings over medium-high heat 30 seconds. Add bell pepper, red onion and bok choy. Cook, stirring occasionally, until crisp-tender. Stir in teriyaki marinade.

4. Return beef to skillet; cook until hot. Meanwhile, cook and drain noodles as directed on package. Serve beef mixture over noodles.

1 Serving: Calories 290 (Calories from Fat 60); Total Fat 6g (Saturated Fat 2.5g; Trans Fat 0g); Cholesterol 45mg; Sodium 2170mg; Total Carbohydrate 38g (Dietary Fiber 1g; Sugars 7g); Protein 20g   **% Daily Value:** Vitamin A 20%; Vitamin C 20%; Calcium 4%; Iron 15%   **Exchanges:** 2 Starch, ½ Other Carbohydrate, 2 Lean Meat   **Carbohydrate Choices:** 2½

beef and kasha mexicana

Prep Time: 25 Minutes   Start to Finish: 25 Minutes   Makes: 6 servings

1	lb extra-lean (at least 90%) ground beef	2	cups frozen whole kernel corn, thawed
1	small onion, chopped (½ cup)	1½	cups water
1	cup uncooked buckwheat kernels or groats (kasha)	1	cup shredded reduced-fat Cheddar cheese (4 oz)
1	can (14.5 oz) diced tomatoes, undrained	2	tablespoons chopped fresh cilantro, if desired
1	can (4.5 oz) chopped green chiles, undrained	2	tablespoons sliced ripe olives, if desired
1	package (1 oz) 40%-less-sodium taco seasoning mix		

1. In 12-inch skillet, cook beef and onion over medium-high heat 5 to 7 minutes, stirring occasionally, until beef is thoroughly cooked; drain. Stir in kasha until kernels are moistened.

2. Stir in tomatoes, chiles, taco seasoning mix, corn and water. Heat to boiling; reduce heat to low. Cover; simmer 5 to 7 minutes, stirring occasionally, until kasha is tender.

3. Sprinkle with cheese. Cover; cook 2 to 3 minutes longer or until cheese is melted. Sprinkle with cilantro and olives.

1 Serving: Calories 300 (Calories from Fat 80); Total Fat 8g (Saturated Fat 3.5g; Trans Fat 0g); Cholesterol 50mg; Sodium 720mg; Total Carbohydrate 33g (Dietary Fiber 4g; Sugars 5g); Protein 23g   **% Daily Value:** Vitamin A 6%; Vitamin C 15%; Calcium 20%; Iron 20%   **Exchanges:** 1½ Starch, ½ Other Carbohydrate, 2½ Lean Meat
Carbohydrate Choices: 2

health smart

If you're trying to get the kids to eat more whole grains, the flavors in this dish are a great way to transition into them. Kasha, also known as buckwheat groats, has a hearty flavor and is a good source of magnesium and fiber.

beef in creamy mushroom sauce

Prep Time: 30 Minutes   Start to Finish: 30 Minutes   Makes: 6 servings

2 tablespoons cornstarch	1 medium bell pepper (any color), cut into 1-inch pieces
1 cup water	3 cups sliced fresh mushrooms (about 8 oz)
1 lb boneless beef sirloin steak, about ½ inch thick	¼ cup brandy or water
1 small onion, chopped (¼ cup)	1 teaspoon beef bouillon granules
1 clove garlic, finely chopped	2 tablespoons low-fat sour cream
¼ teaspoon salt	3 tablespoons chopped fresh chives
⅛ teaspoon pepper	3 cups hot cooked mostaccioli pasta

1. In small bowl, stir cornstarch into water; set aside. Trim excess fat from beef. Cut beef into thin strips, about 1½×½ inch.

2. Spray 10-inch skillet with cooking spray; heat over medium-high heat. Add onion, garlic, salt and pepper; cook about 3 minutes, stirring frequently, until onion is tender. Stir in beef and bell pepper. Cook about 4 minutes, stirring frequently, until beef is no longer pink.

3. Stir in mushrooms. Add brandy; sprinkle bouillon over beef mixture. Heat to boiling; reduce heat. Cover; simmer 1 minute. Stir in sour cream.

4. Stir cornstarch mixture into beef mixture. Cook over medium-high heat about 2 minutes, stirring frequently, until thickened. Stir in chives. Serve over pasta.

1 Serving: Calories 260 (Calories from Fat 40); Total Fat 4g (Saturated Fat 1.5g; Trans Fat 0g); Cholesterol 50mg; Sodium 370mg; Total Carbohydrate 28g (Dietary Fiber 2g; Sugars 2g); Protein 25g   **% Daily Value:** Vitamin A 15%; Vitamin C 25%; Calcium 0%; Iron 15%   **Exchanges:** 1½ Starch, 1 Vegetable, 2½ Lean Meat   **Carbohydrate Choices:** 2

mexican steak stir-fry

Prep Time: 25 Minutes   Start to Finish: 25 Minutes   Makes: 4 servings

¾ lb boneless beef sirloin steak, about ¾ inch thick
1 medium onion, chopped (½ cup)
½ cup chopped bell pepper (any color)
1 cup frozen whole kernel corn
½ cup salsa

1 medium zucchini, sliced (2 cups)
1 cup canned pinto beans, drained, rinsed
1 can (14.5 oz) no-salt-added whole tomatoes, undrained

1. Trim excess fat from beef. Cut beef with grain into 2-inch strips; cut strips across grain into ⅛-inch slices. (Beef is easier to cut if partially frozen, 30 to 60 minutes.)

2. Spray 12-inch skillet with cooking spray; heat over medium-high heat. Cook beef, onion and bell pepper 4 to 5 minutes, stirring frequently, until beef is brown.

3. Stir in remaining ingredients, breaking up tomatoes. Cook about 5 minutes, stirring occasionally, until zucchini is tender and mixture is hot.

1 Serving: Calories 270 (Calories from Fat 35); Total Fat 4g (Saturated Fat 1g; Trans Fat 0g); Cholesterol 55mg; Sodium 440mg; Total Carbohydrate 30g (Dietary Fiber 7g; Sugars 7g); Protein 29g   **% Daily Value:** Vitamin A 10%; Vitamin C 30%; Calcium 8%; Iron 25%   **Exchanges:** 1 Starch, 2 Vegetable, 3 Very Lean Meat, ½ Fat   **Carbohydrate Choices:** 2

szechuan beef and bean sprouts

Prep Time: 20 Minutes   Start to Finish: 30 Minutes   Makes: 4 servings

1 lb boneless beef eye of round steak	⅛ teaspoon crushed red pepper flakes
¼ cup chicken broth with 33% less sodium	4 plum (Roma) tomatoes, cut into eighths
1 tablespoon soy sauce	2 cups fresh bean sprouts (4 oz)
1 tablespoon Szechuan sauce	1 tablespoon chopped fresh cilantro

1. Trim excess fat from beef. Cut beef with grain into 2-inch strips; cut strips across grain into ⅛-inch slices. (Beef is easier to cut if partially frozen, 30 to 60 minutes.) In medium bowl, mix broth, soy sauce, Szechuan sauce and pepper flakes. Stir in beef. Let stand 10 minutes.

2. Drain beef; reserve marinade. Heat 12-inch nonstick skillet over medium-high heat. Add half of the beef to skillet; stir-fry 2 to 3 minutes or until brown. Remove beef from skillet. Repeat with remaining beef. Return all beef to skillet.

3. Add reserved marinade, the tomatoes and bean sprouts to skillet; cook and stir about 1 minute or until sprouts are no longer crisp. Sprinkle with cilantro.

1 Serving: Calories 180 (Calories from Fat 50); Total Fat 6g (Saturated Fat 1.5g; Trans Fat 0g); Cholesterol 60mg; Sodium 420mg; Total Carbohydrate 6g (Dietary Fiber 0g; Sugars 2g); Protein 27g   **% Daily Value:** Vitamin A 10%; Vitamin C 10%; Calcium 2%; Iron 15%   **Exchanges:** 1 Vegetable, 3½ Very Lean Meat, 1 Fat   **Carbohydrate Choices:** ½

serve with
Try serving this Asian dish over a bed of brown or white rice.

270 calories

peppery cajun pork pasta

Prep Time: 30 Minutes Start to Finish: 30 Minutes Makes: 7 servings

8	oz uncooked fettuccine	3	medium plum (Roma) tomatoes, chopped (1 cup)
1	lb pork tenderloin, cut into ¼-inch slices	1	can (15 oz) black-eyed peas, rinsed, drained
4	teaspoons Cajun seasoning	¼	cup lemon juice
1	tablespoon vegetable oil	1	teaspoon dried oregano leaves
1	large red onion, chopped (1½ cups)	¼	teaspoon freshly ground pepper
2	large zucchini, chopped (2½ cups)		Red pepper sauce, if desired
¼	teaspoon salt		

1. Cook and drain fettuccine as directed on package. Meanwhile, sprinkle pork with Cajun seasoning. In 12-inch skillet, heat oil over medium-high heat. Add pork; cook 4 to 6 minutes, turning occasionally, until no longer pink in center. Remove from skillet; keep warm.

2. Spray same skillet with cooking spray; heat over medium-high heat. Cook onion in skillet about 4 minutes, stirring frequently, until it begins to brown. Add zucchini and salt. Cook about 4 minutes, stirring frequently, until vegetables are tender.

3. Stir in remaining ingredients. Cook and stir about 1 minute until hot.

4. Toss vegetable mixture and fettuccine. Serve pork over fettuccine mixture, or toss pork with fettuccine mixture.

1 Serving: Calories 270 (Calories from Fat 40); Total Fat 4.5g (Saturated Fat 1.5g; Trans Fat 0g); Cholesterol 50mg; Sodium 540mg; Total Carbohydrate 37g (Dietary Fiber 4g; Sugars 4g); Protein 21g **% Daily Value:** Vitamin A 6%; Vitamin C 15%; Calcium 4%; Iron 15% **Exchanges:** 2 Starch, 1 Vegetable, 2 Lean Meat **Carbohydrate Choices:** 2½

chinese pork and pasta

Prep Time: 30 Minutes   Start to Finish: 1 Hour 30 Minutes   Makes: 4 servings

1   can (8 oz) chunk pineapple in juice,
      drained, juice reserved
1   tablespoon soy sauce
1   teaspoon honey or packed
      brown sugar
2   cloves garlic, finely chopped
1   tablespoon cornstarch
½   lb pork tenderloin, cut into
      ¼-inch slices

4   oz uncooked vermicelli
2   teaspoons dark sesame oil
¼   cup fat-free chicken broth
½   medium onion, sliced
1   medium bell pepper (any color),
      chopped (1 cup)
4   large stalks bok choy, chopped
4   oz fresh snow pea pods (1 cup), strings
      removed, cut diagonally in half

1. In medium glass bowl, mix reserved pineapple juice, soy sauce, honey, garlic and cornstarch. Stir in pork. Cover and refrigerate at least 1 hour but no longer than 4 hours.

2. Cook and drain vermicelli as directed on package. In wok or 10-inch nonstick skillet, heat oil over medium-high heat. Add pork with marinade; stir-fry 2 minutes. Remove pork from skillet.

3. Add broth, onion, bell pepper and bok choy; cook 6 minutes, stirring frequently. Add pea pods, pineapple and cooked vermicelli. Cook 2 minutes, stirring constantly.

4. Return pork to skillet. Cook and stir about 1 minute until sauce is thickened.

1 Serving: Calories 300 (Calories from Fat 50); Total Fat 6g (Saturated Fat 1.5g; Trans Fat 0g); Cholesterol 25mg; Sodium 340mg; Total Carbohydrate 44g (Dietary Fiber 4g; Sugars 14g); Protein 18g   **% Daily Value:** Vitamin A 60%; Vitamin C 70%; Calcium 8%; Iron 15%   **Exchanges:** 1½ Starch, 1 Other Carbohydrate, 2 Vegetable, 1½ Lean Meat **Carbohydrate Choices:** 3

pork with squash and onions

photo on page C-4

Prep Time: 10 Minutes   Start to Finish: 35 Minutes   Makes: 4 servings

1	teaspoon dried sage leaves	1	acorn squash (about 1½ lb)
¾	teaspoon salt	1	medium onion, cut into ¼-inch slices
½	teaspoon pepper	½	cup chicken broth
2	cloves garlic, finely chopped	1	medium unpeeled cooking apple, cut
4	pork loin or rib chops, ½ inch thick		into eighths
	(about 1 lb)		

1. In small bowl, mix sage, ½ teaspoon of the salt, ¼ teaspoon of the pepper and the garlic; rub on both sides of pork. Heat 10-inch nonstick skillet over medium heat. Cook pork in skillet about 6 minutes, turning once, until brown.

2. Meanwhile, cut squash crosswise into 1-inch slices; remove seeds and fibers. Cut each slice into fourths; set aside.

3. Place onion on pork. Pour broth around pork. Heat to boiling; reduce heat to low. Place squash and apple on pork; sprinkle with the remaining ¼ teaspoon salt and ¼ teaspoon pepper.

4. Cover; simmer about 15 minutes or until pork is no longer pink in center and squash is tender.

1 Serving: Calories 220 (Calories from Fat 45); Total Fat 5g (Saturated Fat 1.5g; Trans Fat 0g); Cholesterol 50mg; Sodium 630mg; Total Carbohydrate 21g (Dietary Fiber 5g; Sugars 7g); Protein 24g   **% Daily Value:** Vitamin A 8%; Vitamin C 10%; Calcium 6%; Iron 8%   **Exchanges:** 1 Other Carbohydrate, 1 Vegetable, 3 Lean Meat   **Carbohydrate Choices:** 1½

health smart

Acorn squash is packed with great nutrients. It's an excellent source of vitamins A and C, plus it contains potassium and fiber.

harvest pork chop dinner

Prep Time: 15 Minutes   **Start to Finish:** 45 Minutes   **Makes:** 4 servings

4 pork loin or rib chops, ½ inch thick (1 to 1¼ lb)	4 small carrots, cut into 1-inch pieces
½ cup beef or chicken broth	2 medium onions, quartered
3 medium unpeeled red potatoes, quartered	¾ teaspoon salt
	¼ teaspoon pepper
	Chopped fresh parsley, if desired

1. Heat 12-inch nonstick skillet over medium-high heat. Cook pork in skillet about 5 minutes, turning once, until brown.

2. Add broth, potatoes, carrots and onions. Sprinkle with salt and pepper. Heat to boiling; reduce heat. Cover; simmer about 30 minutes or until vegetables are tender and pork is no longer pink in center. Sprinkle with parsley.

1 Serving: Calories 290 (Calories from Fat 80); Total Fat 9g (Saturated Fat 3g; Trans Fat 0g); Cholesterol 70mg; Sodium 640mg; Total Carbohydrate 28g (Dietary Fiber 4g; Sugars 6g); Protein 27g   **% Daily Value:** Vitamin A 180%; Vitamin C 15%; Calcium 4%; Iron 8%   **Exchanges:** 1½ Starch, 1 Vegetable, 3 Lean Meat   **Carbohydrate Choices:** 2

mango-pork fried rice

Prep Time: 20 Minutes   Start to Finish: 20 Minutes   Makes: 5 servings

¾ cup diced cooked pork
½ teaspoon cornstarch
1 ripe mango, peeled, pitted and diced
1 can (8 oz) sliced water chestnuts, drained
1 cup sliced fresh mushrooms (3 oz)
1 tablespoon finely chopped gingerroot

1 clove garlic, finely chopped
3 cups cold cooked rice
2 teaspoons reduced-sodium soy sauce
1 cup frozen green peas, thawed
2 medium green onions, sliced (2 tablespoons)
   Dash pepper

1. In medium bowl, mix pork and cornstarch. Spray wok or 12-inch skillet with cooking spray; heat over medium-high heat. Add pork, mango, water chestnuts, mushrooms, gingerroot and garlic; stir-fry 1 minute. Remove mixture from skillet.

2. Spray same skillet with cooking spray; heat over medium-high heat. Add rice; stir-fry 1 minute. Stir in soy sauce. Add pork mixture, peas, onions and pepper; stir-fry 1 minute or until heated through.

1 Serving: Calories 250 (Calories from Fat 25); Total Fat 2.5g (Saturated Fat 1g; Trans Fat 0g); Cholesterol 15mg; Sodium 470mg; Total Carbohydrate 45g (Dietary Fiber 3g; Sugars 7g); Protein 11g   **% Daily Value:** Vitamin A 15%; Vitamin C 15%; Calcium 4%; Iron 10%   **Exchanges:** 2½ Starch, 1 Vegetable, ½ Fat   **Carbohydrate Choices:** 3

health smart

You can substitute ¾ cup diced reduced-fat firm tofu for the pork by preparing as directed except omitting the cornstarch. Tofu is rich in calcium, protein and health-promoting isoflavones, substances that may be good for your bones, your heart and your ability to prevent cancer.

ham with cabbage and apples

Prep Time: 10 Minutes   Start to Finish: 20 Minutes   Makes: 4 servings

4 cups coleslaw mix or shredded cabbage	1 large onion, chopped (1 cup)
1 tablespoon packed brown sugar	1 large green cooking apple, sliced
1 tablespoon cider vinegar	1 cooked ham slice, about ½ inch thick (1 lb)
⅛ teaspoon pepper	

1. Spray 10-inch skillet with cooking spray; heat over medium heat. Add all ingredients except ham. Cook about 5 minutes, stirring frequently, until apple is crisp-tender.

2. Place ham on cabbage mixture; reduce heat to low. Cover; cook 5 to 10 minutes or until ham is hot.

1 Serving: Calories 280 (Calories from Fat 90); Total Fat 10g (Saturated Fat 3.5g; Trans Fat 0g); Cholesterol 65mg; Sodium 1720mg; Total Carbohydrate 19g (Dietary Fiber 3g; Sugars 13g); Protein 27g   **% Daily Value:** Vitamin A 0%; Vitamin C 25%; Calcium 6%; Iron 10%   **Exchanges:** 1 Other Carbohydrate, 1 Vegetable, 3½ Lean Meat
Carbohydrate Choices: 1

halibut and asparagus stir-fry

Prep Time: 25 Minutes   Start to Finish: 25 Minutes   Makes: 4 servings

2 teaspoons olive or canola oil	6 oz uncooked whole wheat vermicelli or angel hair pasta
1 lb halibut or other firm fish fillets, cut into 1-inch pieces	1 package (8 oz) sliced fresh mushrooms (3 cups)
1 medium onion, thinly sliced	1 medium tomato, cut into thin wedges
3 cloves garlic, finely chopped	
1 teaspoon finely chopped gingerroot	2 tablespoons reduced-sodium soy sauce
1 box (9 oz) frozen asparagus cuts, thawed, drained	1 tablespoon lemon juice

1. In 12-inch nonstick skillet, heat oil over medium-high heat. Add halibut, onion, garlic, gingerroot and asparagus; cook 2 to 4 minutes, stirring frequently, or until fish almost flakes with fork. Meanwhile, cook pasta as directed on package, omitting salt.

2. Carefully stir mushrooms, tomato, soy sauce and lemon juice into skillet. Cook 2 to 3 minutes, stirring frequently, until heated through and fish flakes easily with fork.

3. Drain pasta; serve with fish mixture and additional reduced-sodium soy sauce if desired.

1 Serving: Calories 170 (Calories from Fat 35); Total Fat 4g (Saturated Fat 0.5g; Trans Fat 0g); Cholesterol 60mg; Sodium 370mg; Total Carbohydrate 9g (Dietary Fiber 2g; Sugars 4g); Protein 26g   **% Daily Value:** Vitamin A 15%; Vitamin C 20%; Calcium 4%; Iron 6%   **Exchanges:** 1½ Vegetable, 3 Very Lean Meat, ½ Fat   **Carbohydrate Choices:** ½

try this
When asparagus is in season and plentiful, substitute 1 lb fresh for the frozen.

orange roughy with fennel rice

Prep Time: 15 Minutes   **Start to Finish:** 25 Minutes   **Makes:** 4 servings

1 cup chopped fennel bulb	1 lb orange roughy, sole or other
1 small onion, chopped (¼ cup)	delicate- to medium-texture fish
2 tablespoons water	fillets (about ¾ inch thick)
2 cups chicken broth	Paprika
1 cup uncooked regular long-grain	1 tablespoon chopped fresh or
white rice	1 teaspoon dried tarragon leaves
1 cup shredded fresh spinach	Lemon wedges

1. In 10-inch nonstick skillet, cook fennel and onion in water over medium heat about 4 minutes, stirring occasionally, until crisp-tender. Stir in broth, rice and spinach. Heat to boiling; reduce heat. Cover; simmer 10 minutes.

2. Cut fish fillets into 4 serving pieces. Place on rice mixture. Cover; simmer 8 to 10 minutes longer or until fish flakes easily with fork and liquid is absorbed.

3. Sprinkle fish with paprika and tarragon. Serve with lemon wedges.

1 Serving: Calories 300 (Calories from Fat 20); Total Fat 2.5g (Saturated Fat 0.5g; Trans Fat 0g); Cholesterol 55mg; Sodium 620mg; Total Carbohydrate 44g (Dietary Fiber 2g; Sugars 1g); Protein 26g   **% Daily Value:** Vitamin A 20%; Vitamin C 6%; Calcium 6%; Iron 15%   **Exchanges:** 2½ Starch, 1 Vegetable, 2½ Very Lean Meat   **Carbohydrate Choices:** 3

try this

With its broad, bulbous base and green, feathery foliage, fresh fennel has a delicate, sweet flavor with a hint of anise. There is really no substitute for the unique flavor.

lox and cream cheese scramble

Prep Time: 20 Minutes   Start to Finish: 20 Minutes   Makes: 4 servings

8 eggs or 16 egg whites	3 oz salmon lox, chopped
¼ teaspoon dried dill weed	2 tablespoons ⅓-less-fat cream cheese
¼ teaspoon salt	(Neufchâtel)
1 teaspoon canola oil	Reduced-fat sour cream, if desired
2 medium green onions, chopped	Capers, if desired
(2 tablespoons)	

1. In large bowl, beat eggs, dill weed and salt with wire whisk or fork until well blended. In 12-inch nonstick skillet, heat oil over medium heat. Pour egg mixture into skillet. Cook uncovered 4 minutes; as mixture begins to set on bottom and side, gently lift cooked portions with spatula so thin, uncooked portion can flow to bottom. Avoid constant stirring.

2. Gently stir in onions and lox. Drop cream cheese by teaspoonfuls onto mixture. Cook 4 to 5 minutes, stirring gently, until eggs are thickened but still moist. Garnish with sour cream and capers.

1 Serving: Calories 200 (Calories from Fat 130); Total Fat 14g (Saturated Fat 4.5g; Trans Fat 0g); Cholesterol 435mg; Sodium 460mg; Total Carbohydrate 2g (Dietary Fiber 0g; Sugars 2g); Protein 17g   **% Daily Value:** Vitamin A 15%; Vitamin C 0%; Calcium 6%; Iron 8%   **Exchanges:** 2½ Medium-Fat Meat   **Carbohydrate Choices:** 0

health smart

The salmon adds extra color and flavor as well as nutrition to this egg scramble. To reduce the amount of cholesterol in this recipe, use the egg whites instead of whole eggs.

sesame shrimp stir-fry

Prep Time: 25 Minutes   Start to Finish: 1 Hour 25 Minutes   Makes: 4 servings

¾ lb uncooked deveined peeled large shrimp, thawed if frozen, tail shells removed
¼ cup teriyaki marinade (from 12-oz bottle)
½ cup water
1 tablespoon cornstarch
1 tablespoon canola oil

1 medium carrot, sliced (½ cup)
8 oz fresh snow pea pods (2 cups), strings removed, cut diagonally in half
2 cups sliced fresh mushrooms (about 5 oz)
1 cup uncooked instant brown rice
1 tablespoon sesame seed, toasted*

1. Place shrimp in 8-inch square (2-quart) glass baking dish. Pour teriyaki marinade over shrimp. Cover and refrigerate at least 1 hour but no longer than 2 hours.

2. Remove shrimp from marinade; reserve marinade. Stir water and cornstarch into marinade; set aside.

3. In wok or 10-inch nonstick skillet, heat oil over medium-high heat. Add carrot; cook and stir 1 minute. Add shrimp, pea pods and mushrooms; cook 3 to 5 minutes, stirring frequently, or until shrimp are pink and vegetables are crisp-tender. Meanwhile, cook rice as directed on package, omitting butter and salt.

4. Stir marinade mixture into shrimp mixture; heat to boiling. Cook and stir until sauce is thickened. Sprinkle with sesame seed. Serve with rice.

***Note:** To toast sesame seed, bake uncovered in shallow pan at 350°F for 8 to 10 minutes, stirring occasionally, until golden brown.

1 Serving: Calories 250 (Calories from Fat 50); Total Fat 6g (Saturated Fat 0.5g; Trans Fat 0g); Cholesterol 120mg; Sodium 850mg; Total Carbohydrate 33g (Dietary Fiber 4g; Sugars 4g); Protein 19g   **% Daily Value:** Vitamin A 60%; Vitamin C 15%; Calcium 6%; Iron 20%   **Exchanges:** 2 Starch, 1 Vegetable, 1½ Very Lean Meat, ½ Fat   **Carbohydrate Choices:** 2

scallop pad thai

Prep Time: 35 Minutes   Start to Finish: 35 Minutes   Makes: 6 servings

1 package (7 oz) rice stick noodles	2 teaspoons canola oil
3 tablespoons packed brown sugar	½ cup ½-inch pieces green onions (7 medium)
3 tablespoons fish sauce or 3 tablespoons reduced-sodium soy sauce and 1 tablespoon dry sherry	8 oz fresh bean sprouts (4 cups), rinsed, drained
3 tablespoons rice vinegar	1 cup shredded carrots (about 2 medium)
1 tablespoon reduced-sodium soy sauce	½ cup chopped fresh cilantro
1 tablespoon chili puree with garlic	2 tablespoons finely chopped dry-roasted peanuts
1 teaspoon paprika	6 lime wedges
1 lb bay scallops, well drained	

1. Fill 3-quart microwavable bowl half full with water; add noodles. Microwave uncovered on High 3 to 5 minutes or until water is hot. Let stand 5 minutes; drain.

2. Meanwhile, in small bowl, mix brown sugar, fish sauce, vinegar, soy sauce, chili puree and paprika; set aside. Pat scallops dry with paper towels.

3. In 12-inch nonstick skillet or wok, heat oil over medium-high heat. Add scallops and onions; cook about 4 minutes, stirring frequently, until scallops are white and opaque. Stir in bean sprouts; cook 1 minute.

4. Stir fish sauce mixture and noodles into scallop mixture. Cook about 2 minutes or until thoroughly heated and sprouts are no longer crisp.

5. Remove from heat. Toss scallop mixture with carrots and cilantro. Sprinkle with peanuts; serve with lime wedges.

1 Serving: Calories 250 (Calories from Fat 35); Total Fat 4g (Saturated Fat 0g; Trans Fat 0g); Cholesterol 20mg; Sodium 990mg; Total Carbohydrate 42g (Dietary Fiber 3g; Sugars 9g); Protein 12g   **% Daily Value:** Vitamin A 50%; Vitamin C 10%; Calcium 8%; Iron 10%   **Exchanges:** 2 Starch, ½ Other Carbohydrate, 1 Vegetable, ½ Very Lean Meat, ½ Fat **Carbohydrate Choices:** 3

stir-fried broccoli with crabmeat

Prep Time: 20 Minutes   Start to Finish: 20 Minutes   Makes: 4 servings

1	lb fresh broccoli	1	clove garlic, finely chopped
2	green onions (with tops)	¼	cup chicken broth
1	tablespoon cornstarch	1	package (8 oz) frozen salad-style
1	tablespoon cold water		imitation crabmeat, thawed
3	tablespoons vegetable oil	½	teaspoon sesame oil

1. Peel outer layer from broccoli. Cut broccoli lengthwise into 1-inch stems; remove florets. Cut stems diagonally into ¼-inch slices. Place broccoli stems in boiling water; heat to boiling. Cover and cook 30 seconds. Add florets; heat to boiling. Cover and cook 30 seconds; drain. Immediately rinse in cold water; drain.

2. Cut onions into ½-inch pieces; slice lengthwise in half and set aside. In small bowl, mix cornstarch and water; set aside.

3. In wok or 12-inch skillet, heat vegetable oil over high heat. Add broccoli and garlic; stir-fry 1 minute. Add broth; heat to boiling. Stir in cornstarch mixture; cook and stir until thickened. Add imitation crabmeat, onions and sesame oil; cook and stir 1 minute.

1 Serving: Calories 210 (Calories from Fat 110); Total Fat 12g (Saturated Fat 2g; Trans Fat 0g); Cholesterol 15mg; Sodium 590mg; Total Carbohydrate 14g (Dietary Fiber 3g; Sugars 4g); Protein 12g   **% Daily Value:** Vitamin A 15%; Vitamin C 90%; Calcium 6%; Iron 6%   **Exchanges:** ½ Other Carbohydrate, 1 Vegetable, 1½ Lean Meat, 1½ Fat **Carbohydrate Choices:** 1

whole wheat fettuccine with spring vegetables

Prep Time: 25 Minutes   Start to Finish: 1 Hour 25 Minutes   Makes: 6 servings

1	package (12 oz) uncooked whole wheat fettuccine	1	box (9 oz) frozen baby sweet peas
2	cups cut-up fresh asparagus	1	medium tomato, chopped (¾ cup)
1	tablespoon butter or margarine	¼	cup chopped fresh or 2 tablespoons dried basil leaves
1	medium zucchini, cut into julienne strips (2 cups)	¼	teaspoon pepper
		⅓	cup grated Parmesan cheese

1. Cook and drain fettuccine as directed on package. Rinse with cold water; drain.

2. Cook asparagus in enough boiling water to cover 3 to 4 minutes or until crisp-tender; drain.

3. In 10-inch skillet, melt butter over medium-high heat. Add asparagus, zucchini and peas; cook about 4 minutes, stirring frequently, until crisp-tender.

4. In large bowl, toss asparagus mixture, fettuccine, tomato, basil and pepper. Cover and refrigerate about 1 hour or until chilled. Sprinkle with cheese.

1 Serving: Calories 300 (Calories from Fat 45); Total Fat 5g (Saturated Fat 2g; Trans Fat 0g); Cholesterol 10mg; Sodium 135mg; Total Carbohydrate 49g (Dietary Fiber 9g; Sugars 5g); Protein 15g   **% Daily Value:** Vitamin A 35%; Vitamin C 15%; Calcium 10%; Iron 25%   **Exchanges:** 3 Starch, 1 Vegetable, ½ Medium-Fat Meat   **Carbohydrate Choices:** 3½

try this

Short on time? This pasta dish can be served warm, too. Instead of rinsing with cold water, cover the drained pasta to keep it warm while preparing the vegetable mixture.

rigatoni with artichokes

Prep Time: 30 Minutes   Start to Finish: 30 Minutes   Makes: 6 servings

2 cups uncooked rigatoni pasta (6 oz)	2 tablespoons finely chopped sun-dried tomatoes in oil
2 tablespoons butter or margarine	1 teaspoon cornstarch
1½ cups soft bread crumbs (about 2½ slices bread)	¼ teaspoon salt
1 tablespoon chopped fresh parsley	¼ teaspoon crushed red pepper flakes
1 teaspoon olive or vegetable oil	¼ teaspoon pepper
2 cloves garlic, finely chopped	1 can (14 oz) artichoke hearts, drained
¾ cup chicken broth	1 tablespoon grated Romano or Parmesan cheese

1. Cook and drain pasta as directed on package. Meanwhile, in 10-inch skillet, melt butter over medium-high heat. Add bread crumbs; cook 5 to 6 minutes, stirring occasionally, until light brown. Stir in parsley. Remove from skillet; keep warm.

2. In same skillet, heat oil over medium-high heat. Cook garlic in oil, stirring frequently, until golden.

3. In tightly covered container, shake broth, sun-dried tomatoes, cornstarch, salt, pepper flakes and pepper. Gradually stir into garlic. Heat to boiling, stirring constantly. Boil and stir 1 minute.

4. Stir in artichokes. Toss with pasta. Sprinkle with bread crumbs and cheese.

1 Serving: Calories 270 (Calories from Fat 60); Total Fat 7g (Saturated Fat 1.5g; Trans Fat 1.5g); Cholesterol 0mg; Sodium 480mg; Total Carbohydrate 44g (Dietary Fiber 6g; Sugars 2g); Protein 9g   **% Daily Value:** Vitamin A 6%; Vitamin C 6%; Calcium 6%; Iron 10%   **Exchanges:** 3 Starch, 1 Fat   **Carbohydrate Choices:** 3

cuban black beans and rice

Prep Time: 1 Hour   Start to Finish: 1 Hour   Makes: 6 servings

1	large onion, chopped (1 cup)	2	cloves garlic, finely chopped
1	medium bell pepper (any color), chopped (1 cup)	1	can (15 oz) black beans, drained, rinsed
2	medium carrots, chopped (¾ cup)	4	cups hot cooked brown rice
1	cup orange juice	1	cup plain fat-free yogurt
2	teaspoons paprika		Paprika, if desired
1	teaspoon ground coriander	1	lime, cut into wedges
⅛	teaspoon crushed red pepper flakes		
1	can (14.5 oz) whole tomatoes, undrained		

1. In 2-quart saucepan, mix onion, bell pepper, carrots, orange juice, paprika, coriander, pepper flakes, tomatoes and garlic. Heat to boiling; reduce heat. Cover; simmer about 45 minutes, stirring occasionally, until thickened.

2. Remove from heat; stir in beans. Place 1 cup bean mixture in blender or food processor; cover and blend on medium speed about 30 seconds or until smooth.

3. Stir blended mixture into bean mixture in saucepan. Cook over medium heat about 3 minutes or until hot. Serve over rice with yogurt. Sprinkle with paprika. Serve with lime wedges.

1 Serving: Calories 300 (Calories from Fat 15); Total Fat 2g (Saturated Fat 0g; Trans Fat 0g); Cholesterol 0mg; Sodium 700mg; Total Carbohydrate 59g (Dietary Fiber 12g; Sugars 12g); Protein 11g   **% Daily Value:** Vitamin A 60%; Vitamin C 40%; Calcium 15%; Iron 15%   **Exchanges:** 2 Starch, 1½ Other Carbohydrate, 1 Vegetable, ½ Lean Meat **Carbohydrate Choices:** 4

serve with

Try this dish the next time you have an evening that calls for a meatless main dish. It's a great alternative.

creamy quinoa
primavera

Prep Time: 15 Minutes   Start to Finish: 30 Minutes   Makes: 6 servings

1½ cups uncooked quinoa	2 cloves garlic, finely chopped
3 cups vegetable or chicken broth	5 cups thinly sliced or bite-size pieces
1 package (3 oz) cream cheese, cut	assorted fresh vegetables (such
into cubes	as asparagus, broccoli, carrots,
1 tablespoon chopped fresh or	zucchini)
1 teaspoon dried basil leaves	2 tablespoons grated Romano cheese
2 teaspoons butter or margarine	

1. Rinse quinoa thoroughly; drain. In 2-quart saucepan, heat quinoa and broth to boiling; reduce heat. Cover; simmer 10 to 15 minutes or until broth is absorbed. Stir in cream cheese and basil.

2. In 10-inch nonstick skillet, melt butter over medium-high heat. Add garlic; cook and stir about 30 seconds until golden. Stir in vegetables. Cook about 2 minutes, stirring frequently, until vegetables are crisp-tender.

3. Toss vegetables and quinoa mixture. Sprinkle with Romano cheese.

1 Serving: Calories 260 (Calories from Fat 90); Total Fat 10g (Saturated Fat 4.5g; Trans Fat 0g); Cholesterol 20mg; Sodium 570mg; Total Carbohydrate 34g (Dietary Fiber 5g; Sugars 5g); Protein 9g   **% Daily Value:** Vitamin A 45%; Vitamin C 25%; Calcium 8%; Iron 15%   **Exchanges:** 2 Starch, 1 Vegetable, 2 Fat   **Carbohydrate Choices:** 2

serve with
You can use whatever vegetables you have on hand in this tasty, colorful skillet dinner. Serve a salad tossed with sliced apples or pears and some crunchy walnuts on the side.

casseroles
and pot pies

Classic comfort foods, casseroles and pot pies can pack a lot of calories.
Fortunately, "rich and satisfying" doesn't have to mean "heavy and unhealthy."
Try these recipes for some comfort food that won't weigh you down.

lemon chicken with broccoli

Prep Time: 20 Minutes   **Start to Finish:** 1 Hour   **Makes:** 6 servings

2	cups uncooked bow-tie (farfalle) pasta (4 oz)		1	can (10¾ oz) condensed 98% fat-free cream of chicken soup with 45% less sodium
¼	cup crushed round buttery crackers		1	cup chicken broth
1	teaspoon grated lemon peel		½	cup fat-free (skim) milk
1	lb boneless skinless chicken breasts, cut into ¼-inch strips		2	tablespoons lemon juice
2	cloves garlic, finely chopped		⅛	teaspoon pepper
2	cups frozen broccoli florets or broccoli cuts, thawed, drained			

1. Heat oven to 350°F. Spray 13×9-inch (3-quart) glass baking dish with cooking spray.

2. Cook and drain pasta as directed on package. Meanwhile, in small bowl, mix crushed crackers and lemon peel; set aside.

3. Spray 10-inch skillet with cooking spray; heat over medium-high heat. Add chicken and garlic; cook 2 to 3 minutes, stirring frequently, until chicken is brown. Remove from heat; stir in pasta and remaining ingredients. Spoon chicken mixture into baking dish. Sprinkle with crumb mixture.

4. Cover with foil; bake 25 minutes. Bake uncovered 10 to 15 minutes longer or until hot and bubbly.

1 Serving: Calories 260 (Calories from Fat 50); Total Fat 6g (Saturated Fat 1.5g; Trans Fat 0g); Cholesterol 50mg; Sodium 720mg; Total Carbohydrate 26g (Dietary Fiber 2g; Sugars 2g); Protein 25g **% Daily Value:** Vitamin A 15%; Vitamin C 15%; Calcium 6%; Iron 10% **Exchanges:** 1½ Starch, 2½ Lean Meat **Carbohydrate Choices:** 2

try this
If you don't have buttery cracker crumbs, regular cracker crumbs or seasoned dry bread crumbs also work well for the topping.

240 calories

swiss chicken casserole

Prep Time: 15 Minutes   Start to Finish: 1 Hour 15 Minutes   Makes: 8 servings

4   cups boiling water
2   boxes (6 oz each) sun-dried tomato
    Florentine long grain and wild
    rice mix
4   large boneless skinless chicken
    breasts (about 2 lb)

8   thick slices (1¼ oz each) cooked ham
    (from deli)
¼   cup diced bell pepper (any color)
4   slices (1 oz each) Swiss cheese, cut in
    half

1. Heat oven to 350°F. Spray 13×9-inch (3-quart) glass baking dish with cooking spray.
Stir boiling water, rice and seasoning mixes in baking dish.

2. Cut chicken breasts in half lengthwise; wrap a ham slice around each chicken piece.
Stir bell pepper into rice. Place wrapped chicken over rice.

3. Cover with foil. Bake 40 to 45 minutes. Uncover; bake about 10 minutes longer or
until liquid is absorbed and juice of chicken is clear when thickest part is cut (170°F).

4. Top each chicken breast with cheese. Bake uncovered 3 to 4 minutes or until
cheese is melted.

1 Serving: Calories 240 (Calories from Fat 80); Total Fat 8g (Saturated Fat 4g; Trans Fat 0g); Cholesterol 75mg; Sodium
660mg; Total Carbohydrate 13g (Dietary Fiber 0g; Sugars 0g); Protein 28g   **% Daily Value:** Vitamin A 6%; Vitamin C 4%;
Calcium 15%; Iron 8%   **Exchanges:** 1 Starch, 3½ Very Lean Meat, 1 Fat   **Carbohydrate Choices:** 1

5 ways to make a meal healthy

1. Use a nonstick spray, vegetable juice, or broth for sautéing foods. If you
   use fat, try oil instead of butter and use as little as possible.
2. Choose romaine, spinach, or dark-green leafy lettuce—they are filled
   with folic acid, vitamin C, beta-carotene (vitamin A) and potassium.
3. Eat the skin on fruits, potatoes and other veggies—it increases the
   fiber content.
4. Choose whole grains. Buy breads and pastas made with whole grains and
   rice that contains more fiber and disease-fighting phytochemicals.
5. Serve a fruit or vegetable at every meal.

baked chicken and rice with autumn vegetables

Prep Time: 15 Minutes   **Start to Finish:** 45 Minutes   **Makes:** 4 servings

8   chicken drumsticks or thighs (1¼ lb), skin removed
1   box (6 oz) original long-grain and wild rice mix
2   cups cubed (1½ inch) peeled butternut squash

1   medium zucchini, cut lengthwise in half, then cut crosswise into ¾-inch slices
1   medium bell pepper (any color), cut into 1-inch pieces
2   cups water
½   cup garlic-and-herbs spreadable cheese

1. Heat oven to 425°F. Spray 10-inch skillet with cooking spray; heat over medium-high heat. Cook chicken in skillet about 5 minutes, turning once, until brown. Remove chicken from skillet.

2. In ungreased 13×9-inch (3-quart) glass baking dish, mix rice, contents of seasoning packet, squash, zucchini and bell pepper.

3. Add water to skillet; heat to boiling. Pour boiling water over rice mixture; stir to mix. Stir in cheese. Place chicken on rice mixture.

4. Cover with foil. Bake about 30 minutes or until liquid is absorbed and juice of chicken is clear when thickest part is cut to bone (180°F).

1 Serving: Calories 260 (Calories from Fat 100); Total Fat 11g (Saturated Fat 6g; Trans Fat 0g); Cholesterol 90mg; Sodium 290mg; Total Carbohydrate 21g (Dietary Fiber 2g; Sugars 5g); Protein 21g   **% Daily Value:** Vitamin A 150%; Vitamin C 60%; Calcium 8%; Iron 15%   **Exchanges:** 1 Starch, 1 Vegetable, 2 Lean Meat, 1 Fat   **Carbohydrate Choices:** 1½

health smart

It may take a few minutes to remove the skin from the drumsticks and thighs, but it does cut calories and fat. To save time, you can use boneless skinless thighs, but check on the chicken before the end of the bake time because it may take less time for it to get done.

country french chicken

Prep Time: 25 Minutes   Start to Finish: 3 Hours 25 Minutes   Makes: 8 servings

¼ cup chopped sun-dried tomatoes in olive oil, drained	1½ cups sliced fresh mushrooms (about 4 oz)
2 tablespoons herbes de Provence	1 cup uncooked regular long-grain white rice
2 tablespoons olive oil	1 medium carrot, shredded (¾ cup)
2 tablespoons lemon juice	2 cups boiling water
1 tablespoon finely chopped garlic	1 tablespoon chopped fresh Italian (flat-leaf) parsley
1 teaspoon salt	
8 large chicken thighs (about 2 lb), skin removed	2 teaspoons grated lemon peel

1. In shallow glass or plastic dish or resealable food-storage plastic bag, mix tomatoes, herbes de Provence, oil, lemon juice, garlic and ½ teaspoon of the salt. Add chicken and mushrooms; seal bag. Turn to coat chicken and mushrooms in marinade. Refrigerate at least 2 hours but no longer than 24 hours.

2. Heat oven to 375°F. Spray 13×9-inch (3-quart) glass baking dish with cooking spray.

3. Place rice, carrot and remaining ½ teaspoon salt in baking dish; stir in boiling water. Place chicken, mushrooms and marinade evenly over rice mixture.

4. Cover with foil. Bake 50 to 60 minutes or until liquid is absorbed and juice of chicken is clear when thickest part is cut to bone (180°F). Sprinkle with parsley and lemon peel.

1 Serving: Calories 260 (Calories from Fat 90); Total Fat 10g (Saturated Fat 2.5g; Trans Fat 0g); Cholesterol 45mg; Sodium 360mg; Total Carbohydrate 23g (Dietary Fiber 1g; Sugars 1g); Protein 18g   **% Daily Value:** Vitamin A 40%; Vitamin C 6%; Calcium 4%; Iron 20%   **Exchanges:** 1½ Starch, 2 Lean Meat, ½ Fat   **Carbohydrate Choices:** 1½

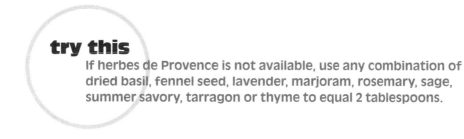

try this

If herbes de Provence is not available, use any combination of dried basil, fennel seed, lavender, marjoram, rosemary, sage, summer savory, tarragon or thyme to equal 2 tablespoons.

baked chicken panzanella

Prep Time: 10 Minutes   **Start to Finish:** 40 Minutes   **Makes:** 6 servings

2	cups chopped cooked chicken	1	package (5 oz) Italian-seasoned croutons
1	can (14.5 oz) diced tomatoes with basil, garlic and oregano, drained	¼	cup Italian dressing
4	medium green onions, sliced (¼ cup)	¾	cup shredded Parmesan cheese (3 oz)
		¼	cup sliced fresh basil leaves

1. Heat oven to 350°F. In ungreased 11×7-inch (2-quart) glass baking dish, layer chicken, tomatoes, onions and croutons. Drizzle with Italian dressing.

2. Cover with foil. Bake 20 minutes. Uncover; top with cheese. Bake about 10 minutes longer or until hot and cheese is melted. Sprinkle with basil.

1 Serving: Calories 290 (Calories from Fat 130); Total Fat 14g (Saturated Fat 4.5g; Trans Fat 1.5g); Cholesterol 50mg; Sodium 830mg; Total Carbohydrate 20g (Dietary Fiber 2g; Sugars 4g); Protein 21g   **% Daily Value:** Vitamin A 6%; Vitamin C 6%; Calcium 20%; Iron 10%   **Exchanges:** 1 Starch, ½ Other Carbohydrate, 2½ Medium-Fat Meat **Carbohydrate Choices:** 1

try this

Any cooked chicken will work in this adaption of the Italian bread salad, panzanella. Use rotisserie chicken or, for a smoky flavor, try grilled chicken.

chicken-noodle casserole

Prep Time: 20 Minutes   Start to Finish: 1 Hour 5 Minutes   Makes: 7 servings

4 cups uncooked egg noodles (8 oz)	1 can (10¾ oz) condensed 98% fat-free cream of chicken soup with 45% less sodium
1 medium onion, chopped (½ cup)	
2 medium stalks celery, sliced (1 cup)	
2½ cups cut-up cooked chicken breast	1 package (9 oz) frozen baby sweet peas
½ teaspoon salt	
¼ teaspoon pepper	1 can (4 oz) sliced mushrooms, drained
1 can (14 oz) chicken broth	

1. Heat oven to 350°F. Spray 3-quart casserole with cooking spray.

2. Cook noodles as directed on package, using minimum cook time. Meanwhile, spray 10-inch skillet with cooking spray. Heat over medium-high heat. Add onion and celery; cook about 5 minutes, stirring occasionally, until tender. Stir in remaining ingredients.

3. Drain noodles; place in casserole. Top with chicken mixture.

4. Cover; bake 30 minutes. Stir; bake uncovered about 15 minutes longer or until liquid is absorbed.

1 Serving: Calories 280 (Calories from Fat 60); Total Fat 7g (Saturated Fat 1.5g; Trans Fat 0g); Cholesterol 70mg; Sodium 880mg; Total Carbohydrate 33g (Dietary Fiber 3g; Sugars 3g); Protein 22g   **% Daily Value:** Vitamin A 20%; Vitamin C 4%; Calcium 4%; Iron 15%   **Exchanges:** 2 Starch, 1 Vegetable, 2 Lean Meat   **Carbohydrate Choices:** 2

try this

This family-favorite casserole is great to have tucked in the freezer for those times when you want to serve a healthy meal but you're short on time. Cover the baked and cooled casserole with foil. Freeze no longer than 2 months; thaw before reheating. About 1 hour before serving, heat oven to 350°F. Bake thawed casserole, covered, for 45 minutes. Uncover and bake 10 to 15 minutes longer or until hot.

chicken enchiladas

Prep Time: 25 Minutes   **Start to Finish:** 50 Minutes   **Makes:** 6 servings

1	cup green tomatillo salsa	2	cups chopped cooked chicken
¼	cup fresh cilantro sprigs	¾	cup shredded mozzarella
¼	cup fresh parsley sprigs		cheese (3 oz)
1	tablespoon lime juice	6	flour tortillas (7 or 8 inch)
2	cloves garlic, peeled	1	medium lime, cut into wedges

1. Heat oven to 350°F. Spray 11×7-inch (2-quart) glass baking dish with cooking spray.

2. In blender or food processor, place salsa, cilantro, parsley, lime juice and garlic. Cover; blend on high speed about 30 seconds or until smooth. Reserve half of mixture.

3. Mix remaining salsa mixture with chicken and ¼ cup of the cheese. Spoon about ¼ cup filling down center of each tortilla; roll up. Place, seam side down, in baking dish.

4. Pour reserved salsa mixture over enchiladas. Sprinkle with remaining ½ cup cheese. Bake uncovered 20 to 25 minutes or until hot. Serve with lime wedges.

1 Serving: Calories 250 (Calories from Fat 100); Total Fat 11g (Saturated Fat 4g; Trans Fat 0.5g); Cholesterol 45mg; Sodium 540mg; Total Carbohydrate 18g (Dietary Fiber 2g; Sugars 2g); Protein 19g   **% Daily Value:** Vitamin A 10%; Vitamin C 8%; Calcium 15%; Iron 10%   **Exchanges:** 1 Starch, 2½ Lean Meat, ½ Fat   **Carbohydrate Choices:** 1

health smart

You'll love these calorie-friendly enchiladas. The green salsa mixture is packed with fresh flavor, and there's just enough cheese to make them satisfying without overdoing it.

chicken and rice casserole

Prep Time: 10 Minutes   Start to Finish: 1 Hour   Makes: 6 servings

2	cups cut-up cooked chicken	1	medium onion, chopped (½ cup)
2	cups cooked rice	1	can (14 oz) chicken broth
½	teaspoon salt	1	package (9 oz) frozen cut green
¼	teaspoon pepper		beans, thawed
2	medium stalks celery, sliced (1 cup)		

1. Heat oven to 350°F. Spray 2-quart casserole with cooking spray. Mix all ingredients in casserole.

2. Cover; bake 45 to 50 minutes or until beans are tender and mixture is hot.

1 Serving: Calories 210 (Calories from Fat 60); Total Fat 7g (Saturated Fat 2g; Trans Fat 0g); Cholesterol 40mg; Sodium 740mg; Total Carbohydrate 20g (Dietary Fiber 2g; Sugars 2g); Protein 16g   **% Daily Value:** Vitamin A 4%; Vitamin C 8%; Calcium 4%; Iron 10%   **Exchanges:** 1 Starch, 1 Vegetable, 1½ Lean Meat, ½ Fat   **Carbohydrate Choices:** 1

serve with

Cooked chicken is available in many forms. Look for rotisserie chicken, frozen cut-up chicken or refrigerated varieties. Leftover chicken is also a great choice if you have it on hand.

chicken-tortilla casserole

Prep Time: 20 Minutes   Start to Finish: 1 Hour 15 Minutes   Makes: 8 servings

1 can (10¾ oz) condensed 98% fat-free cream of chicken soup with 45% less sodium	8 soft corn tortillas (6 inch), torn into bite-size pieces
1 can (4.5 oz) chopped green chiles	1 medium bell pepper (any color), chopped (1 cup)
1 container (8 oz) fat-free sour cream	1 large tomato, chopped (1 cup)
½ cup fat-free (skim) milk	1½ cups shredded sharp Cheddar cheese or Mexican cheese blend (6 oz)
2½ cups shredded cooked chicken breast	

1. Heat oven to 350°F. Spray 13×9-inch (3-quart) glass baking dish with cooking spray.

2. In large bowl, mix soup, chiles, sour cream and milk until blended. Stir in chicken, tortillas and bell pepper. Stir in tomato and 1 cup of the cheese. Spoon and spread mixture in baking dish.

3. Cover with foil. Bake 40 minutes. Uncover; sprinkle with remaining ½ cup cheese. Bake uncovered 5 to 10 minutes longer or until cheese is melted and mixture is bubbly. Let stand 5 minutes before serving.

1 Serving: Calories 270 (Calories from Fat 100); Total Fat 11g (Saturated Fat 5g; Trans Fat 0g); Cholesterol 60mg; Sodium 610mg; Total Carbohydrate 22g (Dietary Fiber 2g; Sugars 4g); Protein 22g   **% Daily Value:** Vitamin A 15%; Vitamin C 15%; Calcium 20%; Iron 8%   **Exchanges:** 1½ Starch, 2½ Very Lean Meat, 1½ Fat   **Carbohydrate Choices:** 1½

home-style turkey and potato bake

Prep Time: 15 Minutes   Start to Finish: 45 Minutes   Makes: 6 servings

1	pouch roasted garlic mashed potato mix (from 7.2-oz box)	2	cups chopped cooked turkey breast
1¼	cups hot water	1	bag (1 lb) frozen mixed vegetables (any combination), thawed, drained
½	cup milk	1	jar (12 oz) home-style turkey gravy
2	tablespoons butter or margarine	¼	teaspoon poultry seasoning
4	medium green onions, sliced (¼ cup)		

1. Heat oven to 350°F. Spray 2-quart casserole with cooking spray.

2. Make mashed potatoes as directed on box, using water, milk and butter. Stir in onions.

3. In 2-quart saucepan, heat turkey, vegetables, gravy and poultry seasoning to boiling over medium-high heat. Pour turkey mixture into casserole. Spoon or pipe potatoes around edge of casserole.

4. Bake uncovered about 30 minutes or until heated through and potatoes are light brown.

1 Serving: Calories 260 (Calories from Fat 110); Total Fat 12g (Saturated Fat 5g; Trans Fat 0g); Cholesterol 50mg; Sodium 510mg; Total Carbohydrate 20g (Dietary Fiber 4g; Sugars 4g); Protein 16g   **% Daily Value:** Vitamin A 70%; Vitamin C 2%; Calcium 6%; Iron 10%   **Exchanges:** 1 Starch, 1 Vegetable, 1½ Lean Meat, 1½ Fat   **Carbohydrate Choices:** 1

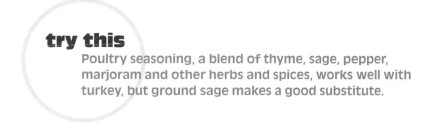

try this

Poultry seasoning, a blend of thyme, sage, pepper, marjoram and other herbs and spices, works well with turkey, but ground sage makes a good substitute.

baked chili with cornmeal crust

Prep Time: 20 Minutes   Start to Finish: 1 Hour   Makes: 8 servings

1	lb lean (at least 80%) ground beef	1	can (15.25 oz) whole kernel corn, drained
1	small onion, chopped (¼ cup)	1	teaspoon salt
1	tablespoon chili powder	¾	cup Original Bisquick mix
1	tablespoon Original Bisquick® mix	¾	cup yellow cornmeal
3	tablespoons water	⅔	cup milk
1	can (14.5 oz) whole tomatoes, undrained	1	egg, slightly beaten

1. Heat oven to 350°F. In 2-quart saucepan, cook beef and onion over medium-high heat 5 to 7 minutes, stirring frequently, until beef is thoroughly cooked; drain.

2. In small bowl, mix chili powder, 1 tablespoon Bisquick mix and the water; add to beef mixture. Stir in tomatoes, corn and salt; break up tomatoes. Heat to boiling, stirring frequently. Pour into ungreased 8-inch square (2-quart) glass baking dish or 2-quart casserole.

3. In medium bowl, stir all remaining ingredients with wire whisk or fork until blended. Pour evenly over beef mixture.

4. Bake uncovered 35 to 40 minutes or until golden brown.

1 Serving: Calories 280 (Calories from Fat 90); Total Fat 10g (Saturated Fat 3.5g; Trans Fat 1g); Cholesterol 65mg; Sodium 680mg; Total Carbohydrate 32g (Dietary Fiber 3g; Sugars 5g); Protein 15g   **% Daily Value:** Vitamin A 10%; Vitamin C 8%; Calcium 8%; Iron 15%   **Exchanges:** 2 Starch, 1½ Lean Meat, 1 Fat   **Carbohydrate Choices:** 2

black-eyed pea casserole

Prep Time: 20 Minutes   Start to Finish: 1 Hour 10 Minutes   Makes: 12 servings

1½ lb lean (at least 80%) ground beef	¾ teaspoon chili powder
2½ teaspoons seasoned salt	2 cans (15 oz each) black-eyed peas, drained, rinsed
½ teaspoon white or black pepper	
1 medium bell pepper (any color), chopped (1 cup)	1 can (14.5 oz) stewed tomatoes, undrained
1 small jalapeño chile, finely chopped	1 cup Original Bisquick mix
⅔ cup chopped onion	1 cup yellow cornmeal
1¼ teaspoons ground cumin	½ cup milk
1 teaspoon garlic powder	½ cup water

1. Heat oven to 375°F. In 10-inch nonstick skillet, cook beef, seasoned salt, pepper, bell pepper, jalapeño chile and onion over medium-high heat 5 to 7 minutes, stirring occasionally, until beef is thoroughly cooked; drain.

2. Stir in cumin, garlic powder, chili powder, black-eyed peas and tomatoes. Spoon into ungreased 13×9-inch (3-quart) glass baking dish.

3. In medium bowl, stir all remaining ingredients with wire whisk or fork until blended. Pour evenly over beef mixture.

4. Bake uncovered 40 to 50 minutes or until light golden brown.

1 Serving: Calories 280 (Calories from Fat 80); Total Fat 8g (Saturated Fat 3g; Trans Fat 1g); Cholesterol 35mg; Sodium 690mg; Total Carbohydrate 33g (Dietary Fiber 4g; Sugars 4g); Protein 17g   **% Daily Value:** Vitamin A 4%; Vitamin C 10%; Calcium 6%; Iron 20%   **Exchanges:** 2 Starch, 1½ Medium-Fat Meat   **Carbohydrate Choices:** 2

health smart

Black-eyed peas are an excellent nutritional value—high in protein and fiber. It's good to rinse them before using to remove excess salt.

philly cheese steak casserole

Prep Time: 25 Minutes   Start to Finish: 1 Hour 15 Minutes   Makes: 6 servings

3 cups uncooked dumpling or wide egg noodles (6 oz)	1 small bell pepper (any color), chopped (½ cup)
1 lb boneless beef sirloin steak, about ¾ inch thick	1 can (14 oz) fat-free beef broth
¼ teaspoon pepper	¼ cup all-purpose flour
1 large onion, chopped (1 cup)	½ cup fat-free half-and-half
	1 tablespoon Dijon mustard
	¾ cup shredded reduced-fat Cheddar cheese (3 oz)

1. Heat oven to 350°F. Spray 11×7-inch (2-quart) glass baking dish with cooking spray.

2. Cook and drain noodles as directed on package. Meanwhile, trim excess fat from beef. Cut beef into ¾-inch pieces. Heat 12-inch nonstick skillet over medium heat. Cook beef and pepper in skillet 2 to 3 minutes, stirring occasionally, until beef is brown.

3. Stir in onion and bell pepper. Cook 2 minutes, stirring occasionally. Spoon into baking dish.

4. In medium bowl, beat broth and flour with wire whisk until smooth. Add to skillet; heat to boiling. Cook, stirring constantly, until mixture thickens. Remove from heat. Stir in half-and-half and mustard. Spoon over beef mixture. Stir in cooked noodles.

5. Cover; bake 40 minutes. Uncover; sprinkle with cheese. Bake about 10 minutes longer or until cheese is melted and casserole is bubbly.

1 Serving: Calories 260 (Calories from Fat 45); Total Fat 5g (Saturated Fat 2g; Trans Fat 0g); Cholesterol 65mg; Sodium 540mg; Total Carbohydrate 30g (Dietary Fiber 2g; Sugars 4g); Protein 24g   **% Daily Value:** Vitamin A 6%; Vitamin C 10%; Calcium 15%; Iron 15%   **Exchanges:** 2 Starch, 2½ Lean Meat   **Carbohydrate Choices:** 2

250 calories

swiss steak casserole

Prep Time: 20 Minutes   Start to Finish: 2 Hours 5 Minutes   Makes: 6 servings

1	lb boneless beef round steak	2	cups sliced fresh mushrooms (6 oz)
3	tablespoons all-purpose flour	1	cup frozen pearl onions
1	teaspoon salt	1	clove garlic, finely chopped
1	teaspoon paprika	4	cups sliced carrots (8 medium)
½	teaspoon pepper	1	can (14.5 oz) stewed tomatoes,
2	tablespoons vegetable oil		undrained

1. Heat oven to 350°F. Trim excess fat from beef; cut beef into ¾-inch cubes. In medium bowl, mix flour, salt, paprika and pepper. Add beef; toss to coat.

2. In 12-inch skillet, heat 1 tablespoon of the oil over medium-high heat. Add beef, reserving remaining flour mixture; cook on all sides until brown. Spoon into ungreased 2½-quart casserole.

3. In same skillet, heat remaining 1 tablespoon oil. Cook mushrooms, onions and garlic 2 to 3 minutes, stirring constantly, until brown. Spoon over beef in casserole. Stir in carrots, tomatoes and reserved flour mixture.

4. Cover; bake 1 hour 30 minutes to 1 hour 45 minutes or until meat and vegetables are tender.

1 Serving: Calories 250 (Calories from Fat 70); Total Fat 8g (Saturated Fat 2g; Trans Fat 0g); Cholesterol 55mg; Sodium 680mg; Total Carbohydrate 20g (Dietary Fiber 4g; Sugars 9g); Protein 25g   **% Daily Value:** Vitamin A 280%; Vitamin C 10%; Calcium 6%; Iron 20%   **Exchanges:** ½ Other Carbohydrate, 2 Vegetable, 3 Lean Meat
Carbohydrate Choices: 1

health smart

Beef round steak is a less tender cut of meat and is lower in fat than some other steaks. It may take longer to cook, but it has fewer calories and comes out juicy and flavorful, making it worth the wait.

 # pastitsio

Prep Time: 20 Minutes   Start to Finish: 1 Hour   Makes: 6 servings

1	cup uncooked elbow macaroni (about 4 oz)	½	teaspoon salt
1	egg white	¼	teaspoon ground cinnamon
¼	cup grated Parmesan cheese	¼	teaspoon ground nutmeg
2	tablespoons milk	1	clove garlic, finely chopped
¾	lb ground lamb	1	cup milk
1½	cups cubed peeled eggplant	1	tablespoon cornstarch
1	can (14.5 oz) whole tomatoes, drained	2	tablespoons grated Parmesan cheese
1	medium onion, chopped (½ cup)	1	egg, beaten

1. Heat oven to 350°F. Cook and drain macaroni as directed on package. Stir in egg white, ¼ cup cheese and 2 tablespoons milk.

2. In 10-inch skillet, cook lamb over medium heat about 10 minutes, stirring occasionally, until no longer pink; drain. Stir in eggplant, tomatoes, onion, salt, cinnamon, nutmeg and garlic, breaking up tomatoes.

3. In 1-quart saucepan, cook 1 cup milk and the cornstarch over medium heat, stirring constantly, until mixture thickens and boils. Stir in 2 tablespoons cheese and the egg.

4. Place half of the macaroni mixture in ungreased 1½-quart casserole. Top with lamb mixture, remaining macaroni mixture and the sauce.

5. Bake uncovered about 40 minutes or until set in center.

1 Serving: Calories 260 (Calories from Fat 100); Total Fat 11g (Saturated Fat 5g; Trans Fat 0g); Cholesterol 80mg; Sodium 510mg; Total Carbohydrate 22g (Dietary Fiber 2g; Sugars 4g); Protein 16g   **% Daily Value:** Vitamin A 4%; Vitamin C 6%; Calcium 10%; Iron 15%   **Exchanges:** 1 Starch, 1 Vegetable, 1½ Medium-Fat Meat, 1 Fat **Carbohydrate Choices:** 1½

 try this
Pastitsio is a popular Greek casserole made up of layers of pasta and lamb with the delicate seasoning blend of cinnamon and nutmeg. You can use ¾ lb lean ground beef instead of the ground lamb, if you wish.

german pork and
cabbage casserole

Prep Time: 20 Minutes   Start to Finish: 1 Hour 5 Minutes   Makes: 6 servings

3	slices bacon	1	can (8 oz) sauerkraut, drained
6	boneless country-style pork ribs	1	medium unpeeled cooking apple, chopped (1 cup)
½	teaspoon salt		
¼	teaspoon pepper	1	cup julienne (matchstick-cut) carrots
5	cups coleslaw mix (from 16-oz bag)	¾	cup apple cider
1	large onion, chopped (1 cup)	1	teaspoon caraway seed

1. Heat oven to 350°F. Spray 13×9-inch (3-quart) glass baking dish with cooking spray.

2. In 12-inch nonstick skillet, cook bacon until crisp; drain on paper towels. Crumble bacon; set aside. Season ribs with salt and pepper. Cook ribs in bacon drippings over high heat 3 to 4 minutes, turning once, until brown. Place in baking dish, reserving drippings in skillet.

3. In same skillet, cook coleslaw mix and onion over medium heat about 3 minutes, stirring occasionally, until softened and wilted. Remove from heat. Add bacon, sauerkraut, apple, carrots, apple cider and caraway seed; mix well. Spoon on top of ribs.

4. Cover with foil. Bake 30 to 45 minutes or until pork is no longer pink and meat thermometer inserted in center reads 160°F.

1 Serving: Calories 280 (Calories from Fat 120); Total Fat 13g (Saturated Fat 4.5g; Trans Fat 0g); Cholesterol 60mg; Sodium 610mg; Total Carbohydrate 18g (Dietary Fiber 4g; Sugars 11g); Protein 21g   **% Daily Value:** Vitamin A 100%; Vitamin C 25%; Calcium 6%; Iron 10%   **Exchanges:** ½ Other Carbohydrate, 2 Vegetable, 2½ Medium-Fat Meat **Carbohydrate Choices:** 1

try this

A medium head of fresh green cabbage can be used instead of the bag of coleslaw mix. Thinly slice enough cabbage to measure 5 cups.

loaded baked potato casserole photo on page C-5

Prep Time: 15 Minutes   Start to Finish: 1 Hour   Makes: 8 servings

1   bag (30 oz) frozen extra-spicy and crispy potato wedges
2   cups chopped cooked ham
8   slices bacon, crisply cooked, crumbled
1   medium bell pepper (any color), chopped (1 cup)

1   cup chopped green onions (about 16 medium)
1   jar (15 oz) cheese dip or process cheese sauce
½   cup sour cream

1. Heat oven to 375°F. Spray 13×9-inch (3-quart) glass baking dish with cooking spray.

2. Arrange potato wedges in baking dish. Bake uncovered 10 to 15 minutes or until thawed and beginning to brown.

3. Top potatoes with half each of the ham, bacon, bell pepper and onions. Spread cheese dip on top. Sprinkle with remaining ham, bacon and bell pepper.

4. Bake 20 to 30 minutes longer or until cheese dip is melted and potatoes are tender. Top with dollops of sour cream and remaining onions.

1 Serving: Calories 300 (Calories from Fat 150); Total Fat 17g (Saturated Fat 8g; Trans Fat 0.5g); Cholesterol 60mg; Sodium 1270mg; Total Carbohydrate 18g (Dietary Fiber 3g; Sugars 6g); Protein 20g   **% Daily Value:** Vitamin A 20%; Vitamin C 25%; Calcium 15%; Iron 10%   **Exchanges:** ½ Starch, ½ Other Carbohydrate, 2½ Medium-Fat Meat, 1 Fat
Carbohydrate Choices: 1

health smart

This casserole is "loaded" with flavor but only 300 calories per serving! To reduce the calories even more, use just 6 slices of bacon and substitue fat-free sour cream for regular.

halibut with
potato succotash

Prep Time: 20 Minutes   Start to Finish: 45 Minutes   Makes: 4 servings

1	halibut or other firm fish fillet (1 to 1½ lb)	1	box (9 oz) frozen baby lima beans
1	tablespoon butter or margarine, melted	1	cup frozen whole kernel corn
1	tablespoon canola oil	½	teaspoon garlic-pepper blend
2	cups frozen potatoes O'Brien with onions and peppers	½	teaspoon seasoned salt
		½	teaspoon dried thyme leaves
		⅛	teaspoon ground red pepper (cayenne)

1. Heat oven to 425°F. Spray 11×7-inch (2-quart) glass baking dish with cooking spray.

2. Cut halibut into 4 serving pieces. Place in baking dish. Brush butter over halibut.

3. In 10-inch nonstick skillet, heat oil over medium-high heat. Cook potatoes in oil 5 minutes, stirring occasionally. Stir in lima beans and corn. Cook 3 to 5 minutes longer or until vegetables are crisp-tender. Spoon mixture around halibut in baking dish. Sprinkle halibut and vegetables with seasonings; stir vegetables slightly.

4. Bake uncovered 20 to 25 minutes or until fish flakes easily with fork and vegetables are tender.

1 Serving: Calories 300 (Calories from Fat 70); Total Fat 8g (Saturated Fat 2.5g; Trans Fat 0g); Cholesterol 70mg; Sodium 340mg; Total Carbohydrate 30g (Dietary Fiber 5g; Sugars 3g); Protein 27g   **% Daily Value:** Vitamin A 8%; Vitamin C 10%; Calcium 4%; Iron 10%   **Exchanges:** 2 Starch, 3 Very Lean Meat, 1 Fat   **Carbohydrate Choices:** 2

290 calories

roasted tilapia and vegetables

Prep Time: 15 Minutes   Start to Finish: 40 Minutes   Makes: 4 servings

- 8 oz fresh asparagus spears, trimmed, cut in half
- 2 small zucchini, halved lengthwise, cut into ½-inch pieces
- 1 medium bell pepper (any color), cut into ½-inch strips
- 1 large onion, cut into ½-inch wedges, separated
- 2 tablespoons olive oil
- 2 teaspoons Montreal steak grill seasoning
- 4 tilapia or other medium-firm fillets (about 1½ lb)
- 1 tablespoon butter or margarine, melted
- ½ teaspoon paprika

1. Heat oven to 450°F. In large bowl, mix asparagus, zucchini, bell pepper, onion and oil. Sprinkle with 1 teaspoon of the grill seasoning; toss to coat. Spread vegetables in ungreased 15×10×1-inch pan. Place on lowest oven rack; bake 5 minutes.

2. Meanwhile, spray 13×9-inch (3-quart) glass baking dish with cooking spray. Pat tilapia fillets dry with paper towels. Brush with butter; sprinkle with paprika and remaining 1 teaspoon grill seasoning. Place in baking dish.

3. Place baking dish on middle oven rack. Bake fish and vegetables uncovered 17 to 18 minutes or until fish flakes easily with fork and vegetables are tender.

1 Serving: Calories 290 (Calories from Fat 110); Total Fat 12g (Saturated Fat 3.5g; Trans Fat 0g); Cholesterol 100mg; Sodium 520mg; Total Carbohydrate 10g (Dietary Fiber 3g; Sugars 5g); Protein 34g   **% Daily Value:** Vitamin A 40%; Vitamin C 45%; Calcium 6%; Iron 8%   **Exchanges:** 2 Vegetable, 4 Lean Meat, ½ Fat   **Carbohydrate Choices:** ½

tuna twist casserole

Prep Time: 10 Minutes   Start to Finish: 30 Minutes   Makes: 6 servings

½ cup refrigerated reduced-fat Alfredo
    pasta sauce (from 10-oz container)
2 eggs
1 clove garlic, finely chopped
4 cups cooked tricolor rotelle pasta

2 cups frozen broccoli, carrots and
    cauliflower (or other combination),
    thawed, drained
1 can (12 oz) tuna in water, drained
1 cup Italian-seasoned croutons

1. Heat oven to 350°F. In ungreased 8-inch square (2-quart) glass baking dish, mix Alfredo sauce, eggs and garlic. Stir in pasta, vegetables and tuna. Press lightly in dish.

2. Cover; bake about 20 minutes or until set. Sprinkle with croutons.

1 Serving: Calories 290 (Calories from Fat 60); Total Fat 6g (Saturated Fat 2.5g; Trans Fat 0g); Cholesterol 90mg; Sodium 480mg; Total Carbohydrate 37g (Dietary Fiber 3g; Sugars 2g); Protein 21g   **% Daily Value:** Vitamin A 15%; Vitamin C 10%; Calcium 8%; Iron 15%   **Exchanges:** 2 Starch, 1 Vegetable, 2 Lean Meat   **Carbohydrate Choices:** 2½

health smart

This lighter twist on a tuna casserole saves 8 grams of fat per serving by using reduced-fat Alfredo sauce instead of the full-fat version and tuna packed in water instead of oil.

shrimp and bow-tie casserole

Prep Time: 15 Minutes   Start to Finish: 1 Hour   Makes: 5 servings

3	cups uncooked bow-tie (farfalle) pasta (6 oz)	1	lb cooked deveined peeled medium shrimp, thawed if frozen, tail shells removed
3	tablespoons onion soup and dip mix	1½	cups frozen baby peas
2	cups fat-free (skim) milk	½	cup shredded Havarti cheese (2 oz)
		¼	teaspoon paprika

1. Heat oven to 350°F. Spray 2-quart casserole with cooking spray.

2. Cook and drain pasta as directed on package. Place pasta in casserole. In same saucepan, heat soup mix and milk over medium heat just to boiling, stirring constantly. Pour over pasta. Add shrimp and peas; stir gently to mix. Sprinkle with cheese and paprika.

3. Cover; bake 35 to 45 minutes or until thoroughly heated and bubbly around edges.

1 Serving: Calories 290 (Calories from Fat 60); Total Fat 6g (Saturated Fat 3.5g; Trans Fat 0g); Cholesterol 215mg; Sodium 840mg; Total Carbohydrate 30g (Dietary Fiber 2g; Sugars 8g); Protein 30g   **% Daily Value:** Vitamin A 20%; Vitamin C 8%; Calcium 25%; Iron 25%   **Exchanges:** 2 Starch, 3½ Very Lean Meat, ½ Fat   **Carbohydrate Choices:** 2

crabmeat and spinach enchiladas

Prep Time: 30 Minutes   **Start to Finish:** 1 Hour 10 Minutes   **Makes:** 8 servings

1 cup chunky-style salsa
¼ cup chili sauce
½ teaspoon ground cumin
¼ cup chopped fresh cilantro
2 packages (8 oz each) refrigerated chunk-style imitation crabmeat
2 cups frozen cut leaf spinach, thawed, squeezed to drain

1 cup shredded Monterey Jack cheese with jalapeño peppers (4 oz)
8 flour tortillas (8 inch)
1 cup shredded reduced-fat mild Cheddar cheese (4 oz)
Additional chopped fresh cilantro, if desired

1. Heat oven to 350°F. Spray 13×9-inch (3-quart) glass baking dish with cooking spray.

2. In small bowl, mix salsa, chili sauce, cumin and ¼ cup cilantro. Break up crabmeat chunks slightly. In medium bowl, mix crabmeat, spinach, Monterey Jack cheese and ¼ cup of the sauce mixture. Spread about ½ cup sauce mixture over bottom of baking dish.

3. Top each tortilla with about ⅔ cup crabmeat mixture; roll up. Place, seam side down, in baking dish. Top with remaining sauce mixture. Sprinkle with Cheddar cheese.

4. Spray sheet of foil with cooking spray. Cover dish with foil, sprayed side down. Bake 35 to 40 minutes or until thoroughly heated. Garnish with cilantro.

1 Serving: Calories 280 (Calories from Fat 70); Total Fat 8g (Saturated Fat 3.5g; Trans Fat 0.5g); Cholesterol 35mg; Sodium 1210mg; Total Carbohydrate 34g (Dietary Fiber 3g; Sugars 3g); Protein 20g   **% Daily Value:** Vitamin A 60%; Vitamin C 8%; Calcium 30%; Iron 15%   **Exchanges:** 2 Starch, 2 Very Lean Meat, 1 Fat   **Carbohydrate Choices:** 2

health smart

Imitation crabmeat is made from pollack, a mild white fish that is extremely low in fat and calories. An acceptable substitute for real crabmeat, imitation crabmeat is readily available and less expensive.

chiles rellenos egg soufflé bake

Prep Time: 20 Minutes   Start to Finish: 1 Hour   Makes: 6 servings

2 cans (4 oz each) peeled whole green chiles, drained	1½ cups milk
4 oz Monterey Jack cheese, cut into 3×½×½-inch strips	½ cup all-purpose flour
1 jar (2 oz) diced pimientos, drained	¼ teaspoon salt
4 eggs, separated	Fresh cilantro sprigs, if desired
	2 cups chunky-style salsa

1. Heat oven to 350°F. Spray 11×7-inch (2-quart) glass baking dish with cooking spray.

2. Stuff chiles with cheese strips; arrange in baking dish. Sprinkle with pimientos.

3. In medium bowl, beat egg yolks and milk with wire whisk. Stir in flour and salt until smooth. In large bowl using electric mixer, beat egg whites on high speed until stiff peaks form. Gently fold yolk mixture into beaten egg whites until no traces of white remain. Spoon mixture evenly over stuffed chiles.

4. Bake uncovered 30 to 40 minutes or until knife inserted in center comes out clean and top is golden brown. Garnish with cilantro sprigs. Serve immediately with salsa.

1 Serving: Calories 230 (Calories from Fat 100); Total Fat 11g (Saturated Fat 6g; Trans Fat 0g); Cholesterol 165mg; Sodium 920mg; Total Carbohydrate 19g (Dietary Fiber 2g; Sugars 8g); Protein 13g   **% Daily Value:** Vitamin A 20%; Vitamin C 20%; Calcium 25%; Iron 10%   **Exchanges:** 1 Starch, 1 Vegetable, 1 Medium-Fat Meat, 1 Fat **Carbohydrate Choices:** 1

individual chicken pot pies

Prep Time: 35 Minutes   Start to Finish: 1 Hour 15 Minutes   Makes: 8 servings

1 tablespoon olive oil	½ cup dry sherry, nonalcoholic wine or chicken broth
1 medium carrot, thinly sliced (½ cup)	1 cup fat-free half-and-half
1 medium stalk celery, thinly sliced (½ cup)	¾ cup water
1 cup diced unpeeled red potatoes	1 teaspoon poultry seasoning
1 medium onion, chopped (½ cup)	1 teaspoon parsley flakes
2 cloves garlic, finely chopped	2 cups cubed cooked chicken breast
2 cans (10¾ oz each) condensed 98% fat-free cream of chicken soup with 45% less sodium	1 cup frozen sweet peas, thawed
	2 sheets frozen phyllo (filo) pastry (18×14 inch), thawed
	Cooking spray

1. Heat oven to 400°F. Lightly spray 8 (8-oz) individual baking dishes (ramekins) with cooking spray.

2. In 3-quart saucepan, heat oil. Add carrot, celery, potatoes, onion and garlic; cook over medium-high heat about 10 minutes, stirring occasionally, until vegetables are tender. Stir in soup, sherry, half-and-half, water, poultry seasoning, parsley, chicken and peas; heat to boiling. Remove from heat.

3. Cover work surface with sheet of plastic wrap the size of phyllo sheets. Place 1 phyllo sheet on plastic wrap; spray with cooking spray. Top with second phyllo sheet; spray with cooking spray. Cut phyllo sheets in half lengthwise into 2 (17×6½-inch) strips; stack strips. Cut stack of strips in half lengthwise again; place 1 stack on other stack. Cut stack of phyllo crosswise into 8 equal stacks.

4. Place ramekins on cookie sheet. Divide chicken mixture evenly among ramekins. Top each ramekin with a phyllo stack, allowing phyllo to hang over side of ramekin.

5. Bake 25 to 35 minutes or until phyllo is golden brown and crispy. Cool 5 minutes before serving.

1 Serving: Calories 200 (Calories from Fat 50); Total Fat 6g (Saturated Fat 1.5g; Trans Fat 0g); Cholesterol 35mg; Sodium 610mg; Total Carbohydrate 21g (Dietary Fiber 3g; Sugars 4g); Protein 15g   **% Daily Value:** Vitamin A 35%; Vitamin C 6%; Calcium 6%; Iron 8%   **Exchanges:** 1½ Starch, 1½ Lean Meat   **Carbohydrate Choices:** 1½

190 calories

impossibly easy chicken primavera pie

Prep Time: 5 Minutes   **Start to Finish:** 45 Minutes   **Makes:** 6 servings

1½ cups cut-up cooked chicken
 1   box (9 oz) frozen asparagus cuts,
     thawed, well drained
 1   cup frozen bell pepper and onion
     stir-fry, thawed, well drained

⅓   cup grated Parmesan cheese
½   cup Original Bisquick mix
 1   cup milk
½   teaspoon salt
 2   eggs

1. Heat oven to 400°F. Spray 9-inch glass pie plate with cooking spray. Layer chicken, asparagus, stir-fry mixture and cheese in pie plate.

2. In medium bowl, stir remaining ingredients with wire whisk or fork until blended. Pour into pie plate.

3. Bake uncovered 30 to 35 minutes or until knife inserted in center comes out clean. Let stand 5 minutes before serving.

1 Serving: Calories 190 (Calories from Fat 70); Total Fat 8g (Saturated Fat 3g; Trans Fat 0.5g); Cholesterol 110mg; Sodium 490mg; Total Carbohydrate 12g (Dietary Fiber 1g; Sugars 4g); Protein 17g   **% Daily Value:** Vitamin A 10%; Vitamin C 15%; Calcium 15%; Iron 6%   **Exchanges:** 1 Starch, 2 Lean Meat   **Carbohydrate Choices:** 1

cheesy italian chicken pie

Prep Time: 20 Minutes   Start to Finish: 1 Hour 10 Minutes   Makes: 8 servings

1½	cups cut-up cooked chicken	½	teaspoon garlic powder
1¼	cups shredded mozzarella cheese (5 oz)	1	can (8 oz) tomato sauce
⅓	cup grated Parmesan cheese	½	cup Original Bisquick mix
½	teaspoon dried oregano leaves	1	cup milk
½	teaspoon dried basil leaves	¼	teaspoon pepper
		2	eggs

1. Heat oven to 400°F. Spray 9-inch glass pie plate with cooking spray.

2. In large bowl, mix chicken, ½ cup of the mozzarella cheese, the Parmesan cheese, oregano, basil, garlic powder and ½ cup of the tomato sauce; spoon into pie plate.

3. In medium bowl, stir Bisquick mix, milk, pepper and eggs with wire whisk or fork until blended. Pour over chicken mixture.

4. Bake uncovered 35 minutes. Sprinkle with remaining ¾ cup mozzarella cheese. Bake 5 to 8 minutes longer or until knife inserted in center comes out clean. Let stand 5 minutes. Serve with remaining tomato sauce, heated if desired.

1 Serving: Calories 250 (Calories from Fat 110); Total Fat 13g (Saturated Fat 6g; Trans Fat 0.5g); Cholesterol 120mg; Sodium 610mg; Total Carbohydrate 12g (Dietary Fiber 1g; Sugars 5g); Protein 23g   **% Daily Value:** Vitamin A 10%; Vitamin C 2%; Calcium 35%; Iron 8%   **Exchanges:** 1 Starch, 3 Lean Meat   **Carbohydrate Choices:** 1

serve with

Serve this hearty cheesy dinner pie with a favorite steamed fresh vegetable, such as green beans.

290 calories

chicken enchilada pie

Prep Time: 15 Minutes   Start to Finish: 50 Minutes   Makes: 6 servings

1   package (9 oz) frozen diced cooked
    chicken, thawed, drained
1   can (4.5 oz) chopped green chiles,
    undrained
½   cup enchilada sauce
½   cup Original Bisquick mix
½   cup cornmeal
½   cup milk

1   egg
1   can (11 oz) vacuum-packed whole
    kernel corn with red and green
    peppers, drained
1   cup shredded Mexican cheese
    blend (4 oz)
1   medium tomato, chopped (¾ cup)

1. Place sheet of foil on lowest oven rack. Heat oven to 400°F.

2. In 10-inch skillet, cook chicken, chiles and enchilada sauce over medium-high heat 3 to 4 minutes, stirring occasionally, until hot and bubbly. Pour into ungreased 9-inch glass pie plate.

3. In medium bowl, stir Bisquick mix, cornmeal, milk and egg with wire whisk or fork until blended. Stir in corn. Spoon over chicken mixture.

4. Place pie plate on rack above foil. Bake uncovered 22 to 27 minutes or until toothpick inserted in topping comes out clean. Top with cheese and tomato. Let stand 5 minutes before serving.

1 Serving: Calories 290 (Calories from Fat 100); Total Fat 11g (Saturated Fat 5g; Trans Fat 0g); Cholesterol 85mg; Sodium 870mg; Total Carbohydrate 29g (Dietary Fiber 2g; Sugars 6g); Protein 20g   **% Daily Value:** Vitamin A 10%; Vitamin C 10%; Calcium 20%; Iron 6%   **Exchanges:** 2 Starch, 2 Very Lean Meat, 1½ Fat   **Carbohydrate Choices:** 2

turkey-spaghetti pie

Prep Time: 30 Minutes   Start to Finish: 1 Hour 20 Minutes   Makes: 6 servings

4   oz uncooked spaghetti
1   tablespoon butter or margarine
½   lb ground turkey breast
1   small bell pepper (any color), chopped (½ cup)
1   small onion, chopped (¼ cup)
1   jar (16 oz) tomato pasta sauce
1   teaspoon chili powder

½   teaspoon salt
¼   teaspoon pepper
2   eggs
1   cup reduced-fat small-curd cottage cheese
½   cup shredded mozzarella cheese (2 oz)

1. Heat oven to 375°F. Spray 10-inch glass deep-dish pie plate with cooking spray.

2. Cook and drain spaghetti as directed on package. Place spaghetti in pie plate, pressing down gently.

3. In 10-inch skillet, melt butter over medium-high heat. Cook turkey, bell pepper and onion in butter, stirring occasionally, until turkey is no longer pink. Stir in pasta sauce, chili powder, salt and pepper. Reduce heat to medium; cook 5 to 6 minutes longer, stirring occasionally, until sauce is thickened.

4. In small bowl, mix eggs and cottage cheese; spread evenly over spaghetti crust. Spoon turkey mixture over cottage cheese mixture. Sprinkle with mozzarella cheese.

5. Bake uncovered 35 to 45 minutes or until center is set. Let stand 5 minutes before cutting.

1 Serving: Calories 300 (Calories from Fat 90); Total Fat 10g (Saturated Fat 3g; Trans Fat 0.5g); Cholesterol 105mg; Sodium 860mg; Total Carbohydrate 30g (Dietary Fiber 2g; Sugars 9g); Protein 23g   **% Daily Value:** Vitamin A 15%; Vitamin C 15%; Calcium 15%; Iron 15%   **Exchanges:** 1 Starch, 1 Other Carbohydrate, 3 Lean Meat   **Carbohydrate Choices:** 2

health smart

This easy family-style recipe is made with regular pasta, but you could try one of the whole-grain varieties instead for a change of pace and a little added fiber.

impossibly easy turkey club pie

Prep Time: 15 Minutes   Start to Finish: 55 Minutes   Makes: 6 servings

8	slices bacon	1	cup milk
1½	cups cut-up cooked turkey breast	2	eggs
1	cup shredded Cheddar cheese (4 oz)		Sliced tomatoes, if desired
½	cup Original Bisquick or Bisquick Heart Smart® mix		Shredded lettuce, if desired

1. Heat oven to 400°F. Line 10-inch microwavable plate with microwavable paper towel. Place bacon on paper towel; cover with another paper towel. Microwave on High 4 to 6 minutes or until crisp; crumble bacon.

2. Spray 9-inch glass pie plate with cooking spray. Sprinkle turkey, bacon and cheese in pie plate. In medium bowl, stir remaining ingredients with wire whisk or fork until blended. Pour into pie plate.

3. Bake uncovered 30 to 35 minutes or until knife inserted in center comes out clean. Let stand 5 minutes before serving. Top with chopped tomatoes and shredded lettuce.

1 Serving: Calories 280 (Calories from Fat 160); Total Fat 18g (Saturated Fat 8g; Trans Fat 0.5g); Cholesterol 135mg; Sodium 500mg; Total Carbohydrate 8g (Dietary Fiber 0g; Sugars 3g); Protein 22g   **% Daily Value:** Vitamin A 8%; Vitamin C 0%; Calcium 20%; Iron 6%   **Exchanges:** ½ Starch, 3 Medium-Fat Meat, ½ Fat   **Carbohydrate Choices:** ½

serve with

This version of a lunch favorite is perfect paired with a dill pickle spear and a piece of fresh fruit.

garlic shepherd's pie

Prep Time: 30 Minutes   Start to Finish: 1 Hour   Makes: 6 servings

1 lb lean (at least 80%) ground beef	½ teaspoon dried basil leaves
1 medium onion, chopped (½ cup)	⅛ teaspoon pepper
1 cup frozen cut green beans	1 pouch roasted garlic mashed potato mix (from 7.2-oz box)
1 cup ready-to-eat baby-cut carrots	1½ cups hot water
1 cup sliced fresh mushrooms (3 oz)	½ cup milk
1 can (14.5 oz) diced tomatoes, undrained	2 teaspoons butter or margarine
1 jar (12 oz) beef gravy	2 teaspoons shredded Parmesan cheese
2 tablespoons chili sauce	

1. Heat oven to 350°F. In 12-inch nonstick skillet, cook beef and onion over medium heat 8 to 10 minutes, stirring occasionally, until beef is thoroughly cooked; drain.

2. Stir in green beans, carrots, mushrooms, tomatoes, gravy, chili sauce, basil and pepper. Heat to boiling; reduce heat. Cover and simmer about 10 minutes or until vegetables are tender. Meanwhile, cook potatoes as directed on box, using hot water, milk and butter. Let stand 5 minutes.

3. Spoon beef mixture into ungreased 8-inch square (2-quart) glass baking dish or 2-quart casserole. Spoon potatoes onto beef mixture around edge of dish. Sprinkle with cheese.

4. Bake uncovered 25 to 30 minutes or until potatoes are firm and beef mixture is bubbly.

1 Serving: Calories 290 (Calories from Fat 120); Total Fat 13g (Saturated Fat 5g; Trans Fat 1g); Cholesterol 55mg; Sodium 800mg; Total Carbohydrate 25g (Dietary Fiber 4g; Sugars 6g); Protein 19g   **% Daily Value:** Vitamin A 80%; Vitamin C 10%; Calcium 8%; Iron 15%   **Exchanges:** 1 Starch, 1 Vegetable, 2 Medium-Fat Meat, ½ Fat   **Carbohydrate Choices:** 1½

ham and pineapple pie

Prep Time: 10 Minutes   Start to Finish: 40 Minutes   Makes: 6 servings

1½ cups chopped cooked ham	1 cup milk
1 can (8 oz) crushed pineapple in juice, drained	2 eggs
4 medium green onions, sliced (¼ cup)	2 teaspoons yellow mustard
1 cup Original Bisquick mix	1 cup shredded Colby–Monterey Jack cheese blend (4 oz)

1. Heat oven to 400°F. Spray 9-inch glass pie plate with cooking spray. Sprinkle ham, pineapple and onions in pie plate.

2. In medium bowl, stir Bisquick mix, milk, eggs and mustard until blended; pour over ham mixture.

3. Bake uncovered about 25 minutes or until knife inserted in center comes out clean. Sprinkle with cheese. Bake 3 to 4 minutes longer or until cheese is melted.

1 Serving: Calories 290 (Calories from Fat 150); Total Fat 16g (Saturated Fat 7g; Trans Fat 0.5g); Cholesterol 115mg; Sodium 770mg; Total Carbohydrate 21g (Dietary Fiber 0g; Sugars 10g); Protein 17g   **% Daily Value:** Vitamin A 8%; Vitamin C 4%; Calcium 25%; Iron 10%   **Exchanges:** 1½ Starch, 1½ Medium-Fat Meat, 1½ Fat   **Carbohydrate Choices:** 1½

canadian bacon and potato quiche

Prep Time: 20 Minutes   Start to Finish: 1 Hour 15 Minutes   Makes: 8 servings

1 refrigerated pie crust (from 15-oz box), softened as directed on box
1 cup frozen country-style shredded hash brown potatoes, thawed
1 cup ½-inch pieces fresh asparagus
1 cup diced Canadian bacon

1½ cups shredded Havarti cheese (6 oz)
4 eggs
1 cup milk
½ teaspoon dried marjoram leaves
¼ teaspoon salt

1. Heat oven to 375°F. Place pie crust in 9-inch glass pie plate as directed on box for One-Crust Filled Pie. Bake about 8 minutes or until light golden brown.

2. Layer potatoes, asparagus, bacon and cheese in partially baked crust. In medium bowl, beat eggs, milk, marjoram and salt with wire whisk until well blended. Pour over mixture in pie plate.

3. Bake 45 to 50 minutes or until knife inserted in center comes out clean. Let stand 5 minutes before cutting.

1 Serving: Calories 290 (Calories from Fat 170); Total Fat 19g (Saturated Fat 8g; Trans Fat 2g); Cholesterol 140mg; Sodium 640mg; Total Carbohydrate 15g (Dietary Fiber 1g; Sugars 3g); Protein 15g   **% Daily Value:** Vitamin A 10%; Vitamin C 4%; Calcium 20%; Iron 6%   **Exchanges:** 1 Starch, 2 High-Fat Meat, ½ Fat   **Carbohydrate Choices:** 1

Chapter 4

meatless
main dishes

Having a meatless meal one or two nights a week is a great way to get your family to eat more veggies. Bonus: it's healthy. And with dishes as delicious as the Sweet Potato Risotto (page 127) and the Family-Favorite Cheese Pizza (page 149), no one will miss the meat.

sage barley-vegetable bake

Prep Time: 25 Minutes   **Start to Finish:** 1 Hour 45 Minutes   **Makes:** 4 servings

1	medium butternut squash, peeled, cut into 1-inch pieces (3 cups)
2	medium parsnips, peeled, cut into 1-inch pieces (2 cups)
2	cans (14 oz each) stewed tomatoes, undrained
2	cups frozen cut green beans (from 12-oz bag)

½   cup coarsely chopped onion
½   cup uncooked quick-cooking barley
½   cup water
1   teaspoon dried sage leaves
½   teaspoon seasoned salt
2   cloves garlic, finely chopped

1. Heat oven to 375°F. In ungreased 3-quart casserole, mix all ingredients, breaking up large pieces of tomatoes.

2. Cover and bake 1 hour to 1 hour 15 minutes or until vegetables and barley are tender.

1 Serving: Calories 250 (Calories from Fat 10); Total Fat 1g (Saturated Fat 0g; Trans Fat 0g); Cholesterol 0mg; Sodium 730mg; Total Carbohydrate 60g (Dietary Fiber 11g; Sugars 20g); Protein 7g   **% Daily Value:** Vitamin A 190%; Vitamin C 40%; Calcium 15%; Iron 15%   **Exchanges:** 2½ Starch, 1 Other Carbohydrate, 1 Vegetable   **Carbohydrate Choices:** 3

health smart

Butternut squash has a peel that ranges from cream to yellow in color, but the inside is bright orange and sweet. Squash is extremely high in vitamin A, so eat up!

baked polenta
with peperonata sauce

Prep Time: 15 Minutes   Start to Finish: 1 Hour 5 Minutes   Makes: 6 servings

Peperonata Sauce

3	tablespoons olive or vegetable oil
3	medium onions, chopped (1½ cups)
1	clove garlic, finely chopped
¾	cup chopped pitted kalamata or ripe olives
1	tablespoon chopped fresh or 1 teaspoon dried basil leaves
½	teaspoon salt

¼	teaspoon pepper
1	can (28 oz) diced tomatoes, drained
1	jar (12 oz) roasted red bell peppers, drained, chopped

Polenta

1	roll (1 lb) refrigerated polenta
1¼	cups grated Romano or Parmesan cheese

1. Heat oven to 350°F. Spray 2-quart casserole or 8-inch square glass baking dish with cooking spray.

2. In 3-quart saucepan, heat oil over medium heat. Add onions and garlic; cook 2 to 3 minutes, stirring occasionally, until onions are crisp-tender. Stir in remaining sauce ingredients. Simmer uncovered about 8 minutes or until slightly thickened.

3. Cut polenta into twelve ½-inch slices. Arrange 6 slices polenta on bottom of casserole. Spread half of the sauce over polenta. Sprinkle with ½ cup of the cheese. Repeat with remaining polenta, sauce and cheese.

4. Bake uncovered 35 to 40 minutes or until heated through and cheese is light brown. Let stand 10 minutes before serving.

1 Serving: Calories 270 (Calories from Fat 140); Total Fat 16g (Saturated Fat 5g; Trans Fat 0g); Cholesterol 20mg; Sodium 1050mg; Total Carbohydrate 22g (Dietary Fiber 3g; Sugars 6g); Protein 11g   **% Daily Value:** Vitamin A 10%; Vitamin C 35%; Calcium 30%; Iron 15%   **Exchanges:** 1 Starch, 1 Vegetable, 1 Medium-Fat Meat, 2 Fat **Carbohydrate Choices:** 1½

try this

If you're short of time, substitute a 32-oz jar of your favorite thick-and-chunky-style tomato pasta sauce. Try to find one flavored with ripe olives for the Peperonata Sauce. You can also make this colorful casserole ahead of time. Cover unbaked casserole and refrigerate it up to 24 hours ahead; just plan on an extra 10 to 15 minutes of baking time.

mostaccioli with sun-dried tomato pesto

Prep Time: 20 Minutes   Start to Finish: 20 Minutes   Makes: 6 servings

3	cups uncooked mostaccioli pasta (9 oz)	2	tablespoons tomato paste
⅓	cup sun-dried tomatoes in oil, drained	1	tablespoon olive or vegetable oil
		1	teaspoon lemon juice
¼	cup firmly packed fresh mint leaves or 4 teaspoons dried mint leaves	½	teaspoon pepper
		1	clove garlic
2	tablespoons chopped walnuts	½	cup crumbled feta cheese (2 oz)

1. Cook and drain pasta as directed on package.

2. Meanwhile, in food processor or blender, place remaining ingredients except cheese. Cover and process until mixture is almost smooth.

3. In large bowl, toss pasta, tomato mixture and cheese.

1 Serving: Calories 260 (Calories from Fat 70); Total Fat 8g (Saturated Fat 2.5g; Trans Fat 0g); Cholesterol 10mg; Sodium 200mg; Total Carbohydrate 37g (Dietary Fiber 3g; Sugars 2g); Protein 8g   **% Daily Value:** Vitamin A 8%; Vitamin C 8%; Calcium 8%; Iron 10%   **Exchanges:** 2 Starch, 1 Vegetable, 1½ Fat   **Carbohydrate Choices:** 2½

fresh tomato
and garlic penne

Prep Time: 15 Minutes   **Start to Finish:** 15 Minutes   **Makes:** 4 servings

2½	cups uncooked penne pasta (about 8 oz)
1	tablespoon olive or vegetable oil
3	cloves garlic, finely chopped
12	medium plum (Roma) tomatoes (2 lb), coarsely chopped

2	tablespoons chopped fresh basil leaves
½	teaspoon salt
¼	teaspoon freshly ground pepper

1. Cook and drain pasta as directed on package.

2. Meanwhile, in 10-inch skillet, heat oil over medium-high heat. Cook garlic in oil 30 seconds, stirring frequently. Stir in tomatoes. Cook 5 to 8 minutes, stirring frequently, until tomatoes are soft and sauce is slightly thickened.

3. Stir in basil, salt and pepper. Cook 1 minute. Serve sauce over pasta.

1 Serving: Calories 290 (Calories from Fat 45); Total Fat 5g (Saturated Fat 0.5g; Trans Fat 0g); Cholesterol 0mg; Sodium 310mg; Total Carbohydrate 52g (Dietary Fiber 5g; Sugars 3g); Protein 9g   **% Daily Value:** Vitamin A 25%; Vitamin C 25%; Calcium 2%; Iron 15%   **Exchanges:** 3 Starch, 1 Vegetable, ½ Fat   **Carbohydrate Choices:** 3½

heart smart

This is a great recipe to experiment with using one of the tasty whole-grain pasta varieties currently available. It's an easy way to add a little extra fiber to the meal.

vegetable curry with couscous

Prep Time: 20 Minutes   Start to Finish: 20 Minutes   Makes: 4 servings

1 tablespoon vegetable oil	1 bag (1 lb) frozen broccoli, cauliflower and carrots (or other combination)
1 medium bell pepper (any color), cut into thin strips	⅓ cup raisins
¼ cup vegetable or chicken broth	⅓ cup chutney
1 tablespoon curry powder	2 cups hot cooked couscous or rice
1 teaspoon salt	¼ cup chopped dry-roasted peanuts

1. In 12-inch skillet, heat oil over medium-high heat. Add bell pepper; cook, stirring frequently, until tender.

2. Stir in broth, curry powder, salt and frozen vegetables. Heat to boiling. Boil about 4 minutes, stirring frequently, until vegetables are crisp-tender.

3. Stir in raisins and chutney. Serve over couscous. Sprinkle with peanuts.

1 Serving: Calories 300 (Calories from Fat 70); Total Fat 8g (Saturated Fat 1g; Trans Fat 0g); Cholesterol 0mg; Sodium 1010mg; Total Carbohydrate 48g (Dietary Fiber 7g; Sugars 18g); Protein 9g   **% Daily Value:** Vitamin A 50%; Vitamin C 60%; Calcium 6%; Iron 10%   **Exchanges:** 2 Starch, 1 Other Carbohydrate, 1 Vegetable, 1½ Fat   **Carbohydrate Choices:** 3

baked asparagus
and couscous

Prep Time: 10 Minutes   Start to Finish: 40 Minutes   Makes: 6 servings

1¼   cups vegetable or chicken broth,
        heated
  1   lb fresh asparagus spears, trimmed,
        cut into 2-inch pieces
  1   cup uncooked couscous
  1   can (10¾ oz) condensed cream of
        asparagus soup
  2   medium carrots, shredded (1½ cups)

  1   tablespoon lemon juice
  1   teaspoon fresh or ½ teaspoon dried
        dill weed
  ½   teaspoon salt
  1   cup soft bread crumbs (about 2 slices
        bread)
  2   tablespoons butter or margarine,
        melted

1. Heat oven to 425°F.

2. In 2-quart casserole, mix broth, asparagus, couscous, soup, carrots, lemon juice, dill weed and salt. Cover and bake 20 minutes or until hot and bubbly.

3. In medium bowl, toss bread crumbs and butter; sprinkle over asparagus mixture. Bake uncovered 8 to 10 minutes or until crumbs are golden brown.

1 Serving: Calories 290 (Calories from Fat 70); Total Fat 8g (Saturated Fat 3.5g; Trans Fat 0g); Cholesterol 10mg; Sodium 950mg; Total Carbohydrate 45g (Dietary Fiber 5g; Sugars 5g); Protein 9g   **% Daily Value:** Vitamin A 110%; Vitamin C 6%; Calcium 8%; Iron 20%   **Exchanges:** 2 Starch, ½ Other Carbohydrate, 1 Vegetable, 1½ Fat
Carbohydrate Choices: 3

try this

This is a great meatless main dish, but the addition of 1 cup cubed cooked turkey ham with the asparagus in step 2 would be a nice variation and makes the dish just a bit heartier.

steamed vegetables in peanut sauce with rice

Prep Time: 20 Minutes   **Start to Finish:** 30 Minutes   **Makes:** 4 servings

1 Japanese or regular eggplant, cut into 2½-inch strips (3 cups)	1 medium onion, thinly sliced
1 medium bell pepper (any color), cut into julienne strips (1½ cups)	½ lb snow pea pods (2 cups)
	2 tablespoons soy sauce
1 large carrot, cut into julienne strips (1 cup)	1 tablespoon creamy peanut butter
	1 tablespoon hoisin sauce
1 cup sliced bok choy (stems and leaves) or celery	1 teaspoon grated gingerroot
	1 clove garlic, finely chopped
	2 cups hot cooked rice

1. Place steamer basket in ½ inch water in saucepan or skillet (water should not touch bottom of basket). Place eggplant, bell pepper, carrot, bok choy and onion in steamer basket. Cover tightly and heat to boiling; reduce heat. Steam 5 to 8 minutes or until vegetables are crisp-tender; add pea pods for the last minute of steaming.

2. In large bowl, beat soy sauce, peanut butter, hoisin sauce, gingerroot and garlic with wire whisk until blended. Add vegetables to peanut butter mixture; toss. Serve over rice.

1 Serving: Calories 210 (Calories from Fat 25); Total Fat 2.5g (Saturated Fat 0.5g; Trans Fat 0g); Cholesterol 0mg; Sodium 870mg; Total Carbohydrate 40g (Dietary Fiber 6g; Sugars 8g); Protein 6g   **% Daily Value:** Vitamin A 130%; Vitamin C 60%; Calcium 6%; Iron 10%   **Exchanges:** 1 Starch, 1 Other Carbohydrate, 2 Vegetable, ½ Fat **Carbohydrate Choices:** 2½

serve with
Treat yourself to basmati rice! It has a strong, nutty aroma and flavor unmatched by any other variety of rice.

sweet potato risotto

Prep Time: 35 Minutes   Start to Finish: 35 Minutes   Makes: 4 servings

2	tablespoons dry white wine or water	3¾	cups vegetable or chicken broth, heated
⅓	cup chopped onion		
1	clove garlic, finely chopped	2	tablespoons grated Parmesan cheese
1	cup uncooked Arborio or other short-grain white rice	½	teaspoon chopped fresh or ¼ teaspoon dried rosemary leaves, crumbled
½	cup mashed cooked sweet potato	⅛	teaspoon ground nutmeg

1. Spray 3-quart nonstick saucepan with cooking spray. Heat wine to boiling in saucepan over medium-high heat. Add onion and garlic; cook 3 to 4 minutes, stirring frequently, until onion is tender.

2. Stir in rice. Cook 1 minute, stirring frequently, until edges of kernels are translucent. Reduce heat to medium.

3. Stir in sweet potato and ½ cup of the broth. Cook uncovered about 3 minutes, stirring frequently, until broth is absorbed. Continue cooking 15 to 20 minutes, adding broth ½ cup at a time and stirring frequently, until rice is just tender and mixture is creamy; remove from heat. Stir in remaining ingredients.

1 Serving: Calories 160 (Calories from Fat 15); Total Fat 1.5g (Saturated Fat 0.5g; Trans Fat 0g); Cholesterol 0mg; Sodium 990mg; Total Carbohydrate 32g (Dietary Fiber 2g; Sugars 5g); Protein 4g   **% Daily Value:** Vitamin A 130%; Vitamin C 6%; Calcium 6%; Iron 10%   **Exchanges:** 1 Starch, 1 Other Carbohydrate, ½ Fat   **Carbohydrate Choices:** 2

health smart

Learn to love sweet potatoes! These deep orange–colored tubers are full of vitamins A and C. You can use either mashed fresh cooked or canned sweet potatoes. For another colorful treat, use mashed cooked carrots instead of sweet potatoes.

180 calories

tortellini with garden vegetables
photo on page C-1

Prep Time: 15 Minutes   Start to Finish: 15 Minutes   Makes: 4 servings

1 package (9 oz) refrigerated cheese-filled tortellini	1 tablespoon grated Parmesan or Romano cheese
1 box (9 oz) broccoli cuts (or other frozen vegetable)	1½ teaspoons olive or vegetable oil
2½ cups quartered cherry tomatoes	4 medium green onions, sliced (¼ cup)
¼ cup chopped fresh basil leaves or parsley	2 medium cloves garlic, finely chopped
	Salt and freshly ground pepper to taste, if desired

1. Cook tortellini as directed on package, adding broccoli for the last 2 to 3 minutes of cook time; drain thoroughly.

2. Add remaining ingredients except salt and pepper; toss. Sprinkle with salt and pepper.

1 Serving: Calories 180 (Calories from Fat 60); Total Fat 6g (Saturated Fat 2.5g; Trans Fat 0g); Cholesterol 60mg; Sodium 65mg; Total Carbohydrate 21g (Dietary Fiber 4g; Sugars 5g); Protein 8g   **% Daily Value:** Vitamin A 35%; Vitamin C 35%; Calcium 10%; Iron 10%   **Exchanges:** 1½ Starch, ½ Medium-Fat Meat, ½ Fat   **Carbohydrate Choices:** 1½

try this
Any variety of tortellini would be delicious in this recipe. Try spinach-, meat- or chicken-filled options.

tortellini with garden vegetables, page 128

180 calories

C-1

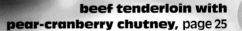

beef tenderloin with
pear-cranberry chutney, page 25
260 calories

italian chicken bracciole, page 20 **250** calories

summer garden
chicken stir-fry, page 50 **200** calories

C-2

peppered pork in
mushroom sauce, page 34 **200** calories

honey-mint lamb chops, page 27

210
calories

moroccan skillet chicken, page 54 **250** calories

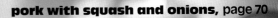
pork with squash and onions, page 70 **220** calories

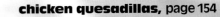
chicken quesadillas, page 154 **280** calories

asparagus and swiss bake, page 146 **270** calories

C-4

loaded baked
potato casserole, page 102
300 calories

fresh vegetable frittata, page 140
260 calories

salsa-shrimp tacos, page 162
190 calories

dilled shrimp and
egg salad wraps, page 163
280 calories

C-5

pesto chicken pizzas, page 181

280
calories

gingered chicken and
fruit salad, page 167
290
calories

C-6
chicken gyro pizza,
page 183
300
calories

chicken and fresh berry salad, page 170

245
calories

vegetarian reuben sandwiches, page 165

230 calories

roasted-vegetable lasagna, page 129

roasted-vegetable
lasagna photo on page C-8

Prep Time: 50 Minutes   Start to Finish: 1 Hour 25 Minutes   Makes: 10 servings

Roasted Vegetables
- 2 medium bell peppers (any color), cut into 1-inch pieces
- 1 medium onion, cut into 8 wedges, separated into pieces
- 2 medium zucchini, sliced (4 cups)
- 8 oz mushrooms, sliced (3 cups)
- ½ teaspoon salt
- ¼ teaspoon pepper

Tomato Sauce
- 1 large onion, chopped (1 cup)
- 2 tablespoons finely chopped garlic
- 1 can (28 oz) crushed tomatoes, undrained
- 3 tablespoons chopped fresh or 1 tablespoon dried basil leaves
- 3 tablespoons chopped fresh or 1 tablespoon dried oregano leaves
- 1 teaspoon sugar
- ½ teaspoon salt
- ½ teaspoon crushed red pepper flakes

Lasagna
- 12 uncooked lasagna noodles
- 3 cups shredded mozzarella cheese (16 oz)
- 1 cup freshly grated Parmesan cheese (4 oz)

1. Heat oven to 450°F. Spray 15×10×1-inch pan with sides with cooking spray. Place bell peppers, onion wedges, zucchini and mushrooms in single layer in pan. Spray vegetables with cooking spray; sprinkle with salt and pepper. Bake uncovered 20 to 25 minutes, turning vegetables once, until vegetables are tender.

2. Meanwhile, prepare Tomato Sauce. Spray 2-quart saucepan with cooking spray. Add chopped onion and garlic; cook over medium heat 2 minutes, stirring occasionally. Stir in remaining sauce ingredients. Heat to boiling; reduce heat. Simmer uncovered 15 to 20 minutes or until slightly thickened.

3. Meanwhile, cook and drain noodles as directed on package. Rinse noodles with cold water; drain. Mix cheeses; set aside.

4. Reduce oven temperature to 400°F. Spray 13×9-inch (3-quart) glass baking dish with cooking spray. Spread ¼ cup of the sauce in baking dish; top with 3 noodles. Layer with ¾ cup sauce, 1¼ cups vegetables and about ¾ cup cheese. Repeat layering with remaining noodles, sauce, vegetables and cheese 3 more times.

5. Bake uncovered 20 to 25 minutes or until hot and bubbly and cheese is light golden brown. Let stand 10 minutes before serving.

1 Serving: Calories 300 (Calories from Fat 100); Total Fat 11g (Saturated Fat 6g; Trans Fat 0g); Cholesterol 25mg; Sodium 690mg; Total Carbohydrate 32g (Dietary Fiber 4g; Sugars 6g); Protein 19g **% Daily Value:** Vitamin A 10%; Vitamin C 30%; Calcium 40%; Iron 15% **Exchanges:** 1½ Starch, 2 Vegetable, 1½ Medium-Fat Meat, ½ Fat **Carbohydrate Choices:** 2

cheesy vegetable-rice skillet

Prep Time: 10 Minutes   Start to Finish: 15 Minutes   Makes: 4 servings

1	can (14 oz) vegetable or chicken broth	1	package (6.2 oz) fast-cooking long-grain and wild rice mix
2	tablespoons butter or margarine	¾	cup shredded Cheddar cheese (3 oz)
1	bag (1 lb) frozen cauliflower, carrots and snow pea pods (or other combination)		

1. In 10-inch skillet, heat broth and butter to boiling over medium-high heat. Stir in frozen vegetables, rice mix and contents of seasoning packet. Heat to boiling; reduce heat.

2. Cover and simmer 5 to 6 minutes or until vegetables and rice are tender. Sprinkle with cheese.

1 Serving: Calories 230 (Calories from Fat 120); Total Fat 13g (Saturated Fat 8g; Trans Fat 0g); Cholesterol 35mg; Sodium 850mg; Total Carbohydrate 19g (Dietary Fiber 3g; Sugars 3g); Protein 9g   **% Daily Value:** Vitamin A 60%; Vitamin C 30%; Calcium 15%; Iron 6%   **Exchanges:** 1 Starch, 1 Vegetable, ½ High-Fat Meat, 1½ Fat   **Carbohydrate Choices:** 1

vegetable paella

Prep Time: 20 Minutes   Start to Finish: 20 Minutes   Makes: 4 servings

2	tablespoons olive or vegetable oil	1	can (14.5 oz) stewed tomatoes, undrained
2	cloves garlic, finely chopped	½	teaspoon saffron threads, crushed
1	large red onion, cut into thin wedges	1	bag (1 lb) frozen corn, broccoli, baby cob corn and carrots (or other combination)
1	cup uncooked instant brown rice		
1	cup vegetable or chicken broth		

1. In 12-inch skillet, heat oil over medium-high heat. Add garlic and onion; cook until onion is tender, stirring frequently.

2. Stir in remaining ingredients. Heat to boiling; reduce heat to medium-low. Cover and cook 5 minutes, stirring occasionally, until hot. Remove from heat; let stand covered 5 minutes.

1 Serving: Calories 250 (Calories from Fat 70); Total Fat 8g (Saturated Fat 1g; Trans Fat 0g); Cholesterol 0mg; Sodium 560mg; Total Carbohydrate 39g (Dietary Fiber 6g; Sugars 9g); Protein 5g   **% Daily Value:** Vitamin A 50%; Vitamin C 40%; Calcium 8%; Iron 10%   **Exchanges:** 1 Starch, 1 Other Carbohydrate, 1 Vegetable, 1½ Fat **Carbohydrate Choices:** 2½

 try this
To satisfy the meat-eaters in the family, remove half of the paella from the skillet; keep warm. Stir 1 cup cubed cooked chicken or turkey breast into the remaining paella in the skillet; heat through.

240 calories

asian rice and lentil burgers

Prep Time: 25 Minutes   **Start to Finish:** 1 Hour 15 Minutes   **Makes:** 4 servings

Patties

½ cup uncooked brown rice
¼ cup dried lentils (2 oz), sorted, rinsed
1½ cups water
¼ cup finely chopped cashews
2 tablespoons unseasoned dry bread crumbs
2 tablespoons stir-fry sauce

4 medium green onions, finely chopped (½ cup)
1 egg or 2 egg whites, beaten

Vegetable Sauce

1 cup frozen mixed vegetables (from 16-oz bag)
½ cup water
2 tablespoons stir-fry sauce

1. In 2-quart saucepan, heat rice, lentils and 1½ cups water to boiling. Reduce heat to low; cover and simmer 30 to 40 minutes, stirring occasionally, until lentils are tender and water is absorbed. Cool slightly.

2. In saucepan, mash rice mixture slightly with fork. Stir in remaining patty ingredients. Shape mixture into 4 patties, about ½ inch thick.

3. Spray 10-inch skillet with cooking spray. Cook patties in skillet about 10 minutes, turning once, until golden brown. Remove from skillet; keep warm.

4. In same skillet, mix sauce ingredients; heat to boiling. Reduce heat to medium; add patties. Cover; cook 5 to 8 minutes until patties are hot and vegetables are crisp-tender. Serve sauce over patties.

1 Serving: Calories 240 (Calories from Fat 60); Total Fat 6g (Saturated Fat 1.5g; Trans Fat 0g); Cholesterol 55mg; Sodium 590mg; Total Carbohydrate 38g (Dietary Fiber 6g; Sugars 6g); Protein 9g   **% Daily Value:** Vitamin A 10%; Vitamin C 4%; Calcium 4%; Iron 15%   **Exchanges:** 2 Starch, ½ Other Carbohydrate, ½ Medium-Fat Meat **Carbohydrate Choices:** 2½

try this

Short on time? Form (but do not cook) the rice and lentil patties up to 24 hours ahead of time, and store tightly wrapped in the refrigerator.

curry lentil and
brown rice casserole

Prep Time: 20 Minutes   **Start to Finish:** 1 Hour 40 Minutes   **Makes:** 4 servings

1 medium dark-orange sweet potato, peeled, cut into ½- to ¾-inch pieces (2 cups)	½ cup raisins
	2½ cups water
	2 tablespoons soy sauce
¾ cup dried lentils (6 oz), sorted, rinsed	2 teaspoons curry powder
½ cup uncooked natural whole-grain brown rice	2 tablespoons slivered almonds, if desired
½ cup chopped red bell pepper	

1. Heat oven to 375°F. In ungreased 2- or 2½-quart casserole, mix all ingredients except almonds.

2. Cover and bake 1 hour to 1 hour 15 minutes or until rice and lentils are tender. Uncover and stir mixture. Let stand 5 minutes before serving. Sprinkle with almonds.

1 Serving: Calories 270 (Calories from Fat 10); Total Fat 1.5g (Saturated Fat 0g; Trans Fat 0g); Cholesterol 0mg; Sodium 470mg; Total Carbohydrate 63g (Dietary Fiber 12g; Sugars 19g); Protein 13g   **% Daily Value:** Vitamin A 110%; Vitamin C 35%; Calcium 6%; Iron 25%   **Exchanges:** 2 Starch, 2 Other Carbohydrate, 1 Very Lean Meat   **Carbohydrate Choices:** 3½

easy ravioli bake

Prep Time: 10 Minutes   Start to Finish: 1 Hour 10 Minutes   Makes: 8 servings

1   jar (26 to 28 oz) tomato pasta sauce
    (any variety)
1   package (25 to 27½ oz) frozen
    cheese-filled ravioli

2   cups shredded mozzarella
    cheese (8 oz)
2   tablespoons grated Parmesan
    cheese

1. Heat oven to 350°F. Spray bottom and sides of 13×9-inch (3-quart) glass baking dish with cooking spray.

2. Spread ¾ cup of the pasta sauce in baking dish. Arrange half of the frozen ravioli in single layer over sauce; top with half of the remaining pasta sauce and 1 cup of the mozzarella cheese. Repeat layers once, starting with ravioli. Sprinkle with Parmesan cheese.

3. Cover with foil. Bake 40 minutes. Remove foil; bake 15 to 20 minutes longer or until bubbly and hot in center. Let stand 10 minutes before cutting.

1 Serving: Calories 290 (Calories from Fat 90); Total Fat 10g (Saturated Fat 6g, Trans Fat 0g); Cholesterol 30mg; Sodium 920mg; Total Carbohydrate 36g (Dietary Fiber 2g, Sugars 6g); Protein 14g %   **Daily Value:** Vitamin A 10%; Vitamin C 6%; Calcium 30%; Iron 10%   **Exchanges:** 1½ Starch, 1 Other Carbohydrate, 1½ Medium-Fat Meat **Carbohydrate Choices:** 2½

try this

To make this super-easy recipe ahead of time, layer the ingredients in the baking dish, cover tightly with foil, and refrigerate up to 24 hours. Bake as directed.

red bean and rice cakes

Prep Time: 30 Minutes   Start to Finish: 45 Minutes   Makes: 8 servings

½   cup uncooked regular long-grain
     white rice
1   cup water
1   cup Fiber One® cereal
2   cans (15 to 16 oz each) red or kidney
     beans, drained, rinsed
1   small onion, finely chopped
¼   cup diced bell pepper (any color)

1   egg or 2 egg whites, beaten
1   tablespoon chili powder
1   teaspoon ground cumin
¼   teaspoon ground red pepper
     (cayenne)
     Salad greens, if desired
½   cup chunky-style salsa

1. Cook rice in water as directed on package. Meanwhile, place cereal in resealable food-storage plastic bag; seal bag and crush with rolling pin or meat mallet (or crush in food processor).

2. In large bowl, place beans; mash with potato masher or fork. Stir in onion, bell pepper, cooked rice, egg, 2 tablespoons of the cereal, the chili powder, cumin and red pepper. Shape into 8 patties; coat patties completely with remaining cereal.

3. Spray 10-inch skillet with cooking spray. Cook 4 patties in skillet over medium heat about 10 minutes, turning once, until brown. Remove patties from skillet. Cover and keep warm while cooking remaining patties.

4. Serve patties on salad greens; top with salsa.

1 Serving: Calories 210 (Calories from Fat 15); Total Fat 1.5g (Saturated Fat 0g; Trans Fat 0g); Cholesterol 25mg; Sodium 300mg; Total Carbohydrate 40g (Dietary Fiber 10g; Sugars 2g); Protein 10g   **% Daily Value:** Vitamin A 10%; Vitamin C 6%; Calcium 8%; Iron 20%   **Exchanges:** 2 Starch, ½ Other Carbohydrate, ½ Very Lean Meat **Carbohydrate Choices:** 2½

health smart
Red and kidney beans are fiber all-stars. One cup of cooked and drained red or kidney beans provides about half of your recommended daily fiber intake.

bean enchiladas

Prep Time: 15 Minutes   Start to Finish: 40 Minutes   Makes: 6 servings

Tomato Sauce
- 1   can (16 oz) whole tomatoes, undrained
- 1   medium onion, chopped (½ cup)
- 1   clove garlic, finely chopped
- ¼   cup chopped fresh cilantro
- ⅛   teaspoon crushed red pepper

Bean Filling
- 1   cup fat free ricotta cheese
- 1   small bell pepper (any color), chopped (½ cup)

- 1   can (15 to 16 oz) pinto beans, rinsed and drained
- 1   teaspoon ground cumin

Enchiladas
- 6   flour tortillas (8 to 10 inch)
- ⅓   cup shredded Cheddar–Monterey Jack cheese blend (about 1½ oz)

1. Heat oven to 375°F. Spray 11×7-inch (2-quart) glass baking dish with cooking spray.

2. Place tomatoes, onion and garlic in blender or food processor. Cover and blend on high speed until smooth. In medium bowl, mix tomato mixture, 2 tablespoons of the cilantro and the red pepper. Spread ½ cup tomato sauce evenly in baking dish.

3. In medium bowl, mix ricotta cheese, bell pepper, beans and cumin and remaining 2 tablespoons cilantro. Spoon ½ cup bean mixture onto one side of each tortilla. Roll up tortillas; place seam sides down on tomato sauce in baking dish.

4. Spoon remaining tomato sauce over tortillas. Sprinkle with cheese. Bake 20 to 25 minutes or until tomato sauce is bubbly and cheese is melted.

1 Serving: Calories 300 (Calories from Fat 60); Total Fat 6g (Saturated Fat 2.5g; Trans Fat 0.5g); Cholesterol 10mg; Sodium 540mg; Total Carbohydrate 44g (Dietary Fiber 6g; Sugars 6g); Protein 16g   **% Daily Value:** Vitamin A 6%; Vitamin C 15%; Calcium 20%; Iron 20%   **Exchanges:** 3 Starch, 1 Lean Meat   **Carbohydrate Choices:** 3

try this
Flour tortillas come in varieties such as whole wheat, pumpkin, spinach, cilantro and tomato. Not only do these tortillas add a flavor twist, but some, such as spinach and tomato, also add a splash of color. Choose your favorite or mix it up to add interest.

garden vegetable frittata

Prep Time: 30 Minutes   Start to Finish: 30 Minutes   Makes: 6 servings

2 tablespoons butter or margarine	1 small tomato, chopped (½ cup)
1 medium onion, chopped (½ cup)	¼ teaspoon salt
1 clove garlic, finely chopped	¼ teaspoon pepper
1 medium bell pepper (any color), chopped (1 cup)	6 eggs or 1½ cups fat-free egg product
2 small zucchini, chopped (2 cups)	¼ cup grated Parmesan cheese

1. Heat oven to 375°F.

2. In 10-inch ovenproof skillet, melt butter over medium-high heat. Add onion and garlic; cook 3 minutes, stirring frequently. Stir in bell pepper; reduce heat to medium. Cook about 2 minutes, stirring occasionally, until crisp-tender. Stir in zucchini, tomato, salt and pepper. Cook 4 minutes, stirring occasionally. In small bowl, beat eggs with wire whisk or fork until blended; pour over vegetable mixture.

3. Bake uncovered 10 to 12 minutes or until center is set. Sprinkle with cheese. Cut into wedges.

1 Serving: Calories 150 (Calories from Fat 90); Total Fat 11g (Saturated Fat 5g; Trans Fat 0g); Cholesterol 225mg; Sodium 270mg; Total Carbohydrate 5g (Dietary Fiber 1g; Sugars 3g); Protein 9g   **% Daily Value:** Vitamin A 15%; Vitamin C 25%; Calcium 10%; Iron 6%   **Exchanges:** 1 Vegetable, 1 Medium-Fat Meat, 1 Fat   **Carbohydrate Choices:** ½

10 powerhouse foods

Keep these delicious foods on hand to add extra nutrients and flavor to your meals.

1. Barley	6. Peanut butter
2. Beans	7. Red bell peppers
3. Blueberries	8. Sweet potatoes
4. Grapes	9. Wild rice
5. Lettuce	10. Yogurt

swiss cheese and bell pepper frittata

Prep Time: 25 Minutes   **Start to Finish:** 25 Minutes   **Makes:** 6 servings

8	eggs or 2 cups fat-free egg product	2	tablespoons butter or margarine
½	teaspoon salt	2	medium bell peppers (any color), chopped (2 cups)
⅛	teaspoon pepper		
½	cup shredded Swiss cheese (2 oz)	1	medium onion, chopped (½ cup)

1. In medium bowl, beat eggs, salt and pepper with wire whisk or fork until blended. Stir in cheese; set aside.

2. In 10-inch ovenproof nonstick skillet, melt butter over medium heat. Add bell peppers and onion; cook about 5 minutes, until onion is tender, stirring occasionally. Pour egg mixture over bell pepper mixture; reduce heat to medium-low. Cover and cook 8 to 10 minutes or until eggs are set and light brown on bottom.

3. Set oven control to broil. Broil frittata with top 4 to 6 inches from heat about 2 minutes or until golden brown. Cut into wedges.

1 Serving: Calories 190 (Calories from Fat 120); Total Fat 14g (Saturated Fat 6g; Trans Fat 0g); Cholesterol 300mg; Sodium 330mg; Total Carbohydrate 5g (Dietary Fiber 1g; Sugars 3g); Protein 11g   **% Daily Value:** Vitamin A 15%; Vitamin C 35%; Calcium 10%; Iron 6%   **Exchanges:** 1 Vegetable, 1 Medium-Fat Meat, 2 Fat   **Carbohydrate Choices:** ½

health smart

Make this a very veggie dinner by tossing in any fresh or frozen (thawed) vegetables you have on hand. Just chop and cook with the peppers in step 2. You'll be adding color, crunch and extra vitamins and minerals.

italian garden frittata

Prep Time: 25 Minutes   **Start to Finish:** 25 Minutes   **Makes:** 4 servings

8 eggs or 2 cups fat-free egg product	1 teaspoon olive or vegetable oil
1 tablespoon coarsely chopped fresh or ½ teaspoon dried sage leaves	1 small zucchini, sliced (1 cup)
½ teaspoon salt	2 medium green onions, sliced (2 tablespoons)
¼ teaspoon pepper	2 plum (Roma) tomatoes, cut lengthwise into thin slices
½ cup grated Parmesan or Romano cheese (2 oz)	

1. In medium bowl, beat eggs, sage, salt and pepper with wire whisk or fork until blended. Stir in ¼ cup of the cheese; set aside.

2. In 10-inch ovenproof nonstick skillet, heat oil over medium heat. Add zucchini and onions; cook and stir about 2 minutes or until zucchini is tender. Add egg mixture; cook about 2 minutes, lifting edges occasionally to allow uncooked egg mixture to flow to bottom of skillet. Do not stir. Cook 4 to 6 minutes until eggs are set and light brown on bottom.

3. Set oven control to broil. Arrange tomato slices on top of eggs; sprinkle with remaining ¼ cup cheese. Broil with top 4 to 6 inches from heat 1 to 3 minutes or until golden brown. Cut into wedges.

1 Serving: Calories 230 (Calories from Fat 140); Total Fat 16g (Saturated Fat 6g; Trans Fat 0g); Cholesterol 435mg; Sodium 660mg; Total Carbohydrate 4g (Dietary Fiber 0g; Sugars 2g); Protein 18g   **% Daily Value:** Vitamin A 20%; Vitamin C 8%; Calcium 25%; Iron 10%   **Exchanges:** 1 Vegetable, 2 Medium-Fat Meat, 1 Fat   **Carbohydrate Choices:** 0

fresh vegetable frittata

photo on page C-5

Prep Time: 25 Minutes   Start to Finish: 25 Minutes   Makes: 4 servings

1	tablespoon vegetable oil	1	tablespoon chopped fresh parsley
1	cup broccoli florets	¼	teaspoon salt
1	medium carrot, shredded (½ cup)	¼	teaspoon red pepper sauce
1	medium onion, chopped (½ cup)	1	cup shredded Cheddar cheese (4 oz)
4	eggs or 1 cup fat-free egg product	1	tablespoon grated Parmesan cheese
¼	cup milk		

1. In 10-inch skillet, heat oil over medium-high heat. Cook broccoli, carrot and onion in oil about 5 minutes, stirring frequently, until vegetables are crisp-tender.

2. In medium bowl, beat eggs, milk, parsley, salt and pepper sauce with wire whisk or fork until blended. Pour egg mixture over vegetable mixture. Sprinkle with cheeses; reduce heat to low.

3. Cover and cook about 10 minutes or until eggs are set and light brown on bottom. Cut into wedges.

1 Serving: Calories 260 (Calories from Fat 170); Total Fat 19g (Saturated Fat 9g; Trans Fat 0g); Cholesterol 245mg; Sodium 440mg; Total Carbohydrate 6g (Dietary Fiber 1g; Sugars 4g); Protein 15g   **% Daily Value:** Vitamin A 60%; Vitamin C 15%; Calcium 25%; Iron 6%   **Exchanges:** 1 Vegetable, 2 Medium-Fat Meat, 2 Fat   **Carbohydrate Choices:** ½

try this

Have some broccoli slaw on hand? Use 1½ cups of this crunchy combo in place of the broccoli florets and carrots.

greek frittata

Prep Time: 25 Minutes   Start to Finish: 25 Minutes   Makes: 4 servings

8	eggs or 2 cups fat-free egg product	1	cup frozen potatoes O'brien with onions and peppers, thawed
½	cup milk		
¼	teaspoon salt	1	tablespoon chopped fresh or 1 teaspoon dried oregano leaves
¼	teaspoon pepper		
¼	cup finely crumbled feta cheese (1 oz)	1½	cups bite-size pieces spinach
1	tablespoon vegetable oil		

1. In medium bowl, beat eggs, milk, salt and pepper with wire whisk or fork until blended. Stir in cheese; set aside.

2. In 10-inch ovenproof nonstick skillet, heat oil over medium heat. Add potatoes and oregano; cook 3 minutes, stirring frequently. Stir in spinach. Cook about 1 minute, stirring frequently, until potatoes are tender and spinach starts to wilt. Reduce heat to medium-low.

3. Pour egg mixture over potato mixture. Cover and cook 7 to 10 minutes or until eggs are set and light brown on bottom.

4. Set oven control to broil. Broil with top about 4 to 6 inches from heat 1 to 3 minutes or until golden brown.

1 Serving: Calories 250 (Calories from Fat 150); Total Fat 17g (Saturated Fat 6g; Trans Fat 0g); Cholesterol 435mg; Sodium 400mg; Total Carbohydrate 8g (Dietary Fiber 0g; Sugars 4g); Protein 15g   **% Daily Value:** Vitamin A 35%; Vitamin C 4%; Calcium 15%; Iron 10%   **Exchanges:** ½ Starch, 2 Medium-Fat Meat, 1½ Fat   **Carbohydrate Choices:** ½

try this
Grated Parmesan cheese or shredded Cheddar cheese can easily be substituted for the feta.

tex-mex scrambled eggs

Prep Time: 20 Minutes   Start to Finish: 20 Minutes   Makes: 4 servings

2	teaspoons vegetable oil	½	medium jalapeño chile seeded, finely chopped (1½ teaspoons)
3	corn tortillas (5 or 6 inch), cut into thin strips	1	cup chunky-style salsa
1	small onion, chopped (¼ cup)	¼	cup low-fat sour cream
8	eggs or 2 cups fat-free egg product	2	medium green onions, chopped (2 tablespoons)

1. In 10-inch skillet, heat oil over medium-high heat. Add tortilla strips and ¼ cup onion; cook about 5 minutes, stirring frequently, until tortillas are crisp. In small bowl, beat eggs with wire whisk or fork until blended; stir in chile. Pour over tortilla mixture; reduce heat to medium.

2. As mixture begins to set at bottom and side, gently lift cooked portions with spatula so that thin, uncooked portion can flow to bottom. Do not stir. Cook 4 to 5 minutes or until eggs are set but still moist.

3. Top each serving with salsa, sour cream and green onions.

1 Serving: Calories 260 (Calories from Fat 140); Total Fat 15g (Saturated Fat 5g; Trans Fat 0g); Cholesterol 430mg; Sodium 530mg; Total Carbohydrate 15g (Dietary Fiber 2g; Sugars 5g); Protein 15g   **% Daily Value:** Vitamin A 15%; Vitamin C 2%; Calcium 10%; Iron 10%   **Exchanges:** 1 Starch, 1½ Medium-Fat Meat, 1½ Fat   **Carbohydrate Choices:** 1

potato-basil scramble

Prep Time: 45 Minutes   Start to Finish: 45 Minutes   Makes: 4 servings

2	medium white potatoes, peeled, cubed (2 cups)	8	eggs or 2 cups fat-free egg product
1	medium onion, finely chopped (½ cup)	2	tablespoons chopped fresh or 2 teaspoons dried basil leaves
1	small bell pepper (any color), chopped (½ cup)	½	teaspoon salt
		⅛	teaspoon ground red pepper (cayenne)

1. In 2-quart saucepan, place potatoes. Add enough water just to cover potatoes. Heat to boiling; reduce heat to low. Cover and simmer 10 to 15 minutes or until tender; drain.

2. Spray 10-inch skillet with cooking spray. Cook potatoes, onion and bell pepper in skillet over medium heat about 5 minutes, stirring frequently, until hot.

3. In small bowl, beat remaining ingredients with wire whisk or fork until blended; pour into skillet. As mixture begins to set at bottom and side, gently lift cooked portions with spatula so that thin, uncooked portion can flow to bottom. Do not stir. Cook 3 to 5 minutes or until eggs are set but still moist.

1 Serving: Calories 120 (Calories from Fat 0); Total Fat 0g (Saturated Fat 0g; Trans Fat 0g); Cholesterol 0mg; Sodium 530mg; Total Carbohydrate 18g (Dietary Fiber 3g; Sugars 4g); Protein 14g   **% Daily Value:** Vitamin A 35%; Vitamin C 35%; Calcium 6%; Iron 15%   **Exchanges:** 1 Starch, 1½ Very Lean Meat   **Carbohydrate Choices:** 1

asian **omelet**

Prep Time: 45 Minutes   Start to Finish: 45 Minutes   Makes: 4 servings

6 eggs or 1½ cups fat-free egg product	1 tablespoon finely chopped carrot
½ cup milk	1 tablespoon finely chopped green onion
½ teaspoon pepper	
1 teaspoon vegetable oil	1 tablespoon finely chopped mushrooms
1 cup cooked brown or white rice, cold	
2 tablespoons finely chopped bell pepper (any color)	1 clove garlic, finely chopped
	1 tablespoon soy sauce

1. In small bowl, beat eggs, milk and pepper slightly with wire whisk or fork; set aside.

2. In 8-inch skillet or omelet pan, heat oil over medium-high heat. Cook remaining ingredients except soy sauce in oil, stirring frequently, until vegetables are crisp-tender. Stir in soy sauce. Remove mixture from skillet; keep warm.

3. Spray same skillet with cooking spray; heat over medium-high heat. Quickly pour about ½ cup of the egg mixture into skillet. Slide skillet back and forth rapidly over heat and, at the same time, quickly stir with fork to spread eggs continuously over bottom of skillet as they thicken. Let stand over heat a few seconds to lightly brown bottom of omelet. (Do not overcook—omelet will continue to cook after folding.)

4. Spoon about ¼ cup of the rice mixture on one side of omelet. Run spatula under unfilled side of omelet; lift over rice mixture. Tilting skillet slightly, turn omelet onto plate. Transfer to serving plate; keep warm. Repeat with remaining egg and rice mixtures.

1 Serving: Calories 190 (Calories from Fat 90); Total Fat 10g (Saturated Fat 3g; Trans Fat 0g); Cholesterol 320mg; Sodium 340mg; Total Carbohydrate 15g (Dietary Fiber 2g; Sugars 3g); Protein 12g   **% Daily Value:** Vitamin A 20%; Vitamin C 6%; Calcium 8%; Iron 8%   **Exchanges:** 1 Starch, 1 Medium-Fat Meat, 1 Fat   **Carbohydrate Choices:** 1

cheese and pesto strata

Prep Time: 15 Minutes   Start to Finish: 9 Hours 5 Minutes   Makes: 12 servings

6 eggs or 1½ cups fat-free egg product	2 cups shredded mozzarella cheese (8 oz)
3½ cups milk	¼ cup basil pesto
1 teaspoon salt	½ cup grated Parmesan cheese (2 oz)
½ teaspoon pepper	
8 cups cubed (1 inch) French bread	

1. Spray 13×9-inch (3-quart) glass baking dish with cooking spray. In large bowl, beat eggs with wire whisk until foamy. Beat in milk until blended; beat in salt and pepper. Set aside.

2. Place bread cubes in baking dish. Sprinkle with mozzarella cheese. Pour egg mixture over top, pressing lightly to moisten bread. Using spoon, swirl pesto through mixture. Sprinkle Parmesan cheese over top. Cover with plastic wrap; refrigerate at least 8 hours but no longer than 24 hours.

3. Heat oven to 350°F. Remove plastic wrap; bake uncovered 40 to 45 minutes or until strata is puffed and knife inserted in center comes out clean. Let stand 5 minutes before serving. Cut into squares.

1 Serving: Calories 240 (Calories from Fat 110); Total Fat 13g (Saturated Fat 6g; Trans Fat 0g); Cholesterol 125mg; Sodium 600mg; Total Carbohydrate 16g (Dietary Fiber 0g; Sugars 4g); Protein 15g   **% Daily Value:** Vitamin A 8%; Vitamin C 0%; Calcium 30%; Iron 6%   **Exchanges:** 1 Starch, 1½ Medium-Fat Meat, 1 Fat   **Carbohydrate Choices:** 1

try this

Use sun-dried tomato pesto instead of the basil pesto for a delicious flavor twist. Prepared pesto can be found in many places at the grocery store.

270 calories

asparagus and swiss bake photo on page C-4

Prep Time: 20 Minutes   Start to Finish: 1 Hour   Makes: 6 servings

½   lb fresh asparagus spears, trimmed, cut into 1-inch pieces, or 1 box (9 oz) frozen asparagus cuts, thawed, drained

1   small bell pepper (any color), chopped (½ cup)

8   medium green onions, sliced (½ cup)

2   cups shredded Swiss cheese (8 oz)

¾   cup Bisquick Heart Smart mix

1   teaspoon lemon-pepper seasoning

1½   cups milk

3   eggs or 1½ cups fat-free egg product

1. Heat oven to 350°F. Spray 8-inch square (2-quart) glass baking dish with cooking spray. In 1-quart saucepan, heat 1 inch water to boiling. Add asparagus; cook uncovered 2 minutes. Drain well.

2. In baking dish, mix asparagus, bell pepper and onions. In medium bowl, stir 1½ cups of the cheese and all remaining ingredients with wire whisk or fork until blended. Pour into baking dish.

3. Bake uncovered 35 minutes. Sprinkle with remaining ½ cup cheese. Bake about 5 minutes longer or until knife inserted between center and edge comes out clean.

1 Serving: Calories 270 (Calories from Fat 130); Total Fat 15g (Saturated Fat 8g; Trans Fat 0g); Cholesterol 145mg; Sodium 310mg; Total Carbohydrate 18g (Dietary Fiber 1g; Sugars 6g); Protein 17g   **% Daily Value:** Vitamin A 20%; Vitamin C 10%; Calcium 45%; Iron 10%   **Exchanges:** 1 Starch, 1 Vegetable, 1½ Lean Meat, 2 Fat   **Carbohydrate Choices:** 1

gruyére vegetable bake

Prep Time: 10 Minutes   Start to Finish: 30 Minutes   Makes: 4 servings

1 bag (1 lb) frozen broccoli, cauliflower and carrots (or other combination)	1 cup milk
2 tablespoons butter or margarine	½ cup shredded Gruyére or Swiss cheese (2 oz)
2 tablespoons all-purpose flour	½ cup soft whole wheat or white bread crumbs (1 slice bread)
¼ teaspoon salt	1 tablespoon butter or margarine, melted
¼ teaspoon onion powder	
¼ teaspoon caraway seed	

1. Heat oven to 350°F. Cook and drain vegetables as directed on package.

2. Meanwhile, in 1½-quart saucepan, melt 2 tablespoons butter over medium heat. Stir in flour, salt, onion powder and caraway seed. Cook, stirring constantly, until mixture is smooth and bubbly; remove from heat. Stir in milk. Heat to boiling, stirring constantly. Boil and stir 1 minute. Stir in cheese until melted. Stir in vegetables.

3. Place vegetable mixture in ungreased 1½-quart casserole. In small bowl, mix bread crumbs and 1 tablespoon butter, sprinkle over to of vegetable mixture. Bake uncovered about 20 minutes or until crumbs are golden.

1 Serving: Calories 270 (Calories from Fat 140); Total Fat 15g (Saturated Fat 9g; Trans Fat 0.5g); Cholesterol 45mg; Sodium 400mg; Total Carbohydrate 21g (Dietary Fiber 4g; Sugars 6g); Protein 11g   **% Daily Value:** Vitamin A 60%; Vitamin C 30%; Calcium 25%; Iron 8%   **Exchanges:** 1 Starch, 1 Vegetable, 1 High-Fat Meat, 1½ Fat   **Carbohydrate Choices:** 1½

try this

For a meaty version of this cheese dish, stir in 1 cup chopped cooked chicken breast with the vegetables in step 2.

cheese quesadillas

Prep Time: 10 Minutes   **Start to Finish:** 15 Minutes   **Makes:** 6 servings (3 wedges each)

2   cups shredded reduced-fat Cheddar cheese (8 oz)

6   reduced-fat flour tortillas (8 to 10 inch)

1   small tomato, chopped (½ cup)

3   medium green onions, chopped (3 tablespoons)

2   tablespoons chopped green chiles (from 4.5-oz can)

Chopped fresh cilantro or parsley, if desired

1. Heat oven to 350°F.

2. Sprinkle ⅓ cup of the cheese evenly over half of each tortilla. Top each with ¼ of the tomato, onions, chiles and cilantro. Fold each tortilla in half over filling; place on ungreased cookie sheet.

3. Bake about 5 minutes or just until cheese is melted. Cut each quesadilla into 3 wedges.

1 Serving: Calories 230 (Calories from Fat 30); Total Fat 3g (Saturated Fat 1.5g; Trans Fat 0g); Cholesterol 10mg; Sodium 830mg; Total Carbohydrate 35g (Dietary Fiber 3g; Sugars 1g); Protein 15g   **% Daily Value:** Vitamin A 4%; Vitamin C 2%; Calcium 35%; Iron 10%   **Exchanges:** 1 Starch, 1½ Other Carbohydrate, 1½ Lean Meat   **Carbohydrate Choices:** 2

try this

Pack these quesadillas with added nutrients by sprinkling canned black beans, sliced bell pepper or onion, spinach leaves or any other chopped veggie of your choosing over the cheese.

family-favorite
cheese pizza

Prep Time: 10 Minutes   **Start to Finish:** 25 Minutes   **Makes:** 8 servings

1½ cups Bisquick Heart Smart mix	2 cups shredded mozzarella cheese (8 oz)
⅓ cup very hot water	5 slices (¾ oz each) reduced-fat American cheese
½ cup pizza sauce	
½ teaspoon Italian seasoning	

1. Move oven rack to lowest rack position; heat oven to 450°F. Spray 12-inch pizza pan with cooking spray.

2. In small bowl, mix Bisquick mix and very hot water with spoon until soft dough forms; beat vigorously 20 strokes. With fingers dipped in Bisquick mix, press dough in pizza pan; pinch edge to form ½-inch rim. Spread pizza sauce over dough. Sprinkle with Italian seasoning and mozzarella cheese.

3. Bake 10 to 12 minutes or until crust is golden and cheese is bubbly.

4. With 2-inch cookie cutters, cut American cheese slices into any shape desired. Arrange shapes on pizza. Let stand 1 to 2 minutes or until American cheese is melted.

1 Serving: Calories 210 (Calories from Fat 80); Total Fat 9g (Saturated Fat 5g; Trans Fat 0g); Cholesterol 20mg; Sodium 580mg; Total Carbohydrate 19g (Dietary Fiber 0g; Sugars 4g); Protein 11g   **% Daily Value:** Vitamin A 8%; Vitamin C 0%; Calcium 40%; Iron 6%   **Exchanges:** 1 Starch, ½ Other Carbohydrate, 1 Medium-Fat Meat, ½ Fat **Carbohydrate Choices:** 1

serve with
Give this pizza a veggie boost! Serve a mixed-greens salad with lots of added chopped veggies on the side.

sandwiches, salads and pizzas

Sandwiches, salads and pizzas are blockbuster hits at the dinner table, and no wonder. Kids and adults alike love them, and they're easy to throw together after a busy day. And with low-cal renditions like the Blue Cheese Burgers (page 157), these favorites can be everyday fare instead of special treats.

grilled honey-mustard chicken sandwiches

Prep Time: 30 Minutes   **Start to Finish:** 30 Minutes   **Makes:** 4 sandwiches

¼ cup Dijon mustard	1 teaspoon water
2 tablespoons honey	4 boneless skinless chicken
1 teaspoon dried oregano leaves	breasts (1¼ lb)
¼ teaspoon garlic powder	4 whole wheat burger buns, split
⅛ to ¼ teaspoon ground red pepper	8 thin slices tomato
(cayenne)	4 leaves leaf lettuce

1. Heat gas or charcoal grill. In small bowl, mix mustard, honey, oregano, garlic powder, red pepper and water; brush half of the mixture over chicken.

2. Place chicken on grill over medium heat. Cover grill; cook 15 to 20 minutes, turning occasionally and brushing with remaining mustard mixture, until juice of chicken is clear when center of thickest part is cut (170°F). Discard any remaining mustard mixture. Serve chicken on buns with tomato and lettuce.

1 Sandwich: Calories 270 (Calories from Fat 50); Total Fat 5g (Saturated Fat 1g; Trans Fat 0g); Cholesterol 50mg; Sodium 570mg; Total Carbohydrate 32g (Dietary Fiber 2g; Sugars 12g); Protein 24g   **% Daily Value:** Vitamin A 45%; Vitamin C 8%; Calcium 10%; Iron 15%   **Exchanges:** 2 Starch, 2 Lean Meat   **Carbohydrate Choices:** 2

try this

This is the perfect recipe for using up some mustard that's been "hiding" in the refrigerator. Just about any variety you have—spicy brown, honey or coarse-grained—will blend with the honey, oregano and ground red pepper flavors of this sandwich.

italian chicken pitas

Prep Time: 20 Minutes   Start to Finish: 20 Minutes   Makes: 6 servings

¾   lb boneless skinless chicken breasts,
     cut into 1-inch pieces
1   small zucchini, sliced
1   medium carrot, shredded
1   small onion, sliced, separated into rings
1   teaspoon chopped fresh or
     ¼ teaspoon dried basil leaves

1   teaspoon chopped fresh or
     ¼ teaspoon dried oregano leaves
¼   teaspoon pepper
1   medium tomato, chopped (¾ cup)
3   pita (pocket) breads (6 inch)
⅓   cup shredded mozzarella cheese

1. Spray 10-inch skillet with cooking spray. Heat over medium-high heat. Add chicken; stir-fry 3 to 4 minutes or until no longer pink in center. Add zucchini, carrot, onion, basil, oregano and pepper; stir-fry 2 to 3 minutes longer or until vegetables are crisp-tender. Stir in tomato.

2. Cut pita breads in half to form pockets; fill with chicken mixture. Sprinkle with cheese.

1 Serving: Calories 160 (Calories from Fat 25); Total Fat 3g (Saturated Fat 1g; Trans Fat 0g); Cholesterol 30mg; Sodium 200mg; Total Carbohydrate 18g (Dietary Fiber 1g; Sugars 2g); Protein 14g   **% Daily Value:** Vitamin A 40%; Vitamin C 6%; Calcium 8%; Iron 6%   **Exchanges:** 1 Starch, 1 Vegetable, 1 Lean Meat   **Carbohydrate Choices:** 1

serve with
These pitas really are a meal in themselves. Serve a scoop of sorbet with some fresh fruit for dessert.

chicken quesadillas
photo on page C-4

Prep Time: 20 Minutes   Start to Finish: 20 Minutes   Makes: 4 quesadillas

1 cup shredded cooked chicken breast	¾ cup shredded reduced-fat Mexican cheese blend (3 oz)
¼ cup chunky-style salsa	Cooking spray
2 tablespoons chopped fresh cilantro	Additional salsa, if desired
½ cup fat-free refried beans	Fat-free sour cream, if desired
4 low-fat whole wheat tortillas (8 inch)	

1. In medium bowl, stir chicken, ¼ cup salsa and cilantro until well mixed. Spread 2 tablespoons beans over half of each tortilla; top bean side with chicken mixture and cheese. Fold tortillas in half over filling.

2. Heat 12-inch nonstick skillet over medium-low heat. Spray both sides of quesadillas with cooking spray; place 2 quesadillas in skillet. Cover; cook 3 to 4 minutes, turning once, until filling is heated and tortillas are lightly browned. Repeat with remaining quesadillas. Cut into wedges. Serve with additional salsa and sour cream.

1 Quesadilla: Calories 280 (Calories from Fat 70); Total Fat 8g (Saturated Fat 3g; Trans Fat 0g); Cholesterol 40mg; Sodium 720mg; Total Carbohydrate 32g (Dietary Fiber 4g; Sugars 4g); Protein 21g   **% Daily Value:** Vitamin A 4%; Vitamin C 0%; Calcium 40%; Iron 10%   **Exchanges:** 2 Starch, 2 Lean Meat   **Carbohydrate Choices:** 2

try this
Try using refried black beans in place of the regular refried beans. They're often available in different varieties such as fat-free and flavored with lime juice.

grilled turkey burgers with garlicky mayonnaise

Prep Time: 25 Minutes   **Start to Finish:** 25 Minutes   **Makes:** 4 sandwiches

Garlicky Mayonnaise
- ¼ cup fat-free or reduced-fat mayonnaise
- 1 teaspoon lemon juice
- ½ teaspoon finely chopped garlic

Burgers
- 1 lb ground turkey breast
- ¼ cup quick-cooking oats
- 1 tablespoon reduced-sodium soy sauce
- 1 teaspoon salt-free seasoning blend
- 1 small onion, finely chopped (¼ cup)
- 1 egg white
- 4 whole wheat burger buns, split
- 4 leaves leaf lettuce
- 4 slices tomato

1. Heat gas or charcoal grill. In small bowl, mix mayonnaise, lemon juice and garlic. Cover; refrigerate until serving time.

2. In large bowl, stir turkey, oats, soy sauce, seasoning blend, onion and egg white until well mixed. Shape mixture into 4 patties, about ¾ inch thick.

3. Place patties on grill over medium heat. Cook uncovered about 15 minutes, turning once, until thermometer inserted in center of patties reads 165°F.

4. Spread 1 tablespoon mayonnaise on bottom of each bun. Top with burgers, lettuce and tomato. Cover with top half of bun.

1 Sandwich: Calories 270 (Calories from Fat 30); Total Fat 3.5g (Saturated Fat 1g; Trans Fat 0g); Cholesterol 75mg; Sodium 520mg; Total Carbohydrate 26g (Dietary Fiber 4g; Sugars 7g); Protein 34g   **% Daily Value:** Vitamin A 4%; Vitamin C 4%; Calcium 8%; Iron 15%   **Exchanges:** 1½ Starch, 4 Very Lean Meat   **Carbohydrate Choices:** 2

try this
Shape the patties up to 4 hours ahead of time. Cover with plastic wrap and refrigerate until you're ready to grill.

greek turkey burgers with yogurt sauce

Prep Time: 20 Minutes   Start to Finish: 20 Minutes   Makes: 4 sandwiches

Yogurt Sauce
½   cup plain fat-free yogurt
¼   cup chopped red onion
¼   cup chopped cucumber

Burgers
1   lb lean ground turkey

½   cup plain fat-free yogurt
1   teaspoon dried oregano leaves
½   teaspoon garlic powder
½   teaspoon salt
½   teaspoon pepper
4   whole wheat burger buns, split

1. Heat gas or charcoal grill. In small bowl, mix sauce ingredients; refrigerate until serving time.

2. In medium bowl, mix all burger ingredients except buns. Shape mixture into 4 patties, about ½ inch thick.

3. Place patties on grill over medium heat. Cover grill; cook 8 to 10 minutes, turning after 5 minutes, until thermometer inserted in center of patties reads 165°F. Serve burgers on buns with yogurt sauce.

1 Sandwich: Calories 280 (Calories from Fat 70); Total Fat 7g (Saturated Fat 2g; Trans Fat 0g); Cholesterol 75mg; Sodium 590mg; Total Carbohydrate 21g (Dietary Fiber 3g; Sugars 8g); Protein 32g   **% Daily Value:** Vitamin A 0%; Vitamin C 0%; Calcium 15%; Iron 10%   **Exchanges:** 1 Starch, ½ Other Carbohydrate, 3½ Lean Meat   **Carbohydrate Choices:** 1½

serve with

Serve these Greek burgers with a side of tabbouleh, a Mediterranean salad made of cracked wheat, parsley, mint, lemon and olive oil.

blue cheese burgers

Prep Time: 25 Minutes   Start to Finish: 25 Minutes   Makes: 6 sandwiches

¼ cup old-fashioned or quick-cooking oats	½ teaspoon Worcestershire sauce
2 tablespoons water	⅛ teaspoon red pepper sauce
1½ lb extra-lean (at least 90%) ground beef	½ teaspoon coarse ground black pepper
½ cup crumbled reduced-fat blue cheese (4 oz)	½ teaspoon ground mustard
¼ cup finely chopped fresh chives	¼ teaspoon salt
	6 leaves leaf lettuce
	6 slices tomato
	6 whole wheat burger buns, split

1. Heat gas or charcoal grill. In large bowl, mix oats and water. Stir in beef, blue cheese, chives, Worcestershire sauce, pepper sauce, pepper, mustard and salt until well mixed. Shape mixture into 6 patties, about ¾ inch thick.

2. Place patties on grill over medium heat. Cover grill; cook 11 to 13 minutes, turning once, until thermometer inserted in center of patties reads 160°F.

3. Layer lettuce, tomato and burgers on bottom halves of buns; cover with top half of buns.

1 Sandwich: Calories 300 (Calories from Fat 90); Total Fat 10g (Saturated Fat 4.5g; Trans Fat 0.5g); Cholesterol 70mg; Sodium 490mg; Total Carbohydrate 22g (Dietary Fiber 4g; Sugars 5g); Protein 30g   **% Daily Value:** Vitamin A 8%; Vitamin C 6%; Calcium 10%; Iron 20%   **Exchanges:** 1½ Starch, 3½ Lean Meat   **Carbohydrate Choices:** 1½

serve with
As long as you have the grill fired up, grill some corn on the cob and a packet of roasted carrots, potatoes and onions to serve with these tasty burgers.

broiled dijon burgers

Prep Time: 10 Minutes   **Start to Finish:** 20 Minutes   **Makes:** 6 sandwiches

2 egg whites or ¼ cup fat-free egg product	1 cup soft bread crumbs (2 slices bread)
2 tablespoons milk	1 small onion, finely chopped (¼ cup)
2 teaspoons Dijon mustard	1 lb extra-lean (at least 90%) ground beef
¼ teaspoon salt	6 burger buns, split, toasted, if desired
⅛ teaspoon pepper	

1. Set oven control to broil. Spray broiler pan rack with cooking spray.

2. In medium bowl, mix egg whites, milk, mustard, salt and pepper. Stir in bread crumbs and onion. Stir in beef. Shape mixture into 6 patties, about ½ inch thick.

3. Place patties on rack in broiler pan. Broil with tops about 5 inches from heat about 10 minutes for medium, turning once, until thermometer inserted in center of patties reads 160°F. Serve burgers on buns.

1 Sandwich: Calories 260 (Calories from Fat 80); Total Fat 8g (Saturated Fat 3g; Trans Fat 0.5g); Cholesterol 45mg; Sodium 450mg; Total Carbohydrate 27g (Dietary Fiber 1g; Sugars 4g); Protein 20g   **% Daily Value:** Vitamin A 0%; Vitamin C 0%; Calcium 8%; Iron 20%   **Exchanges:** 2 Starch, 2 Lean Meat   **Carbohydrate Choices:** 2

pork, onion
and pepper fajitas

Prep Time: 25 Minutes   **Start to Finish:** 8 Hours 25 Minutes   **Makes:** 4 fajitas

½ lb pork tenderloin
¼ cup lime juice
1½ teaspoons ground cumin
¾ teaspoon salt
4 cloves garlic, finely chopped

1 large onion, thinly sliced
3 medium bell peppers (any color),
    thinly sliced
4 fat-free flour tortillas (6 to 8 inch)

1. Trim fat from pork; cut into 2×½-inch strips. Mix pork, lime juice, cumin, salt and garlic in heavy-duty resealable food-storage plastic bag. Seal bag and refrigerate at least 8 hours but no longer than 24 hours.

2. Remove pork from marinade; reserve marinade. Spray 10-inch skillet with cooking spray. Heat over medium-high heat. Add pork; cook 3 minutes, stirring once. Stir in onion, bell peppers and marinade. Cook 5 to 8 minutes longer, stirring occasionally, until onion and peppers are crisp-tender.

3. Place ¼ of pork mixture in center of each tortilla. Fold one end of tortilla up about 1 inch over mixture; fold right and left sides over folded end, overlapping. Fold remaining end down.

1 Fajita: Calories 250 (Calories from Fat 50); Total Fat 6g (Saturated Fat 1.5g; Trans Fat 0.5g); Cholesterol 25mg; Sodium 770mg; Total Carbohydrate 34g (Dietary Fiber 3g; Sugars 5g); Protein 15g   **% Daily Value:** Vitamin A 6%; Vitamin C 70%; Calcium 10%; Iron 15%   **Exchanges:** 1½ Starch, 2 Vegetable, 1 Lean Meat, ½ Fat   **Carbohydrate Choices:** 2

serve with

Serve these fast fajitas with some chopped tomato sprinkled with fresh cilantro, salsa and fat-free sour cream or yogurt.

open-face tuna melts

Prep Time: 10 Minutes   Start to Finish: 20 Minutes   Makes: 4 servings

1 can (5 oz) tuna in water, drained, flaked	½ teaspoon grated lemon peel
¾ cup chopped celery	4 whole wheat English muffins, split, lightly toasted
2 tablespoons finely chopped onion	8 slices tomato
⅓ cup fat-free mayonnaise or salad dressing	1 cup shredded reduced-fat Cheddar or Monterey Jack cheese (4 oz)

1. Heat oven to 350°F. In medium bowl, mix tuna, celery, onion, mayonnaise and lemon peel.

2. Spread about 3 tablespoons tuna mixture on each English muffin half. Top each with tomato; sprinkle with cheese. Place on ungreased cookie sheet.

3. Bake 8 to 10 minutes or until cheese is melted and sandwiches are thoroughly heated.

1 Serving: Calories 270 (Calories from Fat 40); Total Fat 4.5g (Saturated Fat 2g; Trans Fat 0g); Cholesterol 20mg; Sodium 890mg; Total Carbohydrate 33g (Dietary Fiber 6g; Sugars 6g); Protein 24g   **% Daily Value:** Vitamin A 10%; Vitamin C 8%; Calcium 40%; Iron 15%   **Exchanges:** 2 Starch, 2½ Very Lean Meat, ½ Fat   **Carbohydrate Choices:** 2

cucumber-tuna salad pitas

Prep Time: 15 Minutes   Start to Finish: 15 Minutes   Makes: 4 servings

1	pouch (7.06 oz) albacore tuna	2	tablespoons chopped fresh or 1 teaspoon dried dill weed
¼	cup reduced-fat mayonnaise or salad dressing	1	teaspoon salt-free seasoning blend
¼	cup plain fat-free yogurt	2	whole wheat pita (pocket) breads (8 inch)
½	cup chopped cucumber	1	cup shredded lettuce
2	tablespoons chopped red onion	1	small tomato, chopped (½ cup)

1. In medium bowl, mix tuna, mayonnaise, yogurt, cucumber, onion, dill weed and seasoning blend.

2. Cut pita breads in half to form pockets. Fill with tuna mixture. Add lettuce and tomato.

1 Serving: Calories 220 (Calories from Fat 60); Total Fat 7g (Saturated Fat 1g; Trans Fat 0g); Cholesterol 20mg; Sodium 470mg; Total Carbohydrate 23g (Dietary Fiber 3g; Sugars 3g); Protein 18g   **% Daily Value:** Vitamin A 8%; Vitamin C 8%; Calcium 6%; Iron 10%   **Exchanges:** 1 Starch, ½ Other Carbohydrate, 2 Very Lean Meat, 1 Fat **Carbohydrate Choices:** 1½

190 calories

salsa-shrimp tacos *photo on page C-5*

Prep Time: 15 Minutes   Start to Finish: 15 Minutes   Makes: 6 servings

¾ cup chunky-style salsa	12 taco shells
½ cup frozen chopped green bell pepper	¾ cup shredded Mexican cheese blend (3 oz)
¾ lb uncooked deveined peeled medium shrimp, thawed if frozen, tail shells removed	¾ cup shredded lettuce
	¼ cup taco sauce

1. In 12-inch nonstick skillet, heat salsa and bell pepper over medium-high heat, stirring frequently, until warm.

2. Stir in shrimp. Cook 3 to 4 minutes, turning shrimp occasionally, until shrimp are pink.

3. Fill each taco shell with about ¼ cup shrimp mixture. Top with cheese, lettuce and taco sauce.

1 Serving (2 tacos each): Calories 190 (Calories from Fat 80); Total Fat 9g (Saturated Fat 3.5g; Trans Fat 2g); Cholesterol 95mg; Sodium 400mg; Total Carbohydrate 16g (Dietary Fiber 1g; Sugars 1g); Protein 13g
% Daily Value: Vitamin A 6%; Vitamin C 10%; Calcium 10%; Iron 8%   **Exchanges:** 1 Starch, 1 Vegetable, 1 Very Lean Meat, 1 Fat   **Carbohydrate Choices:** 1

dilled shrimp and egg salad wraps photo on page C-5

Prep Time: 10 Minutes   Start to Finish: 10 Minutes   Makes: 4 wraps

4 hard-cooked eggs, chopped	3 tablespoons creamy mustard-
1 cup chopped cooked shrimp	mayonnaise sauce
1 tablespoon chopped fresh dill weed	¼ teaspoon salt
2 tablespoons finely chopped	4 flour tortillas (8 inch)
red onion	2 cups shredded lettuce

1. In medium bowl, mix all ingredients except tortillas and lettuce.

2. Spread shrimp mixture evenly on each tortilla; top with lettuce. Fold 2 ends of tortilla 1 inch over filling; roll tortilla around filling. Cut in half. Serve immediately, or wrap each sandwich in plastic wrap and refrigerate until serving time or up to 24 hours.

1 Wrap: Calories 280 (Calories from Fat 90); Total Fat 10g (Saturated Fat 3g; Trans Fat 0g); Cholesterol 330mg; Sodium 820mg; Total Carbohydrate 25g (Dietary Fiber 0g; Sugars 1g); Protein 22g   **% Daily Value:** Vitamin A 10%; Vitamin C 4%; Calcium 10%; Iron 20%   **Exchanges:** 1½ Starch, 2½ Lean Meat, ½ Fat   **Carbohydrate Choices:** 1½

health smart

An egg is not just an egg anymore. Look closely in your dairy case at the different varieties of eggs available. Some eggs come from chickens fed special diets to produce eggs high in omega-3 fatty acids, lutein and vitamin E.

280 calories

spicy chili bean burgers

Prep Time: 25 Minutes   **Start to Finish:** 25 Minutes   **Makes:** 5 sandwiches

1 cup Fiber One original bran cereal	1 egg, slightly beaten
1 can (15 or 16 oz) spicy chili beans in sauce, undrained	5 whole wheat burger buns, split
½ cup quick-cooking oats	1¼ cups fresh baby spinach leaves
¼ cup chopped green onions (4 medium)	5 slices tomato

1. Place cereal in resealable food-storage plastic bag; seal bag and finely crush with rolling pin or meat mallet.

2. In medium bowl, mash beans with fork until no whole beans remain. Add cereal, oats, onions and egg; mix well. Shape mixture into 5 patties, each about 3½ inches in diameter.

3. Spray 12-inch skillet with cooking spray. Heat over medium heat. Add patties; cook about 10 minutes, turning once, until brown.

4. Place ¼ cup spinach and 1 tomato slice on bottom half of each bun; top with bean burger. Cover with top half of bun.

1 Sandwich: Calories 280 (Calories from Fat 40); Total Fat 4.5g (Saturated Fat 1g; Trans Fat 0g); Cholesterol 40mg; Sodium 800mg; Total Carbohydrate 48g (Dietary Fiber 12g; Sugars 6g); Protein 11g   **% Daily Value:** Vitamin A 25%; Vitamin C 8%; Calcium 15%; Iron 30%   **Exchanges:** 2½ Starch, ½ Other Carbohydrate, ½ Vegetable, ½ Fat **Carbohydrate Choices:** 3

vegetarian reuben sandwiches photo on page C-7

Prep Time: 20 Minutes   Start to Finish: 20 Minutes   Makes: 4 sandwiches

1	cup sliced onion	½	cup sauerkraut, drained, rinsed
8	slices (4½×3½ inch) rye bread	4	slices (¾ oz each) fat-free Swiss
¼	cup reduced-fat Thousand Island		cheese product
	dressing		Cooking spray
8	strips (2×1 inch) roasted red bell		
	pepper (from 7-oz jar), drained		

1. Spray 12-inch skillet with cooking spray; heat over medium-high heat. Add onion; cook 3 to 5 minutes, stirring frequently, until softened. Remove onion from skillet.

2. Spread 4 bread slices with dressing. Top each slice with ¼ of the onion, 2 strips bell pepper, 2 tablespoons sauerkraut and 1 cheese slice. Top with remaining bread slices.

3. Heat same skillet over medium-low heat. Spray outsides of sandwiches with cooking spray; place sandwiches in skillet. Cook 4 to 5 minutes, turning after 2 minutes, until cheese is melted and bread is toasted.

1 Sandwich: Calories 230 (Calories from Fat 45); Total Fat 5g (Saturated Fat 1.5g; Trans Fat 0g); Cholesterol 5mg; Sodium 750mg; Total Carbohydrate 36g (Dietary Fiber 4g; Sugars 9g); Protein 11g   **% Daily Value:** Vitamin A 35%; Vitamin C 45%; Calcium 25%; Iron 10%   **Exchanges:** 2 Starch, 1 Vegetable, ½ Medium-Fat Meat   **Carbohydrate Choices:** 2½

sausalito chicken and seafood salad

Prep Time: 15 Minutes   Start to Finish: 15 Minutes   Makes: 4 servings

6 cups bite-size pieces mixed salad greens	1 can (4 oz) whole green chiles, drained, sliced lengthwise
1 cup diced cooked chicken	1 container (6 oz) frozen guacamole, thawed
1 large avocado, peeled, pitted and sliced	½ cup fat-free sour cream
1 package (8 oz) refrigerated chunk-style imitation crabmeat	1 large tomato, chopped (1 cup) Lime or lemon wedges

1. Divide salad greens among 4 serving plates. Top with chicken, avocado, imitation crabmeat and chiles.

2. In small bowl, mix guacamole and sour cream; spoon over salads. Top with tomato. Garnish with lime wedges.

1 Serving: Calories 270 (Calories from Fat 100); Total Fat 11g (Saturated Fat 1.5g; Trans Fat 0g); Cholesterol 50mg; Sodium 880mg; Total Carbohydrate 21g (Dietary Fiber 7g; Sugars 7g); Protein 23g   **% Daily Value:** Vitamin A 100%; Vitamin C 80%; Calcium 10%; Iron 15%   **Exchanges:** 1 Other Carbohydrate, 1 Vegetable, 3 Lean Meat, ½ Fat **Carbohydrate Choices:** 1½

gingered chicken and fruit salad photo on page C-6

Prep Time: 25 Minutes   **Start to Finish:** 25 Minutes   **Makes:** 4 servings

Ginger Dressing
- ½ teaspoon grated lime peel
- 2 tablespoons fresh lime juice
- 2 tablespoons canola oil
- 1 tablespoon water
- 2 teaspoons honey
- ½ teaspoon ground ginger

Salad
- 6 cups fresh baby spinach leaves
- 2 cups cubed cooked chicken breast
- 1 ripe medium mango, seed removed, peeled and cubed
- 1 cup seedless red grapes, halved
- 2 medium green onions, sliced (2 tablespoons)
- 2 tablespoons coarsely chopped pecans, toasted*

1. In container with tight-fitting lid, shake dressing ingredients until well mixed.

2. Divide spinach among 4 serving plates. Top each with chicken, mango, grapes, onions and pecans. Drizzle with dressing.

*Note: To toast pecans, heat oven to 350°F. Spread pecans in ungreased shallow pan. Bake uncovered 6 to 10 minutes, stirring occasionally until light brown. Or sprinkle in ungreased heavy skillet. Cook over medium heat 5 to 7 minutes, stirring frequently until pecans begin to brown, then stirring constantly until light brown.

1 Serving: Calories 290 (Calories from Fat 110); Total Fat 13g (Saturated Fat 1.5g; Trans Fat 0g); Cholesterol 55mg; Sodium 90mg; Total Carbohydrate 22g (Dietary Fiber 3g; Sugars 16g); Protein 23g   **% Daily Value:** Vitamin A 90%; Vitamin C 60%; Calcium 8%; Iron 15%   **Exchanges:** ½ Fruit, 1 Other Carbohydrate, 3 Lean Meat, 1 Fat
Carbohydrate Choices: 1½

health smart
Mangoes are an excellent source of both vitamins A and C. Vitamin A is important for bone growth and vision, while vitamin C promotes healthy immune function and collagen formation.

chicken and tortellini salad

Prep Time: 20 Minutes   **Start to Finish:** 2 Hours 20 Minutes   **Makes:** 4 servings

1 package (7 oz) dried cheese-filled tortellini	1 teaspoon sugar
⅓ cup chicken broth	½ teaspoon salt
1 tablespoon chopped fresh or 1 teaspoon dried tarragon leaves	¼ teaspoon pepper
2 tablespoons olive or vegetable oil	1½ cups cut-up cooked chicken or turkey
2 tablespoons lemon juice	3 cups bite-size pieces mixed greens
	1 small bell pepper (any color), cut into ½-inch squares

1. Cook tortellini as directed on package. Meanwhile, in container with tight-fitting lid, shake chicken broth, tarragon, oil, lemon juice, sugar, salt and pepper until well mixed. Drain tortellini; rinse with cold water. In large bowl, combine tortellini and chicken. Add dressing and toss to coat. Cover and refrigerate at least 2 hours or overnight.

2. Just before serving, add greens and bell pepper to tortellini mixture; toss to combine.

1 Serving: Calories 300 (Calories from Fat 120); Total Fat 14g (Saturated Fat 3.5g; Trans Fat 0g); Cholesterol 70mg; Sodium 730mg; Total Carbohydrate 23g (Dietary Fiber 1g; Sugars 2g); Protein 21g   **% Daily Value:** Vitamin A 45%; Vitamin C 40%; Calcium 10%; Iron 10%   **Exchanges:** 1 Starch, 1 Vegetable, 2½ Medium-Fat Meat   **Carbohydrate Choices:** 1½

chicken-grapefruit salad

Prep Time: 15 Minutes   Start to Finish: 1 Hour 15 Minutes   Makes: 6 servings

Dressing

⅔ cup plain fat-free yogurt
½ cup finely chopped peeled cucumber
3 tablespoons grapefruit juice
2 tablespoons light mayonnaise or
     salad dressing
1 teaspoon prepared horseradish
¼ teaspoon pepper

Salad

3 cups cubed cooked chicken
2 cups red grapefruit sections (2 large
     grapefruit)
¾ cup chopped peeled cucumber
1 medium avocado, peeled, pitted,
     coarsely chopped
5 cups watercress sprigs (2 large
     bunches) or arugula

1. In large bowl, mix dressing ingredients with wire whisk or spoon. Add chicken, grapefruit, cucumber and avocado; gently toss until evenly coated.

2. Cover and refrigerate about 1 hour or until chilled. Serve on watercress.

1 Serving: Calories 230 (Calories from Fat 70); Total Fat 7g (Saturated Fat 1.5g; Trans Fat 0g); Cholesterol 60mg; Sodium 150mg; Total Carbohydrate 16g (Dietary Fiber 3g; Sugars 10g); Protein 25g   **% Daily Value:** Vitamin A 40%; Vitamin C 70%; Calcium 15%; Iron 6%   **Exchanges:** 1 Fruit, 3 Lean Meat   **Carbohydrate Choices:** 1

more wise food choices

- Use plain fat-free yogurt to replace mayonnaise in salads and dips.
- Replace high-fat, high-calorie cheese, sour cream, half-and-half, cottage cheese and cream cheese with low-fat or nonfat counterparts.
- A small amount of sharp or strong-flavored cheese, such as blue cheese, adds more flavor and fewer calories than a larger amount of a mild cheese.
- Low-fat cheese adds flavor and texture with fewer calories.
- Both fat-free and low-fat milk have fewer calories than whole milk but contain the same amount of calcium.
- Leave the butter, cheese or cream sauce off your veggies.
- Fresh or frozen fruit without sugar syrup are great choices.
- Use low-fat salad dressing or balsamic vinegar for salads or marinades.

chicken and
fresh berry salad
photo on page C-6

Prep Time: 15 Minutes   Start to Finish: 15 Minutes   Makes: 3 servings

5 cups bite-size pieces mixed salad greens
1 package (6 oz) refrigerated grilled chicken breast strips, cut in half if necessary
1 cup fresh strawberry halves
½ cup fresh blueberries
½ cup fresh raspberries
¼ cup vinaigrette dressing
¼ cup honey-roasted peanuts
2 tablespoons crumbled blue cheese

In large bowl, toss all ingredients except peanuts and cheese until evenly coated with dressing. Sprinkle with peanuts and cheese.

1 Serving: Calories 245 (Calories from Fat 100); Total Fat 11g (Saturated Fat 3g; Trans Fat); Cholesterol 50mg; Sodium 430mg; Total Carbohydrate 19g (Dietary Fiber 6g; Sugars); Protein 24g   **% Daily Value:** Vitamin A; Vitamin C; Calcium; Iron 12%   **Exchanges:** 1 Fruit, 1 Vegetable, 3 Lean Meat   **Carbohydrate Choices:** 1

health smart

Berries are nutrition giants. Just 1 cup of raspberries supplies 8 grams of fiber. Blueberries are high in antioxidants, and strawberries are full of vitamin C. So enjoy this salad for how good it tastes as well as how good it is for you.

grilled balsamic-beef salad

Prep Time: 35 Minutes   Start to Finish: 2 Hours 35 Minutes   Makes: 6 servings

Balsamic Vinaigrette
- ½ cup balsamic vinegar
- ¼ cup water
- 1 package Italian dressing mix
- 1 tablespoon olive oil

Salad
- 1 boneless beef sirloin steak,
     1 to 1½ inches thick (1 lb)

- 4 cups fresh baby salad greens
- 2 cups bite-size pieces arugula leaves
- 2 plum (Roma) tomatoes, chopped
- 1½ cups sliced baby portabella
      mushrooms (4 oz)
- ¾ cup shredded reduced-fat mozzarella
     cheese (3 oz)
- ⅔ cup Caesar-flavored croutons

1. In container with tight-fitting lid, shake vinaigrette ingredients until well mixed. Divide dressing mixture in half.

2. Place beef in shallow glass or plastic dish or heavy-duty resealable food-storage plastic bag. Pour half of the vinaigrette mixture over beef; turn beef to coat. Cover dish or seal bag; refrigerate at least 2 hours to marinate. Cover; refrigerate remaining vinaigrette.

3. Heat gas or charcoal grill. Remove beef from marinade; reserve marinade. Place beef on grill. Cover grill; cook over medium heat 15 to 20 minutes, turning and brushing with marinade occasionally, until desired doneness. Discard any remaining marinade. Cut beef into 3×¼-inch slices.

4. Among 6 plates, divide salad greens, arugula, tomatoes and mushrooms. Top with beef; drizzle with remaining vinaigrette. Sprinkle with cheese and croutons.

1 Serving: Calories 200 (Calories from Fat 80); Total Fat 9g (Saturated Fat 3g; Trans Fat 0g); Cholesterol 50mg; Sodium 590mg; Total Carbohydrate 9g (Dietary Fiber 2g; Sugars 4g); Protein 23g   **% Daily Value:** Vitamin A 45%; Vitamin C 15%; Calcium 15%; Iron 15%   **Exchanges:** 1½ Vegetable, 3 Lean Meat   **Carbohydrate Choices:** ½

asian pork salad

Prep Time: 10 Minutes   Start to Finish: 15 Minutes   Makes: 4 servings

2	tablespoons reduced-sodium soy sauce	3	cups coleslaw mix
1	tablespoon chili puree with garlic	1	small bell pepper (any color), cut into ½-inch strips
1	teaspoon sesame oil	1	can (15 oz) black beans, rinsed, drained
½	lb pork tenderloin, cut into 1½×½-inch strips		

1. In container with tight-fitting lid, shake soy sauce, chili puree and oil until well mixed. Remove 1 tablespoon of the soy sauce mixture; reserve remaining mixture. In medium bowl, toss pork with the 1 tablespoon of the soy sauce mixture.

2. Spray 10-inch nonstick skillet with cooking spray; heat over medium-high heat. Cook pork in skillet, stirring occasionally, until no longer pink in center.

3. In large bowl, place pork. Add reserved soy sauce mixture and remaining ingredients; toss until evenly coated.

1 Serving: Calories 220 (Calories from Fat 35); Total Fat 4g (Saturated Fat 1g; Trans Fat 0g); Cholesterol 25mg; Sodium 750mg; Total Carbohydrate 28g (Dietary Fiber 10g; Sugars 4g); Protein 18g   **% Daily Value:** Vitamin A 50%; Vitamin C 60%; Calcium 8%; Iron 15%   **Exchanges:** 1½ Starch, 1 Vegetable, 1½ Lean Meat   **Carbohydrate Choices:** 2

savory poached-salmon salad

Prep Time: 20 Minutes   Start to Finish: 20 Minutes   Makes: 6 servings

Salad

1	lb salmon or other medium-firm fish steaks (1 inch thick)
¼	teaspoon salt
¼	cup dry white wine or chicken broth
6	cups shredded lettuce
½	cup croutons
¼	cup chopped fresh parsley
½	small red onion, sliced, separated into rings

Dijon Vinaigrette

¼	cup vegetable oil
2	tablespoons finely chopped green onions (2 medium)
2	tablespoons lemon juice
2	teaspoons chopped fresh or ½ teaspoon dried tarragon leaves
1	teaspoon Dijon mustard
	Dash freshly ground pepper

1. In 8-inch square microwavable dish, arrange fish, thickest parts to outside edges. Sprinkle with salt. Pour wine over fish. Cover with plastic wrap, folding back one edge or corner to vent steam. Microwave on High 6 to 8 minutes or until fish flakes easily with fork. Let stand covered 3 minutes; drain. Remove skin and bones; break salmon into 1-inch pieces.

2. In large bowl, gently toss salmon with lettuce, croutons, parsley and onion. In container with tight-fitting lid, shake vinaigrette ingredients until well mixed. Drizzle over salad; gently toss until evenly coated.

1 Serving: Calories 210 (Calories from Fat 120); Total Fat 13g (Saturated Fat 2.5g; Trans Fat 0g); Cholesterol 40mg; Sodium 180mg; Total Carbohydrate 5g (Dietary Fiber 1g; Sugars 2g); Protein 14g   **% Daily Value:** Vitamin A 10%; Vitamin C 6%; Calcium 4%; Iron 6%   **Exchanges:** ½ Other Carbohydrate, 2 Medium-Fat Meat, ½ Fat   **Carbohydrate Choices:** ½

tuna, tomato and mozzarella salad

Prep Time: 20 Minutes   Start to Finish: 30 Minutes   Makes: 3 servings

½   lb tuna or other firm fish steaks
1   teaspoon olive or vegetable oil
1   small clove garlic, finely chopped
3   large plum (Roma) tomatoes, sliced lengthwise

4   oz fresh mozzarella cheese, sliced
2   tablespoons balsamic vinaigrette
2   tablespoons chopped fresh basil leaves

1. Heat gas or charcoal grill. Drizzle both sides of tuna steaks with oil; rub with garlic. Let stand at room temperature 15 minutes to marinate.

2. Meanwhile, arrange tomato and cheese slices on large serving plate or platter. Drizzle with vinaigrette; sprinkle with basil. Set aside.

3. Cover and grill tuna 4 to 6 inches from medium heat 8 to 10 minutes or until fish flakes easily with fork, turning once. Cut tuna into slices; place on top of tomatoes and cheese.

1 Serving: Calories 290 (Calories from Fat 160); Total Fat 18g (Saturated Fat 7g, Trans Fat 0g); Cholesterol 65mg; Sodium 320mg; Total Carbohydrate 7g (Dietary Fiber 1g, Sugars 4g); Protein 25g   **% Daily Value:** Vitamin A 30%; Vitamin C 30%; Calcium 30%; Iron 6%   **Exchanges:** 1 Vegetable, 3½ Lean Meat, 1½ Fat   **Carbohydrate Choices:** ½

try this
Serve with rustic whole wheat bread and glasses of sparkling mineral water topped with orange wedges.

tuna-feta salad

Prep Time: 10 Minutes   Start to Finish: 1 Hour 10 Minutes   Makes: 8 servings

Salad

- 2   cans (15 to 16 oz each) cannellini or other white beans, rinsed, drained
- 1   can (9 oz) chunk light tuna in water, drained, flaked
- ⅓   cup crumbled feta cheese
- 1   medium Spanish, Bermuda or red onion, thinly sliced

    Chopped fresh parsley

Red Wine Vinaigrette

- ⅓   cup olive or vegetable oil
- 3   tablespoons red wine vinegar
- ½   teaspoon salt

    Freshly ground pepper

1. In shallow glass or plastic dish, mix beans, tuna, cheese and onion. In container with tight-fitting lid, shake vinaigrette ingredients until well mixed; pour over bean mixture. Cover and refrigerate at least 1 hour or overnight, stirring occasionally.

2. Transfer bean mixture to serving platter with slotted spoon. Sprinkle with parsley.

1 Serving: Calories 250 (Calories from Fat 100); Total Fat 11g (Saturated Fat 2.5g; Trans Fat 0g); Cholesterol 10mg; Sodium 550mg; Total Carbohydrate 23g (Dietary Fiber 5g; Sugars 1g); Protein 14g   **% Daily Value:** Vitamin A 0%; Vitamin C 2%; Calcium 10%; Iron 20%   **Exchanges:** 1½ Starch, 1½ Lean Meat, 1 Fat   **Carbohydrate Choices:** 1½

230 calories

shrimp pasta salad with fresh fruit salsa

Prep Time: 30 Minutes   Start to Finish: 30 Minutes   Makes: 6 servings

Pasta Salad

2 cups uncooked bow-tie (farfalle) pasta (4 oz)
1 head Boston lettuce, separated into leaves
1 medium cucumber, cut lengthwise in half, then sliced crosswise
18 cooked large (21 to 30 count) deveined peeled shrimp with tail shells left on (about ¾ lb)
1 large avocado, pitted, peeled and sliced

Fresh Fruit Salsa

½ cup coarsely chopped pineapple
½ cup coarsely chopped strawberries
2 kiwifruit, peeled, coarsely chopped
1 small jalapeño chile, chopped
2 tablespoons orange juice
1 tablespoon olive or vegetable oil
1 teaspoon grated orange peel
¼ teaspoon salt
⅛ teaspoon white pepper

1. Cook pasta as directed on package. Meanwhile, divide lettuce among serving plates; arrange cucumber, shrimp and avocado on plates.

2. In small bowl, mix salsa ingredients. Drain pasta and rinse in cold water; divide among salads. Serve with salsa.

1 Serving: Calories 230 (Calories from Fat 70); Total Fat 8g (Saturated Fat 1g; Trans Fat 0g); Cholesterol 125mg; Sodium 230mg; Total Carbohydrate 24g (Dietary Fiber 4g; Sugars 6g); Protein 15g   **% Daily Value:** Vitamin A 25%; Vitamin C 40%; Calcium 6%; Iron 20%   **Exchanges:** 1 Starch, ½ Fruit, 1 Vegetable, 1½ Lean Meat, ½ Fat **Carbohydrate Choices:** 1½

shrimp paella salad

Prep Time: 20 Minutes   Start to Finish: 20 Minutes   Makes: 2 servings

2 slices bacon, cut up	1 tablespoon lemon juice
1 clove garlic, finely chopped	⅛ teaspoon paprika
1 cup cooked rice	2 or 3 drops red pepper sauce
½ cup frozen sweet peas, thawed	6 oz cooked peeled deveined medium
2 tablespoons chopped drained	shrimp, thawed if frozen, tail shells
roasted red bell peppers	removed
(from 7-oz jar)	Lettuce leaves

1. In 10-inch skillet, cook bacon until crisp. Drain, reserving 1 tablespoon drippings in skillet. Drain bacon on paper towel.

2. Cook and stir garlic in bacon drippings over medium heat until softened, about 1 minute. Stir in bacon and remaining ingredients except lettuce.

3. Serve shrimp mixture on lettuce. Sprinkle with additional paprika if desired.

1 Serving: Calories 250 (Calories from Fat 45); Total Fat 5g (Saturated Fat 1.5g; Trans Fat 0g); Cholesterol 175mg; Sodium 650mg; Total Carbohydrate 29g (Dietary Fiber 2g; Sugars 3g); Protein 24g   **% Daily Value:** Vitamin A 25%; Vitamin C 25%; Calcium 6%; Iron 25%   **Exchanges:** 2 Starch, 2½ Very Lean Meat, ½ Fat   **Carbohydrate Choices:** 2

try this

Instead of serving the salad on a bed of lettuce, turn it into lettuce wraps. Fill Bibb or iceberg lettuce leaves with the shrimp mixture, roll and enjoy. Double this recipe for guests and let everyone fill their own.

peppered shrimp and mango salad

Prep Time: 15 Minutes   **Start to Finish:** 15 Minutes   **Makes:** 4 servings

20	uncooked deveined peeled large shrimp, thawed if frozen, tail shells removed (about ¾ lb)
½	teaspoon salt
½	teaspoon pepper
1	tablespoon sesame or vegetable oil

1	bag (5 oz) ready-to-eat mixed salad greens
1½	cups diced mangoes (about 1½ medium)
½	cup sliced radishes (about 5 medium)
⅓	cup Asian sesame dressing

1. Toss shrimp with salt and pepper.

2. In 10-inch skillet, heat oil over high heat. Add shrimp; cook about 3 minutes, stirring frequently, until shrimp are pink. Remove from heat.

3. In large bowl, toss salad greens, mangoes, radishes and dressing. Top with shrimp.

1 Serving: Calories 200 (Calories from Fat 120); Total Fat 13g (Saturated Fat 2g; Trans Fat 0g); Cholesterol 60mg; Sodium 590mg; Total Carbohydrate 13g (Dietary Fiber 2g; Sugars 9g); Protein 7g   **% Daily Value:** Vitamin A 45%; Vitamin C 20%; Calcium 4%; Iron 8%   **Exchanges:** 1 Fruit, 2 Vegetable, 1 Very Lean Meat, 2 Fat   **Carbohydrate Choices:** 1

health smart

Choose dark-green greens for your salad. Romaine and spinach top the charts nutritionally. In general, the darker the green, the more nutrients it has to offer.

spicy coconut-crabmeat salad

Prep Time: 15 Minutes   **Start to Finish:** 15 Minutes   **Makes:** 6 servings

Curry Dressing

1	cup light mayonnaise or salad dressing
1	to 2 teaspoons red curry paste (from 4-oz jar)
1	tablespoon fresh lemon juice

Salad

2	packages (8 oz each) refrigerated chunk-style imitation crabmeat
2	cups fresh sugar snap peas, trimmed, cut in half diagonally
1	cup shredded coconut
½	cup sliced green onions (about 8 medium)
6	cups thinly sliced Chinese (napa) cabbage

1. In large bowl, beat dressing ingredients with wire whisk until blended.

2. Add imitation crabmeat, peas, coconut and onions; gently toss until evenly coated with dressing. Serve on cabbage.

1 Serving: Calories 250 (Calories from Fat 90); Total Fat 10g (Saturated Fat 6g; Trans Fat 0g); Cholesterol 35mg; Sodium 1130mg; Total Carbohydrate 25g (Dietary Fiber 3g; Sugars 16g); Protein 14g   **% Daily Value:** Vitamin A 70%; Vitamin C 45%; Calcium 10%; Iron 10%   **Exchanges:** 1 Other Carbohydrate, 2 Vegetable, 1½ Medium-Fat Meat, ½ Fat **Carbohydrate Choices:** 1½

black bean–taco salad

Prep Time: 15 Minutes   Start to Finish: 15 Minutes   Makes: 4 servings

2   cans (15 oz each) black beans, rinsed, drained
1   can (2.25 oz) sliced ripe olives, drained
2   medium tomatoes, chopped (1½ cups)
4   medium green onions, chopped (¼ cup)
⅓   cup shredded Cheddar cheese

¼   cup chopped fresh cilantro
2   tablespoons lime juice
1   teaspoon ground cumin
¼   teaspoon pepper
4   cups chopped fresh spinach

1. In large bowl, mix beans, olives, tomatoes, onions, cheese and cilantro.

2. In container with tight-fitting lid, shake lime juice, cumin and pepper until well mixed; toss with bean mixture. Serve on spinach.

1 Serving: Calories 280 (Calories from Fat 45); Total Fat 5g (Saturated Fat 2.5g; Trans Fat 0g); Cholesterol 10mg; Sodium 710mg; Total Carbohydrate 43g (Dietary Fiber 17g; Sugars 3g); Protein 16g   **% Daily Value:** Vitamin A 70%; Vitamin C 35%; Calcium 20%; Iron 30%   **Exchanges:** 2 Starch, ½ Other Carbohydrate, 1 Vegetable, 1 Lean Meat **Carbohydrate Choices:** 3

try this

Tuck all of the salad ingredients into a whole wheat flatbread. Flatbread comes in many varieties, some containing up to 8 grams of fiber and only 100 calories. Look for different varieties in the deli section or bread aisle of your grocery store and check labels carefully.

 **280** calories

pesto chicken pizzas photo on page C-6

Prep Time: 10 Minutes   Start to Finish: 20 Minutes   Makes: 4 pizzas

1 cup cut-up cooked chicken breast	¼ cup chopped onion
2 tablespoons refrigerated reduced-fat or regular basil pesto	¼ cup chopped bell pepper (any color)
4 whole wheat pita (pocket) breads (6 inch)	¼ cup shredded reduced-fat mozzarella cheese (1 oz)
½ cup pizza sauce	2 tablespoons shredded Parmesan cheese

1. Heat oven to 400°F. In medium bowl, mix chicken and pesto until blended.

2. Place pita breads in single layer on cookie sheet. Spread 2 tablespoons pizza sauce on each pita. Divide chicken mixture evenly among pitas. Top with remaining ingredients.

3. Bake about 10 minutes or until cheese is melted. Cut pizzas into wedges.

1 Pizza: Calories 280 (Calories from Fat 80); Total Fat 9g (Saturated Fat 2.5g; Trans Fat 0g); Cholesterol 35mg; Sodium 490mg; Total Carbohydrate 30g (Dietary Fiber 4g; Sugars 6g); Protein 19g   **% Daily Value:** Vitamin A 8%; Vitamin C 10%; Calcium 15%; Iron 15%   **Exchanges:** 1½ Starch, ½ Other Carbohydrate, 2 Lean Meat, ½ Fat **Carbohydrate Choices:** 2

cowboy bbq chicken pizza

Prep Time: 10 Minutes   Start to Finish: 35 Minutes   Makes: 8 servings

2 cups Original Bisquick mix	¼ cup chopped cooked bacon (about 4 slices from 2.2-oz package)
¼ cup sour cream	
¼ cup very hot water	1½ cups shredded Colby–Monterey Jack cheese (6 oz)
1 container (18 oz) refrigerated fully cooked original barbeque sauce with shredded chicken	

1. Heat oven to 400°F. In medium bowl, stir Bisquick mix, sour cream and hot water with fork until soft dough forms. Place on surface dusted with Bisquick mix. Shape into a ball; knead 5 times. Roll dough into 14-inch circle; fold circle in half. Place on ungreased large cookie sheet and unfold.

2. Spread chicken mixture over dough to within 2 inches of edge. Fold edge just to chicken mixture. Top with half of the bacon. Sprinkle with cheese and remaining bacon.

3. Bake 20 to 25 minutes or until crust is light golden brown and cheese is melted.

1 Serving: Calories 230 (Calories from Fat 120); Total Fat 14g (Saturated Fat 7g; Trans Fat 1g); Cholesterol 30mg; Sodium 600mg; Total Carbohydrate 19g (Dietary Fiber 0g; Sugars 3g); Protein 8g   **% Daily Value:** Vitamin A 6%; Vitamin C 0%; Calcium 20%; Iron 6%   **Exchanges:** 2 Starch, 2 Medium-Fat Meat, 2 Fat   **Carbohydrate Choices:** 1

serve with
Add a salad tossed with ranch dressing and a serving of mixed vegetables to complete the meal.

chicken gyro pizza

photo on page C-6

Prep Time: 20 Minutes   **Start to Finish:** 45 Minutes   **Makes:** 6 servings

2	cups Bisquick Heart Smart mix	1	can (2¼ oz) sliced ripe olives, drained
¼	teaspoon dried oregano leaves	⅓	cup crumbled feta cheese (2 oz)
½	cup cold water	1¼	cups shredded mozzarella cheese (6 oz)
6	slices cooked chicken breast, cut into strips (about ¾ lb)	1	small tomato, chopped (½ cup)
		½	cup chopped cucumber

1. Move oven rack to lowest position. Heat oven to 425°F. Spray 12-inch pizza pan with cooking spray. Stir Bisquick mix, oregano and water; beat vigorously with spoon 20 strokes until soft dough forms. Press dough in pizza pan, using fingers dipped in Bisquick mix; pinch edge to form ½-inch rim. Bake about 15 minutes or until golden brown.

2. Top crust with chicken and olives; sprinkle with feta and mozzarella cheeses.

3. Bake about 10 minutes or until cheese is melted. Sprinkle with tomato and cucumber.

1 Serving: Calories 300 (Calories from Fat 100); Total Fat 11g (Saturated Fat 4.5g; Trans Fat 0g); Cholesterol 45mg; Sodium 660mg; Total Carbohydrate 30g (Dietary Fiber 0g; Sugars 4g); Protein 19g   **% Daily Value:** Vitamin A 6%; Vitamin C 0%; Calcium 45%; Iron 10%   **Exchanges:** 2 Starch, 2 Medium-Fat Meat   **Carbohydrate Choices:** 2

ranch tuna-melt pizza

Prep Time: 15 Minutes   Start to Finish: 25 Minutes   Makes: 6 servings

1½   cups Original Bisquick mix
⅓   cup boiling water
1   can (12 oz) chunk light tuna in water,
     well drained
¼   cup ranch dressing

3   tablespoons finely chopped green
     onions
1   small tomato, cut into 6 slices
3   slices American cheese, cut in half
     diagonally

1. Heat oven to 450°F. In medium bowl, stir Bisquick mix and boiling water until soft dough forms. Gather dough into a ball.

2. Place dough on surface lightly dusted with Bisquick mix. Roll dough into 13-inch round. Place on ungreased 12-inch pizza pan; pinch edge to form ½-inch rim. Bake 6 to 8 minutes or until light brown.

3. Meanwhile, in medium bowl, mix tuna, dressing and onions. Spread tuna mixture over crust. Arrange tomato and cheese slices alternately in a pinwheel pattern on tuna mixture. Bake 1 to 2 minutes or until cheese is melted. Cut into wedges.

1 Serving: Calories 260 (Calories from Fat 120); Total Fat 13g (Saturated Fat 4g; Trans Fat 1g); Cholesterol 25mg; Sodium 810mg; Total Carbohydrate 20g (Dietary Fiber 0g; Sugars 3g); Protein 16g   **% Daily Value:** Vitamin A 6%; Vitamin C 4%; Calcium 10%; Iron 10%   **Exchanges:** 1½ Starch, 1½ Very Lean Meat, 2 Fat   **Carbohydrate Choices:** 1

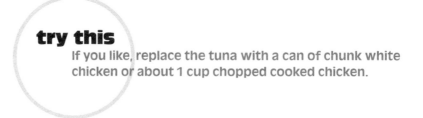

try this
If you like, replace the tuna with a can of chunk white chicken or about 1 cup chopped cooked chicken.

chilly garden pizza

Prep Time: 15 Minutes   Start to Finish: 15 Minutes   Makes: 6 servings

1 container (6.5 oz) 50%-less-fat garlic-and-herbs spreadable cheese	1 large tomato, chopped (1 cup)
	½ cup sliced fresh mushrooms
1 package (10 oz) prebaked thin Italian pizza crust (12 inch)	1 medium carrot, shredded (¾ cup)
	¼ teaspoon salt
¾ cup chopped fresh spinach	⅛ teaspoon pepper
½ cup diced seeded cucumber	1 tablespoon chopped fresh basil leaves

Spread cheese evenly over pizza crust; top with spinach, cucumber, tomato, mushrooms and carrot. Sprinkle with salt, pepper and basil.

1 Serving: Calories 220 (Calories from Fat 80); Total Fat 8g (Saturated Fat 4g; Trans Fat 0g); Cholesterol 15mg; Sodium 420mg; Total Carbohydrate 29g (Dietary Fiber 2g; Sugars 4g); Protein 7g   **% Daily Value:** Vitamin A 70%; Vitamin C 8%; Calcium 6%; Iron 15%   **Exchanges:** 1½ Starch, 1 Vegetable, 1½ Fat   **Carbohydrate Choices:** 2

try this

Instead of using 1 large pizza crust, purchase individual size (6-inch) prebaked pizza crusts. Set out the toppings and let everyone make their own.

soups,
stews and
chilies

Whether it's for lunch or dinner, there's nothing better to fill you up—and warm you up—than a bowl of soup or stew. They're often filled with vegetables, too, so they're a great way to add more vegetables to your diet. Grab a slice of bread and dig into one of the delicious recipes in this chapter.

170 calories

italian chicken noodle soup photo on page C-10

Prep Time: 35 Minutes   **Start to Finish:** 35 Minutes   **Makes:** 6 servings

1	tablespoon olive or canola oil	3	medium carrots, sliced (1½ cups)
2	boneless skinless chicken breasts (about ½ lb), cut into ½-inch pieces	2	cups fresh broccoli florets
		1½	cups uncooked medium egg noodles
1	medium onion, chopped (½ cup)	1	teaspoon dried basil leaves
2	cans (14 oz each) chicken broth	½	teaspoon garlic-pepper blend
2	cups water	¼	cup shredded Parmesan cheese

1. In 4-quart saucepan, heat oil over medium heat. Add chicken; cook 4 to 6 minutes, stirring occasionally, until no longer pink in center. Stir in onion. Cook 2 to 3 minutes, stirring occasionally, until onion is tender.

2. Stir in broth, water and carrots. Heat to boiling. Reduce heat to medium; cook 5 minutes. Stir in broccoli, noodles, basil and garlic-pepper blend. Heat to boiling. Reduce heat; simmer uncovered 8 to 10 minutes, stirring occasionally, until vegetables and noodles are tender.

3. Top each serving with cheese.

1 Serving: Calories 170 (Calories from Fat 60); Total Fat 6g (Saturated Fat 2g; Trans Fat 0g); Cholesterol 35mg; Sodium 730mg; Total Carbohydrate 14g (Dietary Fiber 2g; Sugars 3g); Protein 15g   **% Daily Value:** Vitamin A 110%; Vitamin C 25%; Calcium 10%; Iron 8%   **Exchanges:** ½ Starch, 1 Vegetable, 1½ Very Lean Meat, 1 Fat   **Carbohydrate Choices:** 1

chicken and spinach
tortellini soup

Prep Time: 20 Minutes   Start to Finish: 45 Minutes   Makes: 5 servings

1 tablespoon olive or vegetable oil	2 cups shredded cooked chicken
5 medium green onions, chopped (⅓ cup)	1 cup frozen small cheese-filled tortellini
⅓ cup julienne (matchstick-cut) carrots	¼ teaspoon ground nutmeg, if desired
2 cloves garlic, finely chopped (1 teaspoon)	⅛ teaspoon pepper
6 cups chicken broth	3 cups chopped fresh spinach

1. In 4½- to 5-quart Dutch oven, heat oil over medium-high heat. Cook onions, carrots and garlic in oil 3 to 4 minutes, stirring frequently, until onions are softened.

2. Stir in broth and chicken. Heat to boiling. Stir in tortellini; reduce heat to medium. Cover; cook 3 to 5 minutes or until tortellini are tender.

3. Stir in nutmeg, pepper and spinach. Cover; cook 2 to 3 minutes or until spinach is hot.

1 Serving: Calories 240 (Calories from Fat 100); Total Fat 11g (Saturated Fat 3g; Trans Fat 0g); Cholesterol 80mg; Sodium 1540mg; Total Carbohydrate 10g (Dietary Fiber 1g; Sugars 1g); Protein 25g   **% Daily Value:** Vitamin A 70%; Vitamin C 6%; Calcium 8%; Iron 15%   **Exchanges:** ½ Starch, 1 Vegetable, 3 Lean Meat, ½ Fat   **Carbohydrate Choices:** ½

try this
Dried cheese-filled tortellini can be used in place of the frozen tortellini by adjusting the cooking time according to the package instructions. You can also substitute shredded carrots for the julienne-cut carrots.

thai-style chicken curry soup

Prep Time: 15 Minutes   **Start to Finish:** 15 Minutes   **Makes:** 4 servings

1	carton (32 oz) chicken broth	1	small jalapeño chile, seeded, finely chopped (1 tablespoon)
3	tablespoons packed brown sugar	2	cups chopped cooked chicken
2	tablespoons soy sauce	2	tablespoon chopped fresh cilantro, if desired
2	tablespoons rice vinegar		
2	teaspoons curry powder		
1	small red bell pepper, coarsely chopped (½ cup)		

1. In 3-quart saucepan, stir all ingredients except chicken and cilantro. Heat to boiling over medium-high heat. Reduce heat to medium. Simmer uncovered 3 to 5 minutes or until bell pepper is crisp-tender.

2. Stir in chicken. Cook 1 to 2 minutes or until chicken is hot. Just before serving, add cilantro.

1 Serving: Calories 210 (Calories from Fat 60); Total Fat 7g (Saturated Fat 2g; Trans Fat 0g); Cholesterol 60mg; Sodium 1770mg; Total Carbohydrate 14g (Dietary Fiber 0g; Sugars 11g); Protein 25g   **% Daily Value:** Vitamin A 25%; Vitamin C 30%; Calcium 4%; Iron 10%   **Exchanges:** 1 Other Carbohydrate, 3 Lean Meat   **Carbohydrate Choices:** 1

chicken soup with dumplings

Prep Time: 10 Minutes   **Start to Finish:** 30 Minutes   **Makes:** 6 servings

2 cups cut-up cooked chicken	2 cloves garlic, finely chopped
1 carton (32 oz) 33%-less-sodium chicken broth (4 cups)	1 bag (12 oz) frozen mixed vegetables, thawed, drained
1 tablespoon chopped fresh parsley	1 cup Bisquick Heart Smart mix
1 tablespoon chopped fresh thyme leaves	⅓ cup milk

1. In 3-quart saucepan, heat all ingredients except Bisquick mix and milk to boiling, stirring occasionally.

2. In small bowl, stir Bisquick mix and milk with fork until soft dough forms. Drop dough by 18 teaspoonfuls onto boiling soup. If dumplings sink into soup, carefully bring them to top of broth using slotted spoon. Reduce heat to medium-low.

3. Cook uncovered 10 minutes. Cover and cook 15 minutes longer.

1 Serving: Calories 190 (Calories from Fat 45); Total Fat 5g (Saturated Fat 1g; Trans Fat 0g); Cholesterol 40mg; Sodium 580mg; Total Carbohydrate 19g (Dietary Fiber 1g; Sugars 4g); Protein 18g   **% Daily Value:** Vitamin A 25%; Vitamin C 15%; Calcium 15%; Iron 10%   **Exchanges:** 1 Starch, 2 Lean Meat   **Carbohydrate Choices:** 1

chicken and barley soup

Prep Time: 15 Minutes   Start to Finish: 35 Minutes   Makes: 6 servings

1   carton (32 oz) chicken broth
1   can (14.5 oz) diced tomatoes,
      undrained
2   medium carrots, sliced (1 cup)
2   medium stalks celery, sliced (1 cup)

1   cup sliced fresh mushrooms
      (about 3 oz)
⅓   cup uncooked quick-cooking barley
1   teaspoon dried minced onion
2   cups chopped cooked chicken

1. In 3-quart saucepan, mix all ingredients except chicken. Heat to boiling over medium-high heat. Reduce heat to medium. Cover; simmer 15 to 20 minutes or until barley is tender.

2. Add chicken. Cover; cook about 3 minutes or until chicken is hot.

1 Serving: Calories 180 (Calories from Fat 40); Total Fat 4.5g (Saturated Fat 1g; Trans Fat 0g); Cholesterol 40mg; Sodium 1000mg; Total Carbohydrate 16g (Dietary Fiber 4g; Sugars 3g); Protein 19g   **% Daily Value:** Vitamin A 80%; Vitamin C 10%; Calcium 6%; Iron 10%   **Exchanges:** 1 Starch, 2 Lean Meat   **Carbohydrate Choices:** 1

turkey-spaetzle soup

Prep Time: 25 Minutes   **Start to Finish:** 35 Minutes   **Makes:** 6 servings

2 tablespoons vegetable oil	1 tablespoon chopped fresh or
1 large onion, finely chopped (1 cup)	2 teaspoons dried thyme leaves
1 medium carrot, finely chopped	¼ teaspoon pepper
(½ cup)	2 cups diced cooked turkey
1 medium stalk celery, finely chopped	1 can (49½ oz) chicken broth (6 cups)
(½ cup)	1 bag (12 oz) frozen spaetzle
1 clove garlic, finely chopped	Chopped fresh parsley, if desired
¼ cup all-purpose flour	

1. In 4-quart saucepan, heat oil over medium-high heat. Add onion, carrot, celery and garlic; cook about 2 minutes, stirring frequently, until crisp-tender.

2. Gradually stir in flour, thyme and pepper; cook about 1 minute, stirring constantly. Stir in turkey and broth; heat to boiling.

3. Stir in frozen spaetzle. Cook 2 to 3 minutes, stirring occasionally, until spaetzle are tender. Sprinkle with parsley.

1 Serving: Calories 240 (Calories from Fat 90); Total Fat 10g (Saturated Fat 2.5g; Trans Fat 0g); Cholesterol 70mg; Sodium 1180mg; Total Carbohydrate 17g (Dietary Fiber 2g; Sugars 2g); Protein 21g   **% Daily Value:** Vitamin A 30%; Vitamin C 2%; Calcium 4%; Iron 15%   **Exchanges:** 1 Starch, 2½ Lean Meat, ½ Fat   **Carbohydrate Choices:** 1

try this
If you prefer, substitute 3 cups frozen egg noodles for the spaetzle.

turkey-wild rice soup

Prep Time: 10 Minutes   Start to Finish: 35 Minutes   Makes: 6 servings

3	tablespoons butter or margarine	2	cups water
½	cup all-purpose flour	2	tablespoons instant chopped onion
2	cans (14 oz each) 33%-less-sodium chicken broth	1	box (6 oz) original long-grain and wild rice mix
1	package (8 oz) 98% fat-free oven-roasted turkey breast, cubed (about 2 cups)	2	cups fat-free half-and-half

1. In 5-quart Dutch oven, melt butter over medium heat. Stir in flour with wire whisk until well blended. Slowly stir in broth with wire whisk. Stir in turkey, water, onion, rice and contents of seasoning packet.

2. Heat to boiling over high heat, stirring occasionally. Reduce heat to medium-low. Cover and simmer about 25 minutes or until rice is tender.

3. Stir in half-and-half; heat just to boiling.

1 Serving: Calories 290 (Calories from Fat 70); Total Fat 8g (Saturated Fat 4.5g; Trans Fat 0g); Cholesterol 40mg; Sodium 1200mg; Total Carbohydrate 40g (Dietary Fiber 1g; Sugars 7g); Protein 14g   **% Daily Value:** Vitamin A 4%; Vitamin C 0%; Calcium 10%; Iron 10%   **Exchanges:** 2 Starch, ½ Other Carbohydrate, 1 Lean Meat, 1 Fat **Carbohydrate Choices:** 2½

creamy beef noodle soup

Prep Time: 50 Minutes   Start to Finish: 50 Minutes   Makes: 7 servings

2 tablespoons butter or margarine	6½ cups beef broth
1 medium onion, coarsely chopped (½ cup)	¼ cup ketchup
4 medium cloves garlic, finely chopped (2 teaspoons)	¾ teaspoon salt
	⅛ teaspoon pepper
1 package (8 oz) sliced fresh mushrooms (3 cups)	2 cups uncooked medium egg noodles
1½ lb boneless beef top sirloin steak, cut into 2×¾×¼-inch pieces	1 container (8 oz) reduced-fat sour cream

1. In 5- to 6-quart Dutch oven, melt butter over medium-high heat. Cook onion, garlic and mushrooms in butter 5 to 6 minutes, stirring frequently, until mushrooms are softened.

2. Stir in beef. Cook 5 to 6 minutes, stirring frequently, until beef is no longer pink. Stir in remaining ingredients except noodles and sour cream. Heat to boiling; reduce heat to medium-low. Cover; cook 10 minutes, stirring occasionally. Stir in noodles. Cover; cook 5 to 7 minutes, stirring occasionally, until noodles are tender.

3. Stir in sour cream. Cook 3 to 5 minutes, stirring frequently, until well blended.

1 Serving: Calories 290 (Calories from Fat 110); Total Fat 12g (Saturated Fat 6g; Trans Fat 0g); Cholesterol 95mg; Sodium 1380mg; Total Carbohydrate 14g (Dietary Fiber 1g; Sugars 5g); Protein 31g   **% Daily Value:** Vitamin A 6%; Vitamin C 4%; Calcium 6%; Iron 20%   **Exchanges:** 1 Starch, 4 Lean Meat   **Carbohydrate Choices:** 1

asian beef and noodle soup
photo on page C-11

Prep Time: 45 Minutes   Start to Finish: 1 Hour 10 Minutes   Makes: 6 servings

3 oz uncooked cellophane noodles (bean threads)	6 cups reduced-sodium beef broth
1 tablespoon dark sesame oil	2 cups finely sliced bok choy
1½ lb boneless beef top sirloin steak, cut into bite-size strips	1 cup julienne (matchstick-cut) carrots
2 teaspoons finely chopped garlic	½ teaspoon ground ginger
2 packages (about 3.5 oz each) fresh shiitake or button mushrooms, sliced	⅛ teaspoon pepper
	2 medium green onions, sliced (2 tablespoons)

1. In medium bowl, soak bundle of cellophane noodles in warm water 10 to 15 minutes or until softened; drain. Cut noodle bundle into thirds. Cover and set aside.

2. In 5- to 6-quart Dutch oven, heat oil over medium-high heat. Cook beef, garlic and mushrooms in oil 5 to 6 minutes, stirring occasionally, just until beef is no longer pink.

3. Stir in remaining ingredients except noodles and onions. Heat to boiling; reduce heat to medium-low. Cover; cook 14 to 15 minutes, stirring occasionally, until beef is tender.

4. Stir in noodles. Cover; cook 2 to 3 minutes or until noodles are hot. Sprinkle with onions.

1 Serving: Calories 250 (Calories from Fat 70); Total Fat 8g (Saturated Fat 2g; Trans Fat 0g); Cholesterol 60mg; Sodium 250mg; Total Carbohydrate 17g (Dietary Fiber 2g; Sugars 2g); Protein 29g   **% Daily Value:** Vitamin A 90%; Vitamin C 10%; Calcium 6%; Iron 20%   **Exchanges:** 1 Starch, 3½ Very Lean Meat, 1 Fat   **Carbohydrate Choices:** 1

try this
If you can't find cellophane noodles, you can use vermicelli instead. Simply cook and drain 3 oz vermicelli as directed on the package, and stir into the soup in step 4.

220 **calories**

italian beef and bean soup

photo on page C-10

Prep Time: 20 Minutes   **Start to Finish:** 40 Minutes   **Makes:** 5 servings

2 teaspoons all-purpose flour	1 can (14.5 oz) diced tomatoes with
¼ teaspoon salt	basil, garlic and oregano, undrained
¼ teaspoon pepper	2 cups frozen Italian-blend vegetables
½ lb boneless beef round steak, cut into	(from 1-lb bag)
½-inch cubes	3 cups water
1 tablespoon olive or canola oil	Grated Parmesan cheese, if desired
1 can (15 oz) cannellini beans, drained, rinsed	

1. In 1-quart resealable food-storage plastic bag, place flour, salt and pepper. Seal bag; shake until blended. Add beef; seal bag and shake until beef is evenly coated with flour mixture.

2. In 3-quart heavy saucepan or Dutch oven, heat oil over medium-high heat. Add beef; cook 4 to 5 minutes, stirring occasionally, until brown on all sides.

3. Stir in remaining ingredients except cheese. Heat to boiling. Reduce heat; simmer uncovered 15 to 20 minutes or until vegetables are tender. Serve with cheese.

1 Serving: Calories 220 (Calories from Fat 40); Total Fat 4.5g (Saturated Fat 1g; Trans Fat 0g); Cholesterol 25mg; Sodium 250mg; Total Carbohydrate 25g (Dietary Fiber 7g; Sugars 4g); Protein 19g   **% Daily Value:** Vitamin A 6%; Vitamin C 8%; Calcium 10%; Iron 30%   **Exchanges:** 1½ Starch, 1 Vegetable, 1½ Very Lean Meat, ½ Fat **Carbohydrate Choices:** 1½

cheese-filled tortellini soup

Prep Time: 40 Minutes   Start to Finish: 40 Minutes   Makes: 5 servings

2 tablespoons butter or margarine	2½ cups dried cheese-filled tortellini (10 oz)
1 medium stalk celery, chopped (½ cup)	1 tablespoon chopped fresh parsley
1 medium carrot, chopped (½ cup)	½ teaspoon ground nutmeg
1 small onion, chopped (¼ cup)	¼ teaspoon pepper
1 clove garlic, finely chopped	Freshly grated Parmesan cheese, if desired
6 cups water	
2 extra-large vegetarian vegetable bouillon cubes	

1. In 4-quart Dutch oven, melt butter over medium heat. Add celery, carrot, onion and garlic; cook, stirring frequently, until crisp-tender.

2. Stir in water and bouillon cubes. Heat to boiling. Reduce heat to low; stir in tortellini. Cover; simmer about 20 minutes, stirring occasionally, until tortellini are tender.

3. Stir in parsley, nutmeg and pepper. Sprinkle individual servings with cheese.

1 Serving: Calories 280 (Calories from Fat 90); Total Fat 10g (Saturated Fat 5g; Trans Fat 0g); Cholesterol 55mg; Sodium 1420mg; Total Carbohydrate 38g (Dietary Fiber 2g; Sugars 3g); Protein 11g   **% Daily Value:** Vitamin A 50%; Vitamin C 4%; Calcium 10%; Iron 8%   **Exchanges:** 2½ Starch, ½ High-Fat Meat, 1 Fat   **Carbohydrate Choices:** 2½

health smart

Feel free to add extra vegetables to this soup. Butternut squash cubes, green beans or baby spinach leaves would all add color and flavor plus valuable nutrients. Add the squash during the last 10 minutes of cooking and cook just until tender.

provençal vegetable and pasta soup

Prep Time: 55 Minutes   Start to Finish: 55 Minutes   Makes: 8 servings

2 teaspoons olive oil	3 cups water
1 cup julienne (matchstick-cut) carrots (2 medium)	1 can (15 oz) cannellini beans, drained, rinsed
1 small leek, rinsed, cut in half lengthwise and chopped (½ cup)	1½ lb small fresh green beans, trimmed, cut in half crosswise
1 medium stalk celery, chopped (½ cup)	Pinch of saffron threads, if desired
3 cloves garlic, finely chopped	1 tablespoon parsley flakes
2 tablespoons chopped fresh basil leaves	1 tablespoon herbes de Provence
¼ teaspoon pepper	1 dried bay leaf
1 can (15 oz) tomato sauce	1 cup uncooked mini penne pasta (4 oz)
1 carton (32 oz) reduced-sodium fat-free chicken stock	Freshly grated Romano cheese, if desired

1. In 5-quart stockpot or Dutch oven, heat oil over medium heat. Add carrots, leek and celery; cook 10 minutes, stirring occasionally.

2. Stir in garlic, basil and pepper; cook and stir 30 seconds. Stir in tomato sauce, chicken stock and water; heat to boiling. Stir in cannellini beans, green beans, saffron, parsley, herbes de Provence and bay leaf; heat to boiling. Reduce heat. Simmer uncovered about 15 minutes or until vegetables are tender.

3. Meanwhile, cook and drain pasta as directed on package. Stir pasta into soup. Remove bay leaf. Ladle soup into bowls. Serve with cheese.

1 Serving: Calories 200 (Calories from Fat 15); Total Fat 2g (Saturated Fat 0g; Trans Fat 0g); Cholesterol 0mg; Sodium 590mg; Total Carbohydrate 36g (Dietary Fiber 8g; Sugars 5g); Protein 10g   **% Daily Value:** Vitamin A 50%; Vitamin C 8%; Calcium 10%; Iron 25%   **Exchanges:** 1½ Starch, ½ Other Carbohydrate, 1 Vegetable, ½ Very Lean Meat **Carbohydrate Choices:** 2½

160 calories

tomato basil soup with orzo

Prep Time: 30 Minutes   Start to Finish: 30 Minutes   Makes: 5 servings

1 tablespoon olive or vegetable oil	2 cans (14 oz each) chicken broth
1 large onion, chopped (1 cup)	1 cup water
2 medium carrots, chopped (1 cup)	1 teaspoon red pepper sauce
2 cans (14.5 oz each) fire-roasted diced tomatoes, undrained	½ cup uncooked orzo pasta
	1 teaspoon dried basil leaves

1. In 4-quart saucepan, heat oil over medium heat. Add onion and carrots. Cook 2 to 3 minutes, stirring occasionally, until softened.

2. Stir in tomatoes, broth, water and pepper sauce. Heat to boiling. Stir in pasta. Heat to boiling; reduce heat to medium. Cook uncovered 10 to 15 minutes, stirring occasionally, until pasta and carrots are tender.

3. Stir in basil. Cook about 1 minute, stirring constantly.

1 Serving: Calories 160 (Calories from Fat 40); Total Fat 4g (Saturated Fat 0.5g; Trans Fat 0g); Cholesterol 0mg; Sodium 990mg; Total Carbohydrate 23g (Dietary Fiber 4g; Sugars 7g); Protein 7g   **% Daily Value:** Vitamin A 110%; Vitamin C 25%; Calcium 8%; Iron 10%   **Exchanges:** 1½ Starch, 1 Vegetable, ½ Fat   **Carbohydrate Choices:** 1½

serve with
Serve this slightly smoky-flavored soup with grilled cheese sandwiches. Add fresh veggies on the side for crunch and extra nutrients.

asian wild rice soup

Prep Time: 5 Minutes   Start to Finish: 1 Hour 5 Minutes   Makes: 4 servings

½	cup uncooked wild rice	1½	cups pieces (½ inch) fresh snow pea pods
3	cups water	3	tablespoons soy sauce
1	small red bell pepper, chopped (½ cup)	¼	teaspoon garlic powder
1	can (14 oz) vegetable broth	¼	teaspoon ground ginger
1½	cups sliced fresh mushrooms (4 oz)		Chopped fresh cilantro, if desired

1. In 3-quart saucepan, heat wild rice and water to boiling over high heat. Reduce heat to low; cover and simmer 45 minutes, stirring occasionally.

2. Stir in bell pepper and broth. Cook uncovered over medium heat 5 minutes, stirring occasionally.

3. Stir in remaining ingredients except cilantro. Cook uncovered over medium heat 5 to 8 minutes, stirring occasionally, until vegetables are crisp-tender. Sprinkle each serving with cilantro.

1 Serving: Calories 130 (Calories from Fat 0); Total Fat 0.5g (Saturated Fat 0g; Trans Fat 0g); Cholesterol 0mg; Sodium 1130mg; Total Carbohydrate 24g (Dietary Fiber 3g; Sugars 4g); Protein 6g   **% Daily Value:** Vitamin A 30%; Vitamin C 45%; Calcium 2%; Iron 10%   **Exchanges:** 1½ Starch, 1 Vegetable   **Carbohydrate Choices:** 1½

serve with

This light soup is simply bursting with flavor! Complete the meal by serving it with a variety of rice crackers and cooked shelled edamame.

navy bean soup

Prep Time: 1 Hour 15 Minutes   **Start to Finish:** 2 Hours 15 Minutes   **Makes:** 6 servings

1	bag (16 oz) dried navy beans, sorted, rinsed	2	medium carrots, chopped (1 cup)
8	cups water	1	large onion, chopped (1 cup)
½	cup chili sauce	1	medium stalk celery, chopped (½ cup)
½	teaspoon dried marjoram leaves	1	can (14 oz) vegetable broth
		2	tablespoons chopped fresh parsley

1. In 8-quart Dutch oven, heat beans and water to boiling. Boil uncovered 2 minutes. Remove from heat; cover and let stand 1 hour.

2. Stir in remaining ingredients except parsley. Heat to boiling. Reduce heat to low; cover and simmer about 1 hour, stirring occasionally, until beans are tender. Stir in parsley.

1 Serving: Calories 300 (Calories from Fat 10); Total Fat 1g (Saturated Fat 0g; Trans Fat 0g); Cholesterol 0mg; Sodium 610mg; Total Carbohydrate 56g (Dietary Fiber 14g; Sugars 11g); Protein 16g   **% Daily Value:** Vitamin A 90%; Vitamin C 10%; Calcium 15%; Iron 25%   **Exchanges:** 2½ Starch, 1 Other Carbohydrate, 1 Very Lean Meat   **Carbohydrate Choices:** 4

lentil soup with asparagus and gruyère

Prep Time: 20 Minutes   Start to Finish: 40 Minutes   Makes: 4 servings

1	cup dried lentils (8 oz), sorted, rinsed	½	teaspoon lemon-pepper seasoning salt
1	medium stalk celery with leaves, sliced (about ½ cup)	¾	lb fresh asparagus, cut into ½-inch pieces, or 1 box (9 oz) frozen asparagus cuts
1	small onion, chopped (¼ cup)		
4	cups water	¼	cup shredded Gruyère or Swiss cheese (1 oz)
1	tablespoon chicken bouillon granules		

1. In 4-quart Dutch oven, mix all ingredients except asparagus and cheese. Heat to boiling; reduce heat. Cover; simmer about 20 minutes or until lentils are very soft.

2. Stir in asparagus. Cook over medium heat about 4 minutes, stirring occasionally, until asparagus is crisp-tender. Sprinkle each serving with 1 tablespoon of the cheese.

1 Serving: Calories 300 (Calories from Fat 90); Total Fat 10g (Saturated Fat 6g; Trans Fat 0g); Cholesterol 30mg; Sodium 920mg; Total Carbohydrate 30g (Dietary Fiber 9g; Sugars 2g); Protein 22g   **% Daily Value:** Vitamin A 15%; Vitamin C 10%; Calcium 35%; Iron 25%   **Exchanges:** 1½ Starch, 1 Vegetable, 2 Very Lean Meat, 1½ Fat
Carbohydrate Choices: 2

coffee counter choices

You can't do without your morning coffee but you forgot to grab breakfast. Doughnuts, cream-filled confections, and greasy, but yummy, fried breads beckon you to take them to work with you.

What can you do?
Know your healthy choices so you can start your day the right way, even on the run. Choose yogurt, biscotti, nuts or trail mix, or select a low-fat baked item. Selections with whole grains (like a whole wheat bagel or whole wheat bread) are great choices. While lattes and chais are about 300 calories each, order yours with skim milk, which has many fewer calories and is loaded with calcium. Don't skip breakfast and don't feel guilty—just enjoy the healthier choice instead.

lentil-tofu soup

Prep Time: 15 Minutes   Start to Finish: 1 Hour   Makes: 4 servings

1 tablespoon canola oil	1 carton (32 oz) reduced-sodium
1 medium onion, chopped (½ cup)	vegetable broth (4 cups)
2 teaspoons curry powder	6 oz firm tofu (from 12-oz package),
1 teaspoon ground cumin	cut into ½-inch cubes
2 cloves garlic, finely chopped	1½ cups coarsely chopped broccoli
⅔ cup dried lentils, sorted, rinsed	2 tablespoons chopped fresh parsley

1. In 3-quart nonstick saucepan, heat oil over medium heat. Cook onion, curry powder, cumin and garlic in oil 2 minutes, stirring occasionally. Stir in lentils and broth. Heat to boiling; reduce heat. Cover; simmer 45 minutes.

2. Stir in tofu, broccoli and parsley. Cook over medium heat about 10 minutes, stirring occasionally, until broccoli is crisp-tender.

1 Serving: Calories 200 (Calories from Fat 45); Total Fat 5g (Saturated Fat 0g; Trans Fat 0g); Cholesterol 0mg; Sodium 330mg; Total Carbohydrate 27g (Dietary Fiber 7g; Sugars 5g); Protein 12g   **% Daily Value:** Vitamin A 20%; Vitamin C 30%; Calcium 6%; Iron 25%   **Exchanges:** 2 Starch, 1 Lean Meat   **Carbohydrate Choices:** 2

health smart

Tofu is a great source of soy protein. Be sure to check freshness dates, and store it in the refrigerator for no longer than 1 week.

tortilla soup

Prep Time: 15 Minutes   Start to Finish: 35 Minutes   Makes: 4 servings

3 teaspoons vegetable oil	1 can (10 oz) diced tomatoes with green chiles, undrained
4 corn tortillas (5 or 6 inch), cut into 2×½-inch strips	1 tablespoon lime juice
1 medium onion, chopped (½ cup)	1 tablespoon chopped fresh cilantro or parsley
2 cans (14 oz each) vegetable broth	

1. In 2-quart nonstick saucepan, heat 2 teaspoons oil over medium-high heat. Add tortilla strips; cook 30 to 60 seconds, stirring occasionally, until crisp and light golden brown. Remove from saucepan; drain on paper towels.

2. In same saucepan, cook remaining 1 teaspoon oil and the onion over medium-high heat, stirring occasionally, until onion is tender.

3. Stir in broth and tomatoes. Heat to boiling. Reduce heat to low; simmer uncovered 20 minutes.

4. Stir in lime juice. Serve soup over tortilla strips; sprinkle with cilantro.

1 Serving: Calories 110 (Calories from Fat 35); Total Fat 4g (Saturated Fat 0.5g; Trans Fat 0g); Cholesterol 0mg; Sodium 1100mg; Total Carbohydrate 17g (Dietary Fiber 2g; Sugars 7g); Protein 2g   **% Daily Value:** Vitamin A 15%; Vitamin C 10%; Calcium 6%; Iron 4%   **Exchanges:** ½ Starch, ½ Other Carbohydrate, 1 Fat   **Carbohydrate Choices:** 1

fire-roasted tomato gazpacho photo on page C-10

Prep Time: 15 Minutes   Start to Finish: 1 Hour 15 Minutes   Makes: 4 servings

1 can (14.5 oz) organic fire-roasted diced tomatoes, undrained	2 tablespoons finely chopped red onion
1½ cups tomato juice	2 tablespoons finely chopped fresh cilantro
1 small cucumber, peeled, chopped (1 cup)	2 teaspoons white wine vinegar
¼ cup finely chopped red bell pepper	

1. In food processor, place all ingredients. Cover; process with quick on-and-off motions until mixture is coarsely pureed.

2. Cover; refrigerate at least 1 hour to blend flavors before serving.

1 Serving: Calories 50 (Calories from Fat 0); Total Fat 0g (Saturated Fat 0g; Trans Fat 0g); Cholesterol 0mg; Sodium 480mg; Total Carbohydrate 10g (Dietary Fiber 1g; Sugars 7g); Protein 2g   **% Daily Value:** Vitamin A 25%; Vitamin C 80%; Calcium 4%; Iron 6%   **Exchanges:** 2 Vegetable   **Carbohydrate Choices:** ½

health smart

Tomatoes, especially those that are cooked or pureed, are one of the richest sources of lycopene. This antioxidant gives tomatoes their red color.

french peasant
chicken stew photo on page C-10

Prep Time: 10 Minutes   Start to Finish: 35 Minutes   Makes: 6 servings

2 cups ready-to-eat baby-cut carrots
1 cup sliced fresh mushrooms
     (about 3 oz)
4 small red potatoes, cut into quarters
1 jar (12 oz) chicken gravy
1 can (14 oz) reduced-sodium
     chicken broth

1 teaspoon dried thyme leaves
½ cup frozen baby sweet peas
1 deli rotisserie chicken (2 to 2½ lb),
     cut into serving pieces

1. In 4-quart saucepan, mix all ingredients except peas and chicken.

2. Heat to boiling over medium-high heat. Reduce heat to medium-low. Cover; simmer about 20 minutes or until vegetables are tender.

3. Stir in peas and chicken. Cover; simmer about 5 minutes or until peas are tender.

1 Serving: Calories 290 (Calories from Fat 90); Total Fat 10g (Saturated Fat 2.5g; Trans Fat 0g); Cholesterol 75mg; Sodium 920mg; Total Carbohydrate 22g (Dietary Fiber 4g; Sugars 4g); Protein 28g   **% Daily Value:** Vitamin A 150%; Vitamin C 10%; Calcium 6%; Iron 20%   **Exchanges:** 1½ Starch, 1 Vegetable, 3 Lean Meat   **Carbohydrate Choices:** 1½

chicken-vegetable stew with dumplings

Prep Time: 5 Minutes   Start to Finish: 30 Minutes   Makes: 3 servings

2 cups frozen broccoli, cauliflower and carrots (or other vegetable combination)	1 can (14.5 oz) no-salt-added stewed tomatoes, undrained
1 cup cut-up cooked chicken breast	1 cup Bisquick Heart Smart mix
¾ cup water	⅓ cup fat-free (skim) milk
1 tablespoon ketchup	½ teaspoon parsley flakes
⅛ teaspoon pepper	⅛ teaspoon garlic salt

1. In 2-quart saucepan, heat vegetables, chicken, water, ketchup, pepper and tomatoes to boiling, stirring occasionally.

2. In small bowl, stir Bisquick mix, milk, parsley flakes and garlic salt until dough forms. Drop dough by 6 spoonfuls onto boiling stew; reduce heat.

3. Simmer uncovered 10 minutes; cover and simmer 10 minutes longer.

1 Serving: Calories 300 (Calories from Fat 40); Total Fat 4.5g (Saturated Fat 0.5g; Trans Fat 0g); Cholesterol 40mg; Sodium 450mg; Total Carbohydrate 43g (Dietary Fiber 3g; Sugars 13g); Protein 22g   **% Daily Value:** Vitamin A 40%; Vitamin C 25%; Calcium 25%; Iron 20%   **Exchanges:** 2 Starch, 2 Vegetable, 2 Very Lean Meat, ½ Fat   **Carbohydrate Choices:** 3

dijon steak and potato stew

Prep Time: 20 Minutes   Start to Finish: 45 Minutes   Makes: 4 servings

1	lb boneless beef sirloin, cut into ½-inch pieces	¼	teaspoon dried thyme leaves
½	teaspoon peppered seasoned salt	4	unpeeled small red potatoes, cut into ½- to ¾-inch cubes (about 2 cups)
2	jars (12 oz each) home-style beef gravy	1½	cups frozen cut green beans
1	cup water	2	medium carrots, sliced (1 cup)
2	tablespoons Dijon mustard		

1. Sprinkle beef with peppered seasoned salt. In 4-quart Dutch oven or 12-inch nonstick skillet, cook beef over medium-high heat about 4 minutes, stirring frequently, until brown.

2. Stir in gravy, water, mustard and thyme until well blended. Stir in potatoes, green beans and carrots. Heat to boiling; reduce heat to medium-low.

3. Cover; cook 20 to 22 minutes, stirring occasionally, until potatoes and beans are tender.

1 Serving: Calories 300 (Calories from Fat 70); Total Fat 8g (Saturated Fat 3g; Trans Fat 0g); Cholesterol 65mg; Sodium 1370mg; Total Carbohydrate 28g (Dietary Fiber 5g; Sugars 3g); Protein 32g   **% Daily Value:** Vitamin A 120%; Vitamin C 10%; Calcium 6%; Iron 30%   **Exchanges:** 1½ Starch, 1 Vegetable, 3½ Very Lean Meat, 1 Fat   **Carbohydrate Choices:** 1½

beef-barley stew

Prep Time: 15 Minutes   Start to Finish: 1 Hour 25 Minutes   Makes: 6 servings

1 lb extra-lean (at least 90%) ground beef	¼ teaspoon salt
1 medium onion, chopped (½ cup)	¼ teaspoon pepper
2 cups beef broth	1 can (14.5 oz) whole tomatoes, undrained
⅔ cup uncooked barley	1 can (8 oz) sliced water chestnuts, undrained
2 teaspoons chopped fresh or ½ teaspoon dried oregano leaves	2 cups frozen mixed vegetables

1. Heat oven to 350°F. Spray 10-inch nonstick skillet with cooking spray. Add beef and onion; cook in skillet over medium heat 7 to 8 minutes, stirring occasionally, until beef is brown; drain.

2. In ungreased 3-quart casserole, mix beef mixture and remaining ingredients except frozen vegetables, breaking up tomatoes.

3. Cover; bake 30 minutes. Stir in frozen vegetables. Cover; bake 30 to 40 minutes longer or until barley is tender.

1 Serving: Calories 280 (Calories from Fat 60); Total Fat 7g (Saturated Fat 2.5g; Trans Fat 0g); Cholesterol 45mg; Sodium 590mg; Total Carbohydrate 34g (Dietary Fiber 8g; Sugars 5g); Protein 20g   **% Daily Value:** Vitamin A 50%; Vitamin C 10%; Calcium 6%; Iron 20%   **Exchanges:** 1½ Starch, ½ Other Carbohydrate, 1 Vegetable, 2 Lean Meat **Carbohydrate Choices:** 2

health smart

One cup of cooked barley packs about 6 grams of fiber. This virtually fat-free whole grain also contains complex carbohydrates, B vitamins and protein.

zesty autumn pork stew

Prep Time: 25 Minutes   Start to Finish: 25 Minutes   Makes: 4 servings

1   lb pork tenderloin, cut into 1-inch
     cubes
2   medium dark-orange sweet potatoes,
     peeled, cubed (2 cups)
1   medium green bell pepper, chopped
     (1 cup)

2   cloves garlic, finely chopped
     (1 teaspoon)
1   cup coleslaw mix
1   teaspoon Cajun seasoning
1   can (14 oz) chicken broth

1. Spray 4-quart Dutch oven with cooking spray; heat over medium-high heat. Cook pork in Dutch oven, stirring occasionally, until brown.

2. Stir in remaining ingredients. Heat to boiling; reduce heat. Cover; simmer about 15 minutes, stirring once, until sweet potatoes are tender.

1 Serving: Calories 240 (Calories from Fat 45); Total Fat 5g (Saturated Fat 1.5g; Trans Fat 0g); Cholesterol 70mg; Sodium 640mg; Total Carbohydrate 18g (Dietary Fiber 3g; Sugars 7g); Protein 30g   **% Daily Value:** Vitamin A 280%; Vitamin C 40%; Calcium 4%; Iron 15%   **Exchanges:** 1 Starch, 4 Very Lean Meat, ½ Fat   **Carbohydrate Choices:** 1

try this

Canned sweet potatoes, cubed, can be substituted for the fresh sweet potatoes. Add them after you reduce the heat in step 2. Just remember to stir the mixture gently because canned sweet potatoes are very soft and tender.

fennel-cod stew

Prep Time: 20 Minutes   **Start to Finish:** 1 Hour   **Makes:** 4 servings

2 teaspoons olive oil	1 teaspoon dried marjoram leaves
1 bulb fennel (1 lb), thinly sliced (about 1½ cups)	4 teaspoons grated orange peel
½ medium onion, sliced (½ cup)	¼ teaspoon salt
4 cloves garlic, finely chopped (2 teaspoons)	¼ teaspoon pepper
2 cans (14.5 oz each) diced tomatoes, undrained	1 lb cod or other medium-firm fish fillets, cut into 1½-inch pieces
½ cup dry white wine or chicken broth	¼ cup finely chopped fresh Italian (flat-leaf) parsley

1. In 4-quart Dutch oven, heat oil over medium-high heat. Add fennel, onion and garlic; cook about 5 minutes, stirring frequently, until vegetables are just beginning to brown. Stir in tomatoes with liquid, wine, marjoram and 2 teaspoons of the orange peel. Reduce heat to medium-low. Partially cover; simmer 20 minutes.

2. Sprinkle salt and pepper on fish. Add to Dutch oven, spooning sauce over fish. Cover; simmer about 20 minutes or until fish flakes easily with fork.

3. Meanwhile, in small bowl, mix parsley and remaining 2 teaspoons orange peel. Spoon stew into bowls; sprinkle with parsley mixture.

1 Serving: Calories 190 (Calories from Fat 35); Total Fat 4g (Saturated Fat 0.5g; Trans Fat 0g); Cholesterol 60mg; Sodium 520mg; Total Carbohydrate 14g (Dietary Fiber 4g; Sugars 7g); Protein 24g **% Daily Value:** Vitamin A 15%; Vitamin C 25%; Calcium 10%; Iron 15% **Exchanges:** ½ Other Carbohydrate, 1 Vegetable, 3 Very Lean Meat, ½ Fat
Carbohydrate Choices: 1

health smart

Comparing foods to household items can make visualizing proper portion sizes easier. Three ounces of meat, fish or poultry is roughly the size of a flip-style cell phone. One cup of vegetables or a medium-size piece of fruit is about the size of a tennis ball.

white bean-chicken chili

Prep Time: 20 Minutes   Start to Finish: 20 Minutes   Makes: 6 servings

2 tablespoons butter or margarine	2 cans (10 oz each) diced tomatoes
1 large onion, coarsely chopped (1 cup)	with green chiles, undrained
2 cloves garlic, finely chopped	1 can (15 to 16 oz) great northern
3 cups cubed cooked chicken	beans, drained, rinsed
½ teaspoon ground cumin	Sour cream, if desired
	Chopped fresh cilantro, if desired

1. In 4½- to 5-quart Dutch oven, melt butter over medium-high heat. Cook onion and garlic in butter, stirring occasionally, until onion is tender.

2. Stir in remaining ingredients except sour cream and cilantro. Heat to boiling; reduce heat to low. Simmer uncovered 2 to 3 minutes, stirring occasionally, until hot.

3. Top each serving with sour cream; sprinkle with cilantro.

1 Serving: Calories 280 (Calories from Fat 80); Total Fat 9g (Saturated Fat 3.5g; Trans Fat 0g); Cholesterol 70mg; Sodium 650mg; Total Carbohydrate 23g (Dietary Fiber 6g; Sugars 6g); Protein 27g   **% Daily Value:** Vitamin A 10%; Vitamin C 8%; Calcium 10%; Iron 20%   **Exchanges:** 1 Starch, 1 Vegetable, 3 Lean Meat   **Carbohydrate Choices:** 1½

serve with

Serve the chili along with a corn muffin drizzled with honey, and add a tall glass of cold milk.

taco-corn chili

Prep Time: 30 Minutes   Start to Finish: 30 Minutes   Makes: 5 servings

1 lb extra-lean (at least 90%) ground beef	1 box (9 oz) frozen whole kernel corn, thawed, drained
1 can (15 to 16 oz) kidney beans, rinsed, drained	2 cups water
1 envelope (1 oz) taco seasoning mix	2 teaspoons sugar
1 can (10 oz) diced tomatoes with green chiles, undrained	

1. Spray 4-quart Dutch oven with cooking spray; heat over medium-high heat. Cook beef in Dutch oven 5 to 7 minutes, stirring occasionally, until brown; drain.

2. Stir in remaining ingredients. Heat to boiling; reduce heat. Simmer uncovered about 18 minutes, stirring occasionally.

1 Serving: Calories 300 (Calories from Fat 70); Total Fat 8g (Saturated Fat 3g; Trans Fat 0g); Cholesterol 55mg; Sodium 1030mg; Total Carbohydrate 36g (Dietary Fiber 6g; Sugars 6g); Protein 25g   **% Daily Value:** Vitamin A 8%; Vitamin C 10%; Calcium 6%; Iron 30%   **Exchanges:** 2½ Starch, 2½ Lean Meat   **Carbohydrate Choices:** 2

try this
When you can't find extra-lean ground beef or are in the mood for something different, substitute extra-lean ground pork, turkey or chicken.

sirloin three-bean chili

photo on page C-12

Prep Time: 20 Minutes   Start to Finish: 55 Minutes   Makes: 10 servings

1 tablespoon vegetable oil	1 can (15 to 16 oz) pinto beans, rinsed, drained
2 lb boneless beef sirloin, cut into 1-inch cubes	1 can (15 to 16 oz) kidney beans, rinsed, drained
1 large onion, coarsely chopped (1 cup)	1 can (15 oz) black beans, rinsed, drained
1 medium bell pepper (any color), coarsely chopped (1 cup)	1 cup beef broth
2 cans (28 oz each) diced tomatoes, undrained	1½ tablespoons ground cumin
	1 tablespoon chili powder

1. Heat oil in 4-quart Dutch oven over medium-high heat. Cook 1 lb of beef at a time in oil, stirring occasionally, until brown; remove from Dutch oven.

2. Add onion and bell pepper to Dutch oven. Cook 2 to 3 minutes, stirring occasionally, until crisp-tender. Stir in remaining ingredients except beef.

3. Cover and cook over medium heat 10 minutes. Stir in beef. Cook 3 to 8 minutes or until beef is tender.

1 Serving: Calories 300 (Calories from Fat 50); Total Fat 5g (Saturated Fat 1.5g; Trans Fat 0g); Cholesterol 50mg; Sodium 690mg; Total Carbohydrate 39g (Dietary Fiber 11g; Sugars 6g); Protein 31g   **% Daily Value:** Vitamin A 20%; Vitamin C 30%; Calcium 15%; Iron 35%   **Exchanges:** 2 Starch, 3½ Very Lean Meat, ½ Fat   **Carbohydrate Choices:** 2

health smart

This chili packs a hefty amount of fiber, 11 grams per serving! Beans of all varieties are high in fiber, but the three varieties in this recipe—kidney, pinto and black—are some of the highest.

vegetarian chili

Prep Time: 40 Minutes   Start to Finish: 40 Minutes   Makes: 6 servings

2	medium white or red potatoes, cut into ½-inch pieces (about 10 oz)
1	medium onion, chopped (½ cup)
1	small bell pepper (any color), chopped (½ cup)
2	cans (14.5 oz each) diced tomatoes, undrained

1	can (15 to 16 oz) garbanzo beans
1	can (15 to 16 oz) kidney beans
1	can (8 oz) tomato sauce
1	tablespoon chili powder
1	teaspoon ground cumin
1	medium zucchini, cut into ½-inch slices

1. In a 4-quart Dutch oven, mix all ingredients except the zucchini. Heat to boiling over high heat, stirring occasionally. Reduce heat to low; cover and simmer 10 minutes.

2. Add zucchini; cover and simmer 5 to 7 minutes, stirring occasionally, until potatoes and zucchini are tender.

1 Serving: Calories 280 (Calories from Fat 25); Total Fat 2.5g (Saturated Fat 0g; Trans Fat 0g); Cholesterol 0mg; Sodium 650mg; Total Carbohydrate 51g (Dietary Fiber 12g; Sugars 8g); Protein 14g   **% Daily Value:** Vitamin A 15%; Vitamin C 35%; Calcium 15%; Iron 35%   **Exchanges:** 2½ Starch, ½ Other Carbohydrate, 1 Vegetable, ½ Very Lean Meat **Carbohydrate Choices:** 3½

chili verde

Prep Time: 45 Minutes   Start to Finish: 45 Minutes   Makes: 4 servings

2	small zucchini, cut into ½-inch pieces (2 cups)	½	cup salsa verde (from 12- to 16-oz jar)
1	large bell pepper (any color), cut into ½-inch pieces (1½ cups)	1	can (15.5 oz) white or yellow hominy, drained, rinsed
½	lb small red potatoes, cut into ½-inch pieces (1½ cups)	1	extra-large vegetarian vegetable bouillon cube
2½	cups water	2	teaspoons chili powder
		¼	cup sour cream

1. In 3-quart saucepan, mix all ingredients except sour cream. Heat to boiling over high heat. Reduce heat to low; cover and simmer 15 to 18 minutes, stirring occasionally, until potatoes are tender.

2. Top individual servings with 1 tablespoon sour cream.

1 Serving: Calories 200 (Calories from Fat 40); Total Fat 4.5g (Saturated Fat 2g; Trans Fat 0g); Cholesterol 10mg; Sodium 940mg; Total Carbohydrate 35g (Dietary Fiber 7g; Sugars 5g); Protein 5g   **% Daily Value:** Vitamin A 30%; Vitamin C 60%; Calcium 6%; Iron 15%   **Exchanges:** 1½ Starch, ½ Other Carbohydrate, 1 Vegetable, ½ Fat **Carbohydrate Choices:** 2

serve with

Serve this dish over hot brown rice or with warm corn or flour tortillas. To add more heat, offer red pepper sauce to sprinkle in as desired.

Chapter 7

slow cooker
suppers

Slow cookers seem a bit like magic. You put several simple ingredients in, and a few hours later, you have a hot, delicious meal waiting for you. Now make that a hot, delicious meal with 300 or fewer calories? That's really magical!

chicken cacciatore

Prep Time: 30 Minutes   Start to Finish: 4 Hours 30 Minutes   Makes: 6 servings

1	cut-up whole chicken (3 to 3½ lb), skin removed	1	can (4 oz) sliced mushrooms, drained
⅓	cup all-purpose flour	1½	teaspoons chopped fresh or ½ teaspoon dried oregano leaves
2	tablespoons vegetable oil	1	teaspoon chopped fresh or ¼ teaspoon dried basil leaves
1	medium bell pepper (any color)		
2	medium onions	½	teaspoon salt
1	can (14.5 oz) diced tomatoes, undrained	2	cloves garlic, finely chopped
			Grated Parmesan cheese, if desired

1. Coat chicken with flour. In 12-inch skillet, heat oil over medium-high heat. Add chicken; cook 15 to 20 minutes or until brown on all sides. Drain. Cut bell pepper and onions crosswise in half; cut each half into fourths.

2. Spray 5- to 6-quart slow cooker with cooking spray. Add half of the chicken pieces. Mix bell pepper, onions and remaining ingredients except cheese; spoon half of mixture over chicken. Add remaining chicken; top with remaining vegetable mixture.

3. Cover; cook on Low heat setting 4 to 6 hours or until juice of chicken is clear when thickest piece is cut to bone (170°F for breasts; 180°F for thighs and drumsticks). Serve with cheese.

1 Serving: Calories 270 (Calories from Fat 100); Total Fat 12g (Saturated Fat 2.5g; Trans Fat 0g); Cholesterol 80mg; Sodium 460mg; Total Carbohydrate 14g (Dietary Fiber 2g; Sugars 4g); Protein 28g   **% Daily Value:** Vitamin A 4%; Vitamin C 20%; Calcium 6%; Iron 15%   **Exchanges:** 2 Vegetable, 3 Lean Meat, 1 Fat   **Carbohydrate Choices:** 1

serve with

Serve over hot cooked fettuccine or rice with a fresh green salad on the side.

garlic chicken with mixed rice

Prep Time: 10 Minutes   **Start to Finish:** 5 Hours 10 Minutes   **Makes:** 6 servings

1 box (6 oz) original long-grain and wild rice mix	2 teaspoons olive or vegetable oil
1 small onion, chopped (½ cup)	6 cloves garlic, peeled
½ medium bell pepper (any color), chopped (½ cup)	1 can (14 oz) chicken broth
	6 bone-in chicken breasts, skinned (3 lb)

1. Spray 3½- to 4-quart slow cooker with cooking spray. Mix rice, contents of seasoning packet, onion, bell pepper, oil, garlic and broth in cooker. Place chicken on top.

2. Cover; cook on Low heat setting 5 to 6 hours or until juice of chicken is clear when center of thickest part is cut (170°F).

1 Serving: Calories 270 (Calories from Fat 70); Total Fat 8g (Saturated Fat 2g, Trans Fat 0g); Cholesterol 100mg; Sodium 540mg; Total Carbohydrate 10g (Dietary Fiber 0g; Sugars 0g); Protein 39g   **% Daily Value:** Vitamin A 0%; Vitamin C 10%; Calcium 4%; Iron 10%   **Exchanges:** ½ Starch, 5 Very Lean Meat, 1 Fat   **Carbohydrate Choices:** ½

asian chicken and noodles

Prep Time: 15 Minutes   Start to Finish: 7 Hours 35 Minutes   Makes: 6 servings

2 packages (3 oz each) Oriental-flavor ramen noodle soup mix	1 teaspoon finely chopped gingerroot
1¼ lb boneless skinless chicken thighs, cut into 1-inch pieces	2½ cups water
2 cups ready-to-eat baby-cut carrots	2 tablespoons teriyaki baste and glaze (from 12-oz bottle)
1 medium bell pepper (any color), coarsely chopped (about 1 cup)	8 oz fresh sugar snap peas (about 2 cups)

1. Spray 3½- to 4-quart slow cooker with cooking spray. Mix contents of seasoning packets from noodle mixes, chicken, carrots, bell pepper, gingerroot, water and teriyaki glaze in cooker.

2. Cover; cook on Low heat setting 7 to 8 hours.

3. Add peas. Break up noodles; add to chicken mixture. Increase heat setting to High. Cook 15 to 20 minutes longer or until peas are crisp-tender and noodles are tender.

1 Serving: Calories 290 (Calories from Fat 110); Total Fat 12g (Saturated Fat 3.5g; Trans Fat 1.5g); Cholesterol 60mg; Sodium 660mg; Total Carbohydrate 21g (Dietary Fiber 3g; Sugars 5g); Protein 24g   **% Daily Value:** Vitamin A 180%; Vitamin C 45%; Calcium 6%; Iron 15%   **Exchanges:** 1 Starch, 1 Vegetable, 3 Lean Meat, ½ Fat   **Carbohydrate Choices:** 1½

chicken chow mein

Prep Time: 15 Minutes   Start to Finish: 6 Hours 30 Minutes   Makes: 4 servings

8 boneless skinless chicken thighs (about 1½ lb)	1 cup chicken broth
1 tablespoon vegetable oil	2 tablespoons soy sauce
2 medium carrots, sliced diagonally (1 cup)	½ teaspoon finely chopped gingerroot
2 medium stalks celery, coarsely chopped (1 cup)	2 tablespoons cornstarch
	3 tablespoons cold water
1 medium onion, chopped (½ cup)	1 cup sliced fresh mushrooms (3 oz)
2 cloves garlic, finely chopped	4 oz fresh snow pea pods (1 cup), strings removed, cut diagonally in half
1 can (8 oz) sliced water chestnuts, drained	Chow mein noodles, if desired

1. Remove fat from chicken. Cut chicken into 1-inch pieces. In 10-inch skillet, heat oil over medium-high heat. Cook chicken in oil about 5 minutes, turning once, until brown.

2. Spray 3½- to 4-quart slow cooker with cooking spray. Add carrots, celery, onion, garlic, water chestnuts and chicken. In small bowl, mix broth, soy sauce and gingerroot; pour over chicken.

3. Cover; cook on Low heat setting 6 to 8 hours.

4. In small bowl, mix cornstarch and water until smooth; stir into chicken mixture. Stir in mushrooms and pea pods. Increase heat setting to High. Cook 15 minutes longer or until thickened. Serve over noodles.

1 Serving: Calories 260 (Calories from Fat 80); Total Fat 9g (Saturated Fat 2.5g; Trans Fat 0g); Cholesterol 60mg; Sodium 810mg; Total Carbohydrate 19g (Dietary Fiber 4g; Sugars 4g); Protein 25g   **% Daily Value:** Vitamin A 110%; Vitamin C 15%; Calcium 6%; Iron 15%   **Exchanges:** 3 Vegetable, 3 Lean Meat, ½ Fat   **Carbohydrate Choices:** 1

serve with

Serve this all-in-one meal with orange or apple slices, grapes or melon cubes. Pick up a package of fun fortune cookies for dessert, and share all of your good fortunes!

turkey with wild rice, squash and cranberries

photo on page C-9

Prep Time: 15 Minutes   **Start to Finish:** 7 Hours 15 Minutes   **Makes:** 6 servings

¾	cup uncooked wild rice	½	teaspoon dried thyme leaves
1	medium butternut squash, peeled, seeded and cut into 1-inch pieces	½	teaspoon salt
1	medium onion, cut into wedges	½	teaspoon pepper
1¼	lb turkey breast tenderloins	3	cups chicken broth
		½	cup dried cranberries

1. Spray 3½- to 4-quart slow cooker with cooking spray. Add rice; top with squash, onion and turkey. Sprinkle with thyme, salt and pepper. Pour broth over all ingredients.

2. Cover; cook on Low heat setting 7 to 9 hours or until rice is tender. Stir in cranberries.

1 Serving: Calories 290 (Calories from Fat 20); Total Fat 2g (Saturated Fat 0.5g; Trans Fat 0g); Cholesterol 65mg; Sodium 760mg; Total Carbohydrate 39g (Dietary Fiber 4g; Sugars 13g); Protein 29g   **% Daily Value:** Vitamin A 250%; Vitamin C 15%; Calcium 8%; Iron 15%   **Exchanges:** 2 Starch, 1 Vegetable, 3 Very Lean Meat   **Carbohydrate Choices:** 2½

turkey with wild rice,
squash and cranberries, page 224

290
calories

C-9

italian chicken noodle soup, page 188 **170** calories

french peasant chicken stew, page 207 **290** calories

fire-roasted tomato gazpacho, page 206 **50** calories

C-10

italian beef and bean soup, page 197 **220** calories

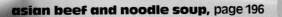
asian beef and noodle soup, page 196

250 calories

C-11

sirloin three-bean chili, page 215
300 calories

cheddar-stuffed chicken breasts, page 253
300 calories

C-12

salmon with spring veggies, page 264
300 calories

seafood jambalaya packets, page 271
300 calories

mediterranean chicken-vegetable kabobs, page 257 **250** calories

**italian steak and vegetables,** page 260 **240** calories

grilled vegetables and ravioli, page 274 **280** calories

double-cheese chicken and vegetables, page 280 **300** calories

honey-mustard turkey with snap peas, page 283
200 calories

white bean and spinach pizza, page 300
240 calories

cornbread chili stacks, page 301
230 calories

orange teriyaki beef with noodles, page 315
270 calories

stuffed chile peppers, page 320

170 calories

220 calories   **cioppino,** page 225

cioppino
photo on page C-16

Prep Time: 20 Minutes   Start to Finish: 4 Hours 5 Minutes   Makes: 8 servings

2	large onions, chopped (2 cups)	¼	teaspoon crushed red pepper
2	medium stalks celery, finely chopped (1 cup)	1	dried bay leaf
5	cloves garlic, finely chopped	1	lb halibut, whitefish, sea bass or other medium-firm fish fillets, cut into 1-inch pieces
1	can (28 oz) diced tomatoes, undrained	¾	lb uncooked deveined peeled medium shrimp, thawed if frozen, tail shells removed
1	bottle (8 oz) clam juice		
1	can (6 oz) tomato paste	1	can (6½ oz) chopped clams with juice, undrained
½	cup dry white wine or water		
1	tablespoon red wine vinegar	1	can (6 oz) crabmeat, drained, cartilage removed and flaked
1	tablespoon olive oil		
2½	teaspoons Italian seasoning	¼	cup chopped fresh parsley
¼	teaspoon sugar		

1. Spray 5- to 6-quart slow cooker with cooking spray. Mix all ingredients except fish, shrimp, clams, crabmeat and parsley in cooker.

2. Cover; cook on High heat setting 3 to 4 hours or until vegetables are tender.

3. Stir in fish, shrimp, clams and crabmeat. Reduce heat setting to Low. Cook 30 to 45 minutes longer or until fish flakes easily with fork. Remove bay leaf. Stir in parsley.

1 Serving: Calories 220 (Calories from Fat 50); Total Fat 6g (Saturated Fat 1g; Trans Fat 0g); Cholesterol 115mg; Sodium 560mg; Total Carbohydrate 14g (Dietary Fiber 3g; Sugars 7g); Protein 26g   **% Daily Value:** Vitamin A 20%; Vitamin C 20%; Calcium 10%; Iron 50%   **Exchanges:** ½ Other Carbohydrate, 1 Vegetable, 3 Lean Meat
Carbohydrate Choices: 1

serve with
Serve this tasty fish stew over brown or white rice, and add some melon wedges on the side. Start the rice at the same time as the stew and they'll both be done together.

chicken and pinto tostadas

Prep Time: 20 Minutes Start to Finish: 8 Hours 40 Minutes Makes: 8 servings

1	package (20 oz) boneless skinless chicken thighs	8	tostada shells, heated if desired
½	cup chunky-style salsa	1	cup shredded lettuce
¼	cup water	½	cup sour cream
2	tablespoons taco seasoning mix	½	cup refrigerated guacamole (from 12-oz container)
1	can (15 to 16 oz) pinto beans, drained, rinsed		

1. Spray 3½- to 4-quart slow cooker with cooking spray. Add chicken. In small bowl, mix salsa, water and taco seasoning mix; pour over chicken.

2. Cover; cook on Low heat setting 8 to 10 hours or until juice of chicken is clear when center of thickest part is cut (180°F).

3. Remove chicken from cooker; place on cutting board. Using 2 forks, pull into shreds. Return chicken to juices in cooker. Stir in beans. Increase heat setting to High. Cover; cook 15 to 20 minutes longer or until thoroughly heated.

4. Spoon chicken mixture over tostada shells. Top with lettuce, sour cream and guacamole.

1 Serving: Calories 290 (Calories from Fat 120); Total Fat 13g (Saturated Fat 4.5g; Trans Fat 0g); Cholesterol 55mg; Sodium 570mg; Total Carbohydrate 24g (Dietary Fiber 5g; Sugars 2g); Protein 20g **% Daily Value:** Vitamin A 6%; Vitamin C 6%; Calcium 6%; Iron 15% **Exchanges:** 1½ Starch, 2 Lean Meat, 1 Fat **Carbohydrate Choices:** 1½

try this

If you don't have tostada shells, just break crispy corn taco shells in half. Place the halves on each plate, and top with the chicken and bean mixture.

garden harvest chicken soup

Prep Time: 25 Minutes   Start to Finish: 7 Hours 45 Minutes   Makes: 6 servings

1   lb boneless skinless chicken thighs, cut into ¾-inch pieces
1   teaspoon peppered seasoned salt
2   medium unpeeled red potatoes, cut into ½-inch pieces (2 cups)
2   medium carrots, sliced (1 cup)
1   medium onion, coarsely chopped (½ cup)

2   cans (14 oz each) chicken broth
2   cups fresh small broccoli florets
1   medium yellow summer squash, coarsely chopped (1½ cups)
2   tablespoons chopped fresh basil leaves

1. Heat 10-inch nonstick skillet over medium-high heat. Add chicken; sprinkle with peppered seasoned salt. Cook 6 to 8 minutes, stirring occasionally, until brown.

2. Spray 3½- to 4-quart slow cooker with cooking spray. Mix chicken, potatoes, carrots, onion and broth in cooker.

3. Cover; cook on Low heat setting 7 to 8 hours.

4. Stir in broccoli, squash and basil. Increase heat setting to High. Cook 15 to 20 minutes longer or until vegetables are tender.

1 Serving: Calories 200 (Calories from Fat 60); Total Fat 7g (Saturated Fat 2g; Trans Fat 0g); Cholesterol 45mg; Sodium 850mg; Total Carbohydrate 16g (Dietary Fiber 4g; Sugars 3g); Protein 21g   **% Daily Value:** Vitamin A 90%; Vitamin C 35%; Calcium 6%; Iron 15%   **Exchanges:** ½ Starch, 1 Vegetable, 2½ Lean Meat   **Carbohydrate Choices:** 1

health smart
Soup is soothing to the body as well as the soul. This soup is a great choice, rich with lots of vitamin A, vitamin C and iron from the chicken and vegetables.

lime chicken with rice

Prep Time: 10 Minutes   Start to Finish: 8 Hours 10 Minutes   Makes: 6 servings

1¼	lb bone-in skinless chicken thighs	½	teaspoon dried thyme leaves
¼	cup fresh lime juice (2 limes)	¼	teaspoon pepper
1½	cups chicken broth	2	tablespoons butter or margarine
2	cloves garlic, finely chopped	1	cup uncooked instant rice

1. Spray 3½- to 4-quart slow cooker with cooking spray. Add chicken and remaining ingredients except rice.

2. Cover; cook on Low heat setting 8 to 10 hours or until juice of chicken is clear when thickest part is cut to bone (180°F). During last 15 minutes of cooking, stir in rice.

3. Remove chicken from slow cooker. Place cooked rice on each serving plate; top with chicken. Spoon any remaining juices over chicken.

1 Serving: Calories 210 (Calories from Fat 80); Total Fat 9g (Saturated Fat 4g, Trans Fat 0g); Cholesterol 50mg; Sodium 320mg; Total Carbohydrate 15g (Dietary Fiber 0g; Sugars 0g); Protein 15g   **% Daily Value:** Vitamin A 4%; Vitamin C 2%; Calcium 2%; Iron 15%   **Exchanges:** 1 Starch, 1½ Lean Meat, 1 Fat   **Carbohydrate Choices:** 1

barbecued beans
with turkey sausage

Prep Time: 10 Minutes   Start to Finish: 5 Hours 10 Minutes   Makes: 12 servings

2   cans (15 to 16 oz each) great northern
      beans, rinsed, drained
2   cans (15 oz each) black beans, rinsed,
      drained
1   large onion, chopped (1 cup)
1   cup barbecue sauce
¼   cup packed brown sugar

1   tablespoon ground mustard
1   tablespoon Worcestershire sauce
2   teaspoons chili powder
1   ring (1 lb) fully cooked turkey smoked
      sausage or 1 ring (14 oz) fully cooked
      turkey kielbasa

1. Spray 3½- to 4-quart slow cooker with cooking spray. Mix all ingredients except sausage in cooker. Place sausage ring over bean mixture.

2. Cover; cook on Low heat setting 5 to 6 hours or until heated through.

1 Serving: Calories 270 (Calories from Fat 40); Total Fat 4g (Saturated Fat 1g; Trans Fat 0g); Cholesterol 20mg; Sodium 840mg; Total Carbohydrate 45g (Dietary Fiber 8g; Sugars 13g); Protein 17g   **% Daily Value:** Vitamin A 4%; Vitamin C 2%; Calcium 10%; Iron 25%   **Exchanges:** 2 Starch, 1 Other Carbohydrate, 1½ Lean Meat   **Carbohydrate Choices:** 2½

health smart
Using lower-fat turkey sausage in place of full-fat pork sausage helps cut the fat by over half without losing out on flavor.

jambalaya

Prep Time: 20 Minutes   Start to Finish: 8 Hours 20 Minutes   Makes: 8 servings

1 large onion, chopped (1 cup)	1 tablespoon parsley flakes
1 medium bell pepper (any color), chopped (1 cup)	½ teaspoon dried thyme leaves
2 medium stalks celery, chopped (1 cup)	½ teaspoon salt
3 cloves garlic, finely chopped	¼ teaspoon pepper
1 can (28 oz) diced tomatoes, undrained	¼ teaspoon red pepper sauce
2 cups chopped cooked turkey smoked sausage	¾ lb uncooked deveined peeled medium shrimp, thawed if frozen, tail shells removed
	4 cups hot cooked rice

1. Spray 3½- to 4-quart slow cooker with cooking spray. Mix all ingredients except shrimp and rice in cooker.

2. Cover; cook on Low heat setting 7 to 8 hours (or High heat setting 3 to 4 hours) or until vegetables are tender.

3. Stir in shrimp. Cook on Low heat setting about 1 hour longer or until shrimp are pink and firm. Serve jambalaya with rice.

1 Serving: Calories 280 (Calories from Fat 100); Total Fat 11g (Saturated Fat 4g; Trans Fat 0g); Cholesterol 80mg; Sodium 770mg; Total Carbohydrate 31g (Dietary Fiber 2g; Sugars 5g); Protein 14g   **% Daily Value:** Vitamin A 8%; Vitamin C 25%; Calcium 8%; Iron 20%   **Exchanges:** 1½ Starch, 1 Vegetable, 1 High-Fat Meat, ½ Fat   **Carbohydrate Choices:** 2

try this

If you like your food with a bit of a kick, choose a spicy sausage and diced tomatoes with green chiles.

couscous-stuffed peppers

Prep Time: 20 Minutes   Start to Finish: 4 Hours 20 Minutes   Makes: 4 servings

4 large bell peppers (any color)	¼ teaspoon ground cinnamon
½ lb lean (at least 80%) ground beef	⅛ teaspoon ground red pepper
½ cup chopped onion	(cayenne)
1 clove garlic, finely chopped	⅔ cup uncooked couscous
1 can (15 oz) tomato sauce	½ cup water
½ teaspoon ground cumin	Pine nuts, if desired
¼ teaspoon salt	Fresh cilantro, if desired

1. Cut thin slice from stem end of each bell pepper to remove top of pepper. Remove seeds and membranes; rinse peppers. Set aside.

2. In 10-inch skillet over medium heat, cook beef, onion and garlic about 5 minutes, stirring occasionally, until beef is brown; drain. Stir in tomato sauce, cumin, salt, cinnamon and red pepper. Stir in couscous. Divide mixture evenly among peppers.

3. Spray 5- to 6-quart slow cooker with cooking spray. Add water; stand peppers upright in cooker.

4. Cover; cook on Low heat setting 5 to 7 hours or until peppers are tender. Sprinkle with pine nuts and cilantro.

1 Serving: Calories 280 (Calories from Fat 60); Total Fat 7g (Saturated Fat 2.5g; Trans Fat 0g); Cholesterol 35mg; Sodium 740mg; Total Carbohydrate 38g (Dietary Fiber 6g; Sugars 10g); Protein 16g   **% Daily Value:** Vitamin A 20%; Vitamin C 120%; Calcium 6%; Iron 20%   **Exchanges:** 2 Starch, 1 Vegetable, 1 High-Fat Meat   **Carbohydrate Choices:** 2½

cabbage roll casserole

Prep Time: 15 Minutes   Start to Finish: 4 Hours 15 Minutes   Makes: 6 servings

1	lb lean (at least 80%) ground beef	2	teaspoons paprika
1	medium onion, chopped (½ cup)	½	teaspoon salt
5	cups coleslaw mix	¼	teaspoon pepper
½	cup uncooked instant rice	1	can (15 oz) Italian-style tomato sauce
¼	cup water		

1. In 10-inch skillet over medium heat, cook beef and onion, stirring occasionally, until beef is brown; drain.

2. Spray 3½- to 4-quart slow cooker with cooking spray. Mix beef mixture and remaining ingredients in cooker. (Cooker will be very full, but cabbage will cook down.)

3. Cover; cook on Low heat setting 4 to 6 hours or until cabbage is tender.

1 Serving: Calories 270 (Calories from Fat 100); Total Fat 11g (Saturated Fat 3.5g; Trans Fat 0.5g); Cholesterol 45mg; Sodium 600mg; Total Carbohydrate 26g (Dietary Fiber 3g; Sugars 10g); Protein 16g   **% Daily Value:** Vitamin A 80%; Vitamin C 20%; Calcium 6%; Iron 15%   **Exchanges:** 1½ Starch, 1½ Vegetable, 1 High-Fat Meat   **Carbohydrate Choices:** 2

try this

You can substitute 4½ cups shredded cabbage and 1 shredded carrot for the coleslaw mix. If you own a food processor with a shredding attachment, this is a great time to use it.

country french beef stew

Prep Time: 25 Minutes   Start to Finish: 7 Hours 55 Minutes   Makes: 12 servings

6	slices bacon, cut into ½-inch pieces	¼	teaspoon pepper
1	boneless beef chuck roast (3 lb)	1	can (14.5 oz) diced tomatoes, undrained
1	large onion, cut into ½-inch wedges	1	package (8 oz) sliced fresh mushrooms (3 cups)
3	cups ready-to-serve baby-cut carrots	½	cup julienne-cut sun-dried tomatoes (not oil-packed)
1	cup red Zinfandel wine or nonalcoholic red wine		Hot cooked egg noodles, if desired
¾	cup beef broth		Chopped fresh parsley or basil leaves, if desired
3	tablespoons all-purpose flour		
1	teaspoon dried basil leaves		
½	teaspoon dried thyme leaves		
½	teaspoon salt		

1. In 12-inch nonstick skillet, cook bacon over medium-high heat, stirring occasionally, until crisp. Remove bacon with slotted spoon; set aside. Drain, reserving 1 tablespoon drippings in skillet.

2. Trim excess fat from beef; cut into 1-inch pieces. Cook beef in bacon drippings 2 to 3 minutes, stirring occasionally, until brown. Add onion. Cook and stir 1 minute.

3. Spray 5- to 6-quart slow cooker with cooking spray. Mix bacon, beef mixture, carrots, wine, broth, flour, basil, thyme, salt, pepper and canned tomatoes in cooker.

4. Cover; cook on Low heat setting 7 to 8 hours or until meat is tender.

5. Stir in mushrooms and sun-dried tomatoes. Cook on Low heat setting 20 to 30 minutes longer or until sun-dried tomatoes are tender. Serve beef mixture over noodles; sprinkle with parsley.

1 Serving: Calories 270 (Calories from Fat 140); Total Fat 15g (Saturated Fat 6g; Trans Fat 0.5g); Cholesterol 70mg; Sodium 430mg; Total Carbohydrate 9g (Dietary Fiber 2g; Sugars 4g); Protein 25g   **% Daily Value:** Vitamin A 100%; Vitamin C 6%; Calcium 4%; Iron 20%   **Exchanges:** 1 Vegetable, 3½ Lean Meat, 1 Fat   **Carbohydrate Choices:** ½

health smart
Beef may have more calories than some other types of meat, but you can still enjoy it by making a hearty stew loaded with vegetables. A bowl of this flavorful stew is only 270 calories.

southwestern pot roast

Prep Time: 15 Minutes   Start to Finish: 8 Hours 15 Minutes   Makes: 8 servings

8	small red potatoes, halved	2	tablespoons all-purpose flour
1	boneless beef arm pot roast (3 lb)	1	jar (16 oz) chunky-style salsa
1	bag (16 oz) ready-to-eat baby-cut carrots		

1. Spray 3½- to 4-quart slow cooker with cooking spray. Add potatoes. Trim excess fat from beef; place over potatoes. Arrange carrots around beef. Sprinkle with flour. Pour salsa over all ingredients.

2. Cover; cook on Low heat setting 8 to 10 hours or until meat and vegetables are tender.

3. Remove beef from cooker; place on cutting board. Using 2 forks, pull beef into serving pieces. To serve, spoon cooking juices over meat and vegetables.

1 Serving: Calories 300 (Calories from Fat 70); Total Fat 8g (Saturated Fat 3g; Trans Fat 0g); Cholesterol 65mg; Sodium 360mg; Total Carbohydrate 30g (Dietary Fiber 5g; Sugars 6g); Protein 27g   **% Daily Value:** Vitamin A 220%; Vitamin C 25%; Calcium 6%; Iron 25%   **Exchanges:** 2 Starch, 1 Vegetable, 3 Very Lean Meat, ½ Fat   **Carbohydrate Choices:** 2

beef and potatoes with rosemary

Prep Time: 20 Minutes   Start to Finish: 8 Hours 20 Minutes   Makes: 8 servings

1 lb medium red potatoes, quartered	1 teaspoon chopped fresh or
1 cup ready-to-eat baby-cut carrots	½ teaspoon dried thyme leaves
1 boneless beef chuck roast (3 lb)	1 teaspoon salt
3 tablespoons Dijon mustard	½ teaspoon pepper
2 tablespoons chopped fresh or	1 small onion, finely chopped (¼ cup)
1½ teaspoons dried rosemary	1½ cups beef broth
leaves, crumbled	

1. Spray 5- to 6-quart slow cooker with cooking spray. Arrange potatoes and carrots around outer edge of cooker.

2. Trim excess fat from beef. Mix mustard, rosemary, thyme, salt and pepper; spread evenly over beef. Place in slow cooker (it will overlap vegetables slightly). Sprinkle onion over beef. Pour broth evenly over beef and vegetables.

3. Cover; cook on Low heat setting 8 to 9 hours or until meat is tender.

4. Remove beef and vegetables from slow cooker with slotted spoon. Slice beef. To serve, spoon beef juices from slow cooker over meat and vegetables.

1 Serving: Calories 290 (Calories from Fat 110); Total Fat 12g (Saturated Fat 4.5g; Trans Fat 0g); Cholesterol 55mg; Sodium 700mg; Total Carbohydrate 25g (Dietary Fiber 3g; Sugars 2g); Protein 21g   **% Daily Value:** Vitamin A 50%; Vitamin C 10%; Calcium 4%; Iron 20%   **Exchanges:** 1 Starch, ½ Other Carbohydrate, 2½ Medium-Fat Meat   **Carbohydrate Choices:** 1½

try this

If your family likes gravy, you may want to thicken the beef juices. Put 2 tablespoons cornstarch and ¼ cup cold water in a tightly covered container and shake to mix. Then add it and the beef juices to a saucepan, and cook over medium heat until thickened.

mexicali round steak

Prep Time: 10 Minutes   Start to Finish: 8 Hours 10 Minutes   Makes: 6 servings

1½   lb boneless beef round steak
1   cup frozen whole kernel corn, thawed
1   cup chopped fresh cilantro
½   cup beef broth
3   medium stalks celery, thinly sliced (1½ cups)

1   large onion, sliced
1   jar (20 oz) chunky-style salsa
1   can (15 oz) black beans, rinsed, drained
1   cup shredded Monterey Jack cheese with jalapeño peppers (4 oz), if desired

1. Trim excess fat from beef; cut into 6 serving pieces. Spray 3½- to 4-quart slow cooker with cooking spray. Place beef in cooker. Mix remaining ingredients except cheese; pour over beef.

2. Cover; cook on Low heat setting 8 to 9 hours or until meat is tender. Sprinkle with cheese.

1 Serving: Calories 270 (Calories from Fat 70); Total Fat 8g (Saturated Fat 3g; Trans Fat 0g); Cholesterol 35mg; Sodium 710mg; Total Carbohydrate 29g (Dietary Fiber 9g; Sugars 5g); Protein 19g   **% Daily Value:** Vitamin A 10%; Vitamin C 6%; Calcium 8%; Iron 20%   **Exchanges:** 1½ Starch, 1 Vegetable, 1½ Medium-Fat Meat   **Carbohydrate Choices:** 2

roast beef hash

Prep Time: 15 Minutes   Start to Finish: 8 Hours 40 Minutes   Makes: 6 servings

2	lb boneless beef top round steak	1	cup water
1	large onion, chopped (1 cup)	3½	cups frozen potatoes O'Brien
½	teaspoon salt		with onions and peppers
½	teaspoon pepper		(from 28-oz bag)
1	package (0.87 to 1.2 oz) brown	1	cup frozen green peas
	gravy mix		

1. Trim excess fat from beef; cut into ½-inch cubes. Spray 3½- to 4-quart slow cooker with cooking spray. Layer onion, beef, salt, pepper and gravy mix (dry) in cooker. Pour water over all ingredients.

2. Cover; cook on Low heat setting 8 to 9 hours. Meanwhile, thaw potatoes in refrigerator.

3. About 30 minutes before serving, stir thawed potatoes and frozen peas into beef mixture. Increase heat setting to High. Cook 25 to 30 minutes longer or until potatoes and peas are tender.

1 Serving: Calories 290 (Calories from Fat 45); Total Fat 5g (Saturated Fat 1.5g; Trans Fat 0g); Cholesterol 75mg; Sodium 510mg; Total Carbohydrate 29g (Dietary Fiber 4g; Sugars 3g); Protein 31g   **% Daily Value:** Vitamin A 8%; Vitamin C 15%; Calcium 4%; Iron 25%   **Exchanges:** 2 Starch, 3½ Very Lean Meat, ½ Fat   **Carbohydrate Choices:** 2

burn off those calories

Check these out and count the extra calories you burn—without even trying!

ACTIVITY	CALORIES BURNED PER MINUTE
Cleaning house	3
Climbing stairs, light to moderate	8
Cooking	3
Driving car	3
E-mailing	2
Eating	3
Gardening	6–9
Mowing lawn	6
Playing piano	2

swiss steak supper

Prep Time: 15 Minutes   Start to Finish: 7 Hours 15 Minutes   Makes: 6 servings

1½ lb boneless beef round steak
½ teaspoon peppered seasoned salt
6 to 8 small potatoes, quartered
1½ cups ready-to-eat baby-cut carrots
1 small onion, sliced

1 can (14.5 oz) diced tomatoes with basil, garlic and oregano, undrained
1 jar (12 oz) home-style beef gravy
  Chopped fresh parsley, if desired

1. Trim excess fat from beef; cut into 6 serving pieces. Spray 12-inch skillet with cooking spray; heat over medium-high heat. Sprinkle beef with peppered seasoned salt. Cook in skillet 6 to 8 minutes, turning once, until brown.

2. Spray 5- to 6-quart slow cooker with cooking spray. Layer potatoes, carrots, beef and onion in cooker. Mix tomatoes and gravy; spoon over mixture in cooker.

3. Cover; cook on Low heat setting 7 to 8 hours or until meat and vegetables are tender. Sprinkle with parsley.

1 Serving: Calories 300 (Calories from Fat 80); Total Fat 9g (Saturated Fat 3.5g; Trans Fat 0g); Cholesterol 35mg; Sodium 680mg; Total Carbohydrate 37g (Dietary Fiber 5g; Sugars 5g); Protein 18g   **% Daily Value:** Vitamin A 110%; Vitamin C 20%; Calcium 6%; Iron 20%   **Exchanges:** 2 Starch, ½ Other Carbohydrate, 1½ Medium-Fat Meat **Carbohydrate Choices:** 2½

serve with
Serve the meat mixture over hot cooked egg noodles. Try the frozen home-style variety for a change of pace.

150 calories

hearty steak and tater soup

Prep Time: 20 Minutes   Start to Finish: 8 Hours 50 Minutes   Makes: 9 servings

1 lb boneless beef round steak	2 cloves garlic, finely chopped
1 lb small red potatoes, cut into ¼-inch slices (4 cups)	1 tablespoon beef bouillon granules
2 medium stalks celery, chopped (1 cup)	½ teaspoon pepper
2 medium carrots, chopped (1 cup)	4 cans (14.5 oz each) beef broth
1 medium onion, chopped (½ cup)	1 jar (6 oz) sliced mushrooms, drained
	½ cup water
	½ cup all-purpose flour

1. Trim excess fat from beef; cut into 1×¼-inch pieces. Spray 5- to 6-quart slow cooker with cooking spray. Mix beef and remaining ingredients except water and flour in cooker.

2. Cover; cook on Low heat setting 8 to 9 hours or until meat is tender.

3. In small bowl, mix water and flour; gradually stir into soup until blended. Increase heat setting to High. Cook about 30 minutes longer or until slightly thickened.

1 Serving: Calories 150 (Calories from Fat 20); Total Fat 2.5g (Saturated Fat 1g; Trans Fat 0g); Cholesterol 25mg; Sodium 1200mg; Total Carbohydrate 18g (Dietary Fiber 3g; Sugars 2g); Protein 15g   **% Daily Value:** Vitamin A 50%; Vitamin C 8%; Calcium 4%; Iron 15%   **Exchanges:** 1 Starch, 1 Vegetable, 1½ Very Lean Meat   **Carbohydrate Choices:** 1

orange pork tenderloin with butternut squash

Prep Time: 20 Minutes   Start to Finish: 7 Hours 20 Minutes   Makes: 6 servings

3	lb butternut squash, peeled, cut into 2-inch pieces (6 cups)	2	pork tenderloins (¾ to 1 lb each)
½	teaspoon salt	¼	cup orange marmalade
		2	cloves garlic, finely chopped

1. Spray 3½- to 4-quart slow cooker with cooking spray. Arrange squash around edge of slow cooker. Sprinkle with salt. Top with pork (it will overlap squash slightly). Mix marmalade and garlic; spread evenly over pork.

2. Cover; cook on Low heat setting 7 to 8 hours or until pork has slight blush of pink in center and thermometer inserted in center reads 160°F.

3. Remove pork from cooker; place on cutting board. Cut pork into slices; serve with squash.

1 Serving: Calories 260 (Calories from Fat 60); Total Fat 6g (Saturated Fat 2g, Trans Fat 0g); Cholesterol 65mg; Sodium 490mg; Total Carbohydrate 20g (Dietary Fiber 3g; Sugars 11g); Protein 30g   **% Daily Value:** Vitamin A 130%; Vitamin C 10%; Calcium 4%; Iron 6%   **Exchanges:** 1 Starch, ½ Other Carbohydrate, 4 Very Lean Meat, ½ Fat   **Carbohydrate Choices:** 1

health smart
Watching your salt intake? Omit the salt, and season to taste with pepper instead.

pork chop supper

Prep Time: 15 Minutes   Start to Finish: 6 Hours 30 Minutes   Makes: 6 servings

6	pork loin or rib chops, ½ inch thick (4 oz each)
1½	lb medium potatoes, cut into eighths (about 6 potatoes)
1	can (10¾ oz) condensed cream of mushroom soup
1	can (4 oz) mushroom pieces and stems, drained
2	tablespoons dry white wine
¼	teaspoon dried thyme leaves
½	teaspoon garlic powder
½	teaspoon Worcestershire sauce
3	tablespoons all-purpose flour
1	tablespoon diced pimientos
2	cups frozen green peas

1. Spray 10-inch skillet with cooking spray; heat over medium-high heat. Cook pork in skillet, turning once, until brown.

2. Spray 5- to 6-quart slow cooker with cooking spray. Add potatoes. In medium bowl, mix soup, mushrooms, wine, thyme, garlic powder, Worcestershire sauce and flour; spoon half of soup mixture over potatoes. Place pork over potatoes; cover with remaining soup mixture.

3. Cover; cook on Low heat setting 6 to 7 hours or until pork is no longer pink in center.

4. Remove pork from slow cooker; keep warm. Stir pimientos and peas into cooker. Cook on Low heat setting about 15 minutes or until peas are tender. Serve vegetable mixture with pork.

1 Serving: Calories 300 (Calories from Fat 80); Total Fat 9g (Saturated Fat 3g; Trans Fat 0g); Cholesterol 55mg; Sodium 290mg; Total Carbohydrate 31g (Dietary Fiber 4g; Sugars 4g); Protein 23g   **% Daily Value:** Vitamin A 20%; Vitamin C 10%; Calcium 4%; Iron 15%   **Exchanges:** 2 Starch, 2½ Lean Meat   **Carbohydrate Choices:** 2

corn, ham and potato scallop

Prep Time: 10 Minutes   Start to Finish: 7 Hours 10 Minutes   Makes: 6 servings

6 cups cubed (1 inch) peeled baking potatoes	2 teaspoons dried minced onion
1½ cups cubed cooked ham	1 can (10¾ oz) condensed Cheddar cheese soup
1½ cups frozen whole kernel corn, thawed	½ cup milk
¼ cup chopped bell pepper (any color)	2 tablespoons all-purpose flour

1. Spray 3½- to 4-quart slow cooker with cooking spray. Mix potatoes, ham, corn, bell pepper and onion in cooker.

2. In small bowl, beat soup, milk and flour with wire whisk until smooth. Pour over potato mixture; stir gently to mix.

3. Cover; cook on Low heat setting 7 to 9 hours or until vegetables are tender.

1 Serving: Calories 300 (Calories from Fat 70); Total Fat 8g (Saturated Fat 3.5g; Trans Fat 0.5g); Cholesterol 30mg; Sodium 980mg; Total Carbohydrate 43g (Dietary Fiber 3g; Sugars 4g); Protein 14g   **% Daily Value:** Vitamin A 25%; Vitamin C 20%; Calcium 8%; Iron 8%   **Exchanges:** 2 Starch, 1 Other Carbohydrate, 1 Lean Meat, ½ Fat   **Carbohydrate Choices:** 3

split pea and sweet potato soup

Prep Time: 10 Minutes   Start to Finish: 8 Hours 10 Minutes   Makes: 8 servings

7 cups water	1 medium onion, finely chopped (½ cup)
¾ teaspoon salt	
½ teaspoon Italian seasoning	1 bag (16 oz) dried yellow split peas (2 cups), sorted, rinsed
¼ teaspoon pepper	
2 small sweet potatoes (¾ lb), peeled, cut into ½-inch pieces	1 package (6 oz) sliced Canadian bacon, coarsely chopped
1 medium potato, peeled, cut into ½-inch pieces (1 cup)	

1. Spray 3½- to 4-quart slow cooker with cooking spray. Mix all ingredients in cooker.

2. Cover; cook on Low heat setting 8 to 9 hours or until split peas are tender. Stir well before serving.

1 Serving: Calories 240 (Calories from Fat 20); Total Fat 2g (Saturated Fat 0.5g; Trans Fat 0g); Cholesterol 10mg; Sodium 500mg; Total Carbohydrate 39g (Dietary Fiber 16g; Sugars 3g); Protein 17g   **% Daily Value:** Vitamin A 100%; Vitamin C 6%; Calcium 4%; Iron 15%   **Exchanges:** 2½ Starch, 1 Lean Meat   **Carbohydrate Choices:** 2½

make-ahead sausage scrambled eggs

Prep Time: 30 Minutes   Start to Finish: 1 Hour   Makes: 12 servings

8	oz bulk pork sausage	½	teaspoon dried thyme leaves
1	package (8 oz) sliced fresh mushrooms (about 3 cups)	½	teaspoon salt
½	cup finely chopped bell pepper (any color)	¼	teaspoon pepper
3	tablespoons butter or margarine	1	can (10¾ oz) condensed 98% fat-free cream of mushroom soup with 30% less sodium
16	eggs	2	cups shredded Cheddar cheese (8 oz)
1	cup half-and-half or milk		

1. In 12-inch nonstick skillet, cook sausage over medium-high heat 5 to 7 minutes, stirring occasionally, until no longer pink. Add mushrooms and bell pepper; cook 4 to 5 minutes, stirring frequently, until vegetables are tender. Remove mixture from skillet; drain. Wipe skillet clean with paper towel.

2. In same skillet, melt butter over medium heat. Meanwhile, in large bowl, beat eggs. Stir in half-and-half, thyme, salt and pepper. Add egg mixture to butter in skillet. Cook over medium heat about 7 minutes, stirring constantly, until mixture is firm but still moist. Stir in soup.

3. Spray 3½- to 4-quart slow cooker with cooking spray. Add half of egg mixture. Top with half each of the sausage mixture and cheese. Repeat layers.

4. Cover; cook on Low heat setting 30 minutes or until cheese is melted. Mixture can be kept warm on Low heat setting up to 2 hours.

1 Serving: Calories 280 (Calories from Fat 200); Total Fat 22g (Saturated Fat 10g; Trans Fat 0g); Cholesterol 325mg; Sodium 490mg; Total Carbohydrate 5g (Dietary Fiber 0g; Sugars 3g); Protein 16g   **% Daily Value:** Vitamin A 15%; Vitamin C 8%; Calcium 15%; Iron 8%   **Exchanges:** ½ Other Carbohydrate, 2½ High-Fat Meat   **Carbohydrate Choices:** ½

try this

Try using Italian-style soy-protein crumbles in place of the sausage for a vegetarian variation. In a nonstick skillet, cook the mushrooms and bell pepper in 1 teaspoon oil until tender. Stir in the crumbles; cook until warm. Remove mixture from the skillet, and continue with step 2.

savory chicken and vegetables

Prep Time: 20 Minutes   Start to Finish: 8 Hours 50 Minutes   Makes: 8 servings

8	boneless skinless chicken thighs (about 1½ lb)	1	bag (16 oz) ready-to-eat baby-cut carrots
2	cups chicken broth	4	sprigs fresh parsley
1	teaspoon salt	4	sprigs fresh or 1 teaspoon dried thyme leaves
¼	teaspoon pepper	2	dried bay leaves
8	oz pearl onions, peeled	1	lb small fresh white mushrooms
6	slices bacon, crisply cooked, crumbled	2	tablespoons all-purpose flour
2	cloves garlic, finely chopped	2	tablespoons cold water

1. Spray 5- to 6-quart slow cooker with cooking spray. Add chicken, broth, salt, pepper, onions, bacon, garlic and carrots. Tie parsley, thyme and bay leaves in a cheesecloth bag or place in tea ball; add to chicken mixture.

2. Cover; cook on Low heat setting 8 to 10 hours or until juice of chicken is clear when center of thickest part is cut (180°F).

3. Skim any fat from surface. Remove cheesecloth bag. Stir in mushrooms. Mix flour and water; stir into chicken mixture. Increase heat setting to High. Cook about 30 minutes longer or until thickened.

1 Serving: Calories 210 (Calories from Fat 80); Total Fat 9g (Saturated Fat 3g; Trans Fat 0g); Cholesterol 50mg; Sodium 710mg; Total Carbohydrate 12g (Dietary Fiber 3g; Sugars 5g); Protein 20g   **% Daily Value:** Vitamin A 210%; Vitamin C 6%; Calcium 4%; Iron 15%   **Exchanges:** 2 Vegetable, 2 Lean Meat, ½ Fat   **Carbohydrate Choices:** 1

marinara sauce with spaghetti

Prep Time: 25 Minutes   Start to Finish: 8 Hours 25 Minutes   Makes: 12 servings

2	cans (28 oz each) crushed tomatoes with Italian herbs, undrained	2	teaspoons dried basil leaves
1	can (6 oz) tomato paste	1	teaspoon dried oregano leaves
1	large onion, chopped (1 cup)	1	teaspoon salt
8	cloves garlic, finely chopped	1	teaspoon pepper
1	tablespoon olive or vegetable oil	24	oz uncooked spaghetti
2	teaspoons sugar		Shredded Parmesan cheese, if desired

1. Spray 3½- to 4-quart slow cooker with cooking spray. Mix all ingredients except spaghetti and cheese in cooker.

2. Cover; cook on Low heat setting 8 to 10 hours.

3. Cook spaghetti as directed on package; drain. Serve sauce over spaghetti. Sprinkle with cheese if desired.

1 Serving: Calories 260 (Calories from Fat 20); Total Fat 2.5g (Saturated Fat 0g; Trans Fat 0g); Cholesterol 0mg; Sodium 510mg; Total Carbohydrate 51g (Dietary Fiber 5g; Sugars 5g); Protein 9g   **% Daily Value:** Vitamin A 15%; Vitamin C 20%; Calcium 6%; Iron 20%   **Exchanges:** 3 Starch, 1 Vegetable   **Carbohydrate Choices:** 3½

try this
This all-purpose sauce is so easy to make that you'll want to cook it often and keep a few extra containers in the freezer. Ladle the cooked sauce into airtight freezer containers; cover and freeze up to 1 month.

tomato-rotini soup

Prep Time: 15 Minutes   Start to Finish: 8 Hours 35 Minutes   Makes: 6 servings

4 cups vegetable broth	1 medium onion, chopped (½ cup)
4 cups tomato juice	1 cup sliced fresh mushrooms
1 tablespoon dried basil leaves	2 cloves garlic, finely chopped
1 teaspoon salt	1 can (28 oz) diced tomatoes,
½ teaspoon dried oregano leaves	undrained
¼ teaspoon pepper	1½ cups uncooked rotini pasta (4½ oz)
2 medium carrots, sliced (1 cup)	Shredded Parmesan cheese,
2 medium stalks celery, chopped	if desired
(1 cup)	

1. Spray 5- to 6-quart slow cooker with cooking spray. Mix all ingredients except pasta and cheese in cooker.

2. Cover; cook on Low heat setting 8 to 9 hours or until vegetables are tender.

3. Stir in pasta. Increase heat setting to High. Cook 15 to 20 minutes longer or until pasta is tender. Sprinkle each serving with cheese.

1 Serving: Calories 180 (Calories from Fat 10); Total Fat 1g (Saturated Fat 0g; Trans Fat 0g); Cholesterol 0mg; Sodium 1670mg; Total Carbohydrate 37g (Dietary Fiber 5g; Sugars 13g); Protein 6g   **% Daily Value:** Vitamin A 100%; Vitamin C 40%; Calcium 10%; Iron 20%   **Exchanges:** 2 Starch, 1 Vegetable   **Carbohydrate Choices:** 2½

serve with
This vegetarian soup is wonderful with a hearty, whole-grain bread and slices of low-fat cheese.

lentil and mixed-vegetable casserole

Prep Time: 5 Minutes Start to Finish: 2 Hours 35 Minutes Makes: 8 servings

1 lb dried lentils (2 cups), sorted, rinsed
2 cans (14 oz each) vegetable broth
½ teaspoon salt
¼ teaspoon pepper

1 bag (1 lb) frozen broccoli, carrots and cauliflower (or other combination), thawed, drained
1 can (10¾ oz) condensed golden mushroom soup

1. Spray 3½- to 4-quart slow cooker with cooking spray. Mix lentils, broth, salt and pepper in cooker.

2. Cover; cook on Low heat setting 2 hours to 2 hours 30 minutes.

3. Stir in vegetables and soup. Cook on Low heat setting about 30 minutes longer or until vegetable are tender.

1 Serving: Calories 220 (Calories from Fat 10); Total Fat 1g (Saturated Fat 0g; Trans Fat 0g); Cholesterol 0mg; Sodium 700mg; Total Carbohydrate 37g (Dietary Fiber 11g; Sugars 3g); Protein 16g **% Daily Value:** Vitamin A 40%; Vitamin C 20%; Calcium 4%; Iron 30% **Exchanges:** 2 Starch, 1 Vegetable, 1 Very Lean Meat **Carbohydrate Choices:** 2½

health smart

Lentils are often used as a tasty meat substitute. They are delicious, easy to cook and very versatile. They're also a good source of iron and phosphorus, and they contain calcium and vitamins A and B.

mediterranean bulgur and lentils

Prep Time: 15 Minutes   Start to Finish: 3 Hours 30 Minutes   Makes: 8 servings

1 cup uncooked bulgur or cracked wheat	2 cans (14 oz each) vegetable or chicken broth
½ cup dried lentils, sorted, rinsed	2 medium tomatoes, chopped (1½ cups)
1 teaspoon ground cumin	½ cup pitted kalamata olives
¼ teaspoon salt	1 cup crumbled reduced-fat feta cheese (4 oz)
3 cloves garlic, finely chopped	
1 can (15.25 oz) whole kernel corn, drained	

1. Spray 3½- to 4-quart slow cooker with cooking spray. Mix all ingredients except tomatoes, olives and cheese in cooker.

2. Cover; cook on Low heat setting 3 to 4 hours or until lentils are tender.

3. Stir in tomatoes and olives. Increase heat setting to High. Cook 15 minutes longer. Top with cheese.

1 Serving: Calories 210 (Calories from Fat 35); Total Fat 4g (Saturated Fat 1.5g; Trans Fat 0g); Cholesterol 0mg; Sodium 880mg; Total Carbohydrate 33g (Dietary Fiber 7g; Sugars 4g); Protein 10g   **% Daily Value:** Vitamin A 20%; Vitamin C 8%; Calcium 8%; Iron 15%   **Exchanges:** 2 Starch, ½ Very Lean Meat, ½ Fat   **Carbohydrate Choices:** 2

serve with

You have a little of everything in this dish including grains, vegetables and cheese. Use warmed pita bread wedges to scoop up every bit. A green salad with a drizzle of olive oil and a spritz of lemon juice is a nice addition.

grilling good and easy

Smoke, fire and food: What could be better than that? These recipes allow you to maximize your enjoyment with big flavors—and a small calorie count.

lemon chicken with grilled fennel and onion

Prep Time: 40 Minutes   Start to Finish: 55 Minutes   Makes: 6 servings

6	bone-in chicken breasts (about 3 lb)	½	teaspoon salt
¼	cup olive or vegetable oil	2	medium bulbs fennel, cut into ½-inch slices
1	teaspoon grated lemon peel		
¼	cup lemon juice	1	medium red onion, cut into ½-inch slices
2	tablespoons chopped fresh or 2 teaspoons dried oregano leaves		

1. Place chicken in shallow glass or plastic dish. In small bowl, mix oil, lemon peel, lemon juice, oregano and salt; pour over chicken. Cover and let stand 15 minutes.

2. Heat gas or charcoal grill. Remove chicken from marinade; reserve marinade. Brush fennel and onion with marinade.

3. Place chicken (skin side down), fennel and onion on grill over medium heat. Cover grill; cook 15 to 20 minutes, turning once and brushing frequently with marinade, or until juice of chicken is clear when thickest part is cut to bone (170°F). Discard any remaining marinade.

1 Serving: Calories 240 (Calories from Fat 100); Total Fat 11g (Saturated Fat 2g; Trans Fat 0g); Cholesterol 75mg; Sodium 310mg; Total Carbohydrate 8g (Dietary Fiber 3g; Sugars 3g); Protein 28g   **% Daily Value:** Vitamin A 6%; Vitamin C 10%; Calcium 6%; Iron 8%   **Exchanges:** 1 Vegetable, 4 Lean Meat, 1 Fat   **Carbohydrate Choices:** ½

try this
Use whatever fresh herbs you have on hand—chopped fresh thyme and rosemary are both delicious.

cheddar-stuffed
chicken breasts photo on page C-12

Prep Time: 35 Minutes   **Start to Finish:** 35 Minutes   **Makes:** 4 servings

4	boneless skinless chicken breasts (about 1¼ lb)
¼	teaspoon salt
¼	teaspoon pepper
3	oz Cheddar cheese or Monterey Jack cheese with jalapeño peppers

1	tablespoon butter or margarine, melted
⅓	cup sour cream
¼	cup chunky-style salsa
	Chopped fresh cilantro, if desired

1. Heat gas or charcoal grill. Between sheets of plastic wrap or waxed paper, place each chicken breast smooth side down; gently pound with flat side of meat mallet or rolling pin until about ¼ inch thick. Sprinkle chicken with salt and pepper.

2. Cut cheese into 4 slices, about 3×1×¼ inch. Place 1 slice in center of each chicken breast. Roll chicken around cheese, folding in sides. Brush rolls with butter.

3. Carefully brush grill rack with oil. Place chicken rolls seam side down on grill over medium heat. Cover grill; cook 15 to 20 minutes, turning after 10 minutes, or until juice of chicken is clear when center of thickest part is cut (170°F).

4. Serve chicken with sour cream and salsa. Sprinkle with cilantro.

1 Serving: Calories 300 (Calories from Fat 160); Total Fat 18g (Saturated Fat 9g; Trans Fat 0.5g); Cholesterol 115mg; Sodium 440mg; Total Carbohydrate 2g (Dietary Fiber 0g; Sugars 2g); Protein 33g   **% Daily Value:** Vitamin A 10%; Vitamin C 2%; Calcium 15%; Iron 6%   **Exchanges:** 4½ Lean Meat, 1 Fat   **Carbohydrate Choices:** 0

health smart
Try fat-free sour cream or fat-free plain yogurt in place of the sour cream to save on fat and calories.

italian chicken packets

Prep Time: 35 Minutes   Start to Finish: 35 Minutes   Makes: 4 servings

4   boneless skinless chicken breasts
      (about 1¼ lb)
1   medium bell pepper (any color),
      cut into 4 wedges

4   plum (Roma) tomatoes, cut in half
1   small red onion, cut into 8 wedges
½   cup fat-free Italian dressing

1. Heat gas or charcoal grill. Cut 4 (18×12-inch) sheets of heavy-duty foil; spray with cooking spray.

2. Place 1 chicken breast half on center of each sheet; top each with 1 bell pepper wedge, 2 tomato halves, 2 onion wedges and 2 tablespoons dressing.

3. Bring up 2 sides of foil so edges meet. Seal edges, making tight ½-inch fold; fold again, allowing space for heat circulation and expansion. Fold other sides to seal.

4. Place packets on grill over medium heat. Cover grill; cook 18 to 22 minutes, rotating packets ½ turn after 10 minutes, or until juice of chicken is clear when center of thickest part is cut (170°F).

5. To serve, cut large X across top of each packet; carefully fold back foil to allow steam to escape.

1 Serving: Calories 250 (Calories from Fat 90); Total Fat 10g (Saturated Fat 2g; Trans Fat 0g); Cholesterol 85mg; Sodium 470mg; Total Carbohydrate 8g (Dietary Fiber 1g; Sugars 5g); Protein 32g   **% Daily Value:** Vitamin A 10%; Vitamin C 60%; Calcium 2%; Iron 8%   **Exchanges:** 1 Vegetable, 4½ Very Lean Meat, 1½ Fat   **Carbohydrate Choices:** ½

try this

If you have time, marinate the chicken in additional fat-free Italian dressing for 1 to 2 hours before grilling. It will add more flavor but not more calories.

sweet-and-sour chicken packets

Prep Time: 30 Minutes   Start to Finish: 30 Minutes   Makes: 4 servings

4   boneless skinless chicken breasts
    (about 1¼ lb)
½   cup sweet-and-sour sauce
1   can (8 oz) chunk pineapple in juice,
    drained

1   medium bell pepper (any color), cut
    into strips
¼   small onion, cut into small wedges
½   cup chow mein noodles, if desired

1. Heat gas or charcoal grill. Cut 4 (18×12-inch) sheets of heavy-duty foil; spray with cooking spray.

2. Place 1 chicken breast half on center of each sheet; top each with 1 tablespoon sweet-and-sour sauce and ¼ of the pineapple, bell pepper and onion. Top with remaining sauce.

3. Bring up 2 sides of foil so edges meet. Seal edges, making tight ½-inch fold; fold again, allowing space for heat circulation and expansion. Fold other sides to seal.

4. Place packets on grill over medium heat. Cover grill; cook 15 to 20 minutes, rotating packets ½ turn after 10 minutes, or until juice of chicken is clear when center of thickest part is cut (170°F).

5. To serve, cut large X across top of each packet; carefully fold back foil to allow steam to escape. Top with chow mein noodles.

1 Serving: Calories 230 (Calories from Fat 45); Total Fat 5g (Saturated Fat 1g; Trans Fat 0g); Cholesterol 75mg; Sodium 180mg; Total Carbohydrate 19g (Dietary Fiber 1g; Sugars 15g); Protein 27g   **% Daily Value:** Vitamin A 2%; Vitamin C 20%; Calcium 2%; Iron 8%   **Exchanges:** 1 Fruit, 4 Very Lean Meat, ½ Fat   **Carbohydrate Choices:** 1

spanish chicken supper

Prep Time: 1 Hour 5 Minutes **Start to Finish:** 1 Hour 5 Minutes **Makes:** 6 servings

Heavy-duty foil bag (5- to 6-serving size)

3 medium unpeeled baking potatoes, cut into ½-inch cubes (4 cups)

2 medium bell peppers (any color), chopped (2 cups)

1 large onion, coarsely chopped (1 cup)

12 large pimiento-stuffed green olives, coarsely chopped

1 can (14.5 oz) diced tomatoes with roasted garlic, undrained

1 tablespoon all-purpose flour

3 teaspoons chili powder

1 teaspoon salt

1½ lb uncooked chicken breast tenders (not breaded)

1. Heat gas or charcoal grill. Place foil bag on cookie sheet; spray inside of bag with cooking spray and sprinkle bottom with flour.

2. In large bowl, mix potatoes, bell peppers, onion, olives and tomatoes. Stir in flour, 2 teaspoons of the chili powder and ½ teaspoon of the salt. Spoon mixture into foil bag. Sprinkle remaining 1 teaspoon chili powder and ½ teaspoon salt over chicken. Arrange chicken on top of vegetables. Seal bag as directed on box.

3. Slide foil bag from cookie sheet onto grill. Cover grill; cook over medium-high heat 30 to 35 minutes, rotating bag ½ turn after 15 minutes, or until potatoes are tender and chicken is no longer pink in center.

4. Carefully open bag as directed on box, allowing steam to escape.

1 Serving: Calories 260 (Calories from Fat 50); Total Fat 6g (Saturated Fat 1.5g; Trans Fat 0g); Cholesterol 70mg; Sodium 720mg; Total Carbohydrate 28g (Dietary Fiber 5g; Sugars 5g); Protein 29g **% Daily Value:** Vitamin A 20%; Vitamin C 50%; Calcium 6%; Iron 15% **Exchanges:** 1½ Starch, 1 Vegetable, 3 Very Lean Meat, ½ Fat **Carbohydrate Choices:** 1½

mediterranean chicken-vegetable kabobs
photo on page C-13

Prep Time: 25 Minutes   Start to Finish: 55 Minutes   Makes: 4 servings

Rosemary-Lemon Marinade

¼   cup lemon juice
3   tablespoons olive or vegetable oil
2   teaspoons chopped fresh or
     1 teaspoon dried rosemary
     leaves, crushed
½   teaspoon salt
¼   teaspoon pepper
4   cloves garlic, finely chopped

Chicken and Vegetables

1   lb boneless skinless chicken breasts,
     cut into 1½-inch pieces
1   medium bell pepper (any color), cut
     into 1-inch pieces
1   medium zucchini or yellow summer
     squash, cut into 1-inch pieces
1   medium red onion, cut into wedges
1   lb fresh asparagus spears
¼   cup crumbled feta cheese (1 oz)

1. In shallow glass or plastic dish or in resealable plastic food-storage bag, mix all marinade ingredients. Add chicken; stir to coat with marinade. Cover dish or seal bag; refrigerate at least 30 minutes but no longer than 6 hours to marinate, stirring chicken occasionally.

2. Heat gas or charcoal grill. Remove chicken from marinade; reserve marinade. On each of 4 (15-inch) metal skewers, alternately thread chicken, bell pepper, zucchini and onion, leaving ¼-inch space between each piece. Brush vegetables with marinade.

3. Place kabobs on grill over medium heat. Cover grill; cook 10 to 15 minutes, turning and brushing frequently with marinade, or until chicken is no longer pink in center. Add asparagus to grill for last 5 minutes of grilling, turning occasionally, until crisp-tender. Discard any remaining marinade.

4. Sprinkle cheese over kabobs. Serve with asparagus.

1 Serving: Calories 250 (Calories from Fat 80); Total Fat 9g (Saturated Fat 3g; Trans Fat 0g); Cholesterol 80mg; Sodium 250mg; Total Carbohydrate 11g (Dietary Fiber 4g; Sugars 6g); Protein 30g   **% Daily Value:** Vitamin A 40%; Vitamin C 45%; Calcium 10%; Iron 20%   **Exchanges:** 2 Vegetable, 3 Lean Meat   **Carbohydrate Choices:** 1

health smart

Sauces and marinades that have been in contact with raw or partially cooked poultry, fish or meat carry bacteria and are not safe to eat. If you want to serve these sauces or marinades, bring them to a full boil and cook for 1 minute to kill any bacteria.

caribbean chicken kabobs

Prep Time: 35 Minutes   Start to Finish: 35 Minutes   Makes: 8 servings

1¾	lb boneless skinless chicken breasts, cut into 1½-inch pieces
¼	cup vegetable oil
3	tablespoons Key West–style coarsely ground seasoning blend

1	small pineapple, peeled, cut into 1-inch cubes
1	medium bell pepper (any color), cut into 1-inch pieces
1	small red onion, cut into 1-inch pieces

1. Heat gas or charcoal grill. Brush chicken with 2 tablespoons of the oil. Place chicken and seasoning in resealable plastic food-storage bag. Shake bag to coat chicken with seasoning.

2. On each of 8 (12-inch) metal skewers, alternately thread chicken, pineapple, bell pepper and onion, leaving ¼-inch space between each piece. Brush kabobs with remaining 2 tablespoons oil.

3. Carefully brush grill rack with oil. Place kabobs on grill over medium heat. Cover grill; cook 15 to 20 minutes, turning once, or until chicken is no longer pink in center.

1 Serving: Calories 210 (Calories from Fat 45); Total Fat 5g (Saturated Fat 1g; Trans Fat 0g); Cholesterol 60mg; Sodium 85mg; Total Carbohydrate 17g (Dietary Fiber 2g; Sugars 12g); Protein 23g   **% Daily Value:** Vitamin A 10%; Vitamin C 60%; Calcium 2%; Iron 6%   **Exchanges:** 1 Other Carbohydrate, 3 Lean Meat   **Carbohydrate Choices:** 1

pizza-chicken kabobs

Prep Time: 30 Minutes   Start to Finish: 30 Minutes   Makes: 6 servings

1½   lb uncooked chicken breast tenders
       (not breaded)
 1   medium bell pepper (any color),
       cut into 1-inch pieces
 1   package (8 oz) fresh whole
       mushrooms

⅓   cup Italian dressing
 2   teaspoons pizza seasoning or
        1 teaspoon Italian seasoning
¼   cup grated Parmesan cheese
½   cup pizza sauce

1. Heat gas or charcoal grill. On each of 6 (11-inch) metal skewers, alternately thread chicken, bell pepper and mushrooms, leaving ¼-inch space between each piece. Brush kabobs with dressing; sprinkle with pizza seasoning.

2. Place kabobs on grill over medium heat. Cover grill; cook 9 to 11 minutes, turning once, or until chicken is no longer pink in center. Immediately sprinkle with cheese.

3. While kabobs are grilling, heat pizza sauce in small saucepan over low heat. Serve kabobs with warm sauce.

1 Serving: Calories 220 (Calories from Fat 80); Total Fat 9g (Saturated Fat 2g; Trans Fat 0g); Cholesterol 75mg; Sodium 400mg; Total Carbohydrate 6g (Dietary Fiber 1g; Sugars 4g); Protein 29g   **% Daily Value:** Vitamin A 15%; Vitamin C 25%; Calcium 8%; Iron 8%   **Exchanges:** ½ Starch, 3 Lean Meat   **Carbohydrate Choices:** ½

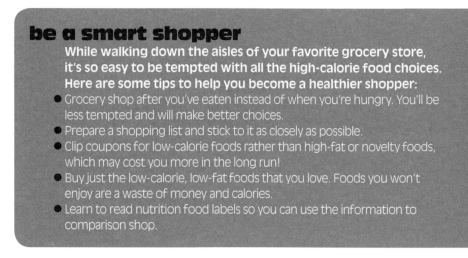

be a smart shopper

While walking down the aisles of your favorite grocery store, it's so easy to be tempted with all the high-calorie food choices. Here are some tips to help you become a healthier shopper:

- Grocery shop after you've eaten instead of when you're hungry. You'll be less tempted and will make better choices.
- Prepare a shopping list and stick to it as closely as possible.
- Clip coupons for low-calorie foods rather than high-fat or novelty foods, which may cost you more in the long run!
- Buy just the low-calorie, low-fat foods that you love. Foods you won't enjoy are a waste of money and calories.
- Learn to read nutrition food labels so you can use the information to comparison shop.

italian steak and vegetables

photo on page C-13

Prep Time: 25 Minutes   Start to Finish: 40 Minutes   Makes: 4 servings

½ cup balsamic vinaigrette dressing	1 lb fresh asparagus spears, cut into 2-inch pieces
¼ cup chopped fresh basil leaves	
1½ teaspoons peppered seasoned salt	1 medium red onion, cut into thin wedges
2 boneless beef top loin steaks (New York, Kansas City or strip steaks), 8 to 10 oz each	1 bell pepper (any color), cut into 8 pieces

1. In large bowl, mix 2 tablespoons of the dressing, 2 tablespoons of the basil and ¾ teaspoon of the peppered seasoned salt; set aside for vegetables. In shallow glass or plastic dish or in resealable food-storage plastic bag, mix remaining dressing, basil and peppered seasoned salt; add beef. Cover dish or seal bag and refrigerate 15 minutes.

2. Heat gas or charcoal grill. Add asparagus, onion and bell pepper to reserved dressing mixture; toss to coat. Place in grill basket (grill "wok"). Reserve dressing in bowl. Remove beef from marinade; reserve marinade.

3. Place grill basket on grill over medium heat. Cook uncovered 5 minutes. Add steaks to grill next to pan. Cover grill; cook beef and vegetables 10 to 12 minutes, turning steaks once and stirring vegetables occasionally, until meat is desired doneness and vegetables are tender. Brush beef with reserved marinade during last 5 minutes of grilling.

4. Add vegetables to bowl with reserved dressing; toss to coat. Cut beef into thin slices. Discard any remaining marinade. Serve vegetables with beef. Drizzle with additional dressing if desired.

1 Serving: Calories 240 (Calories from Fat 80); Total Fat 9g (Saturated Fat 3.5g; Trans Fat 0g); Cholesterol 75mg; Sodium 580mg; Total Carbohydrate 9g (Dietary Fiber 2g; Sugars 6g); Protein 30g   **% Daily Value:** Vitamin A 20%; Vitamin C 60%; Calcium 4%; Iron 20%   **Exchanges:** 1½ Vegetable, 4 Very Lean Meat, 1½ Fat   **Carbohydrate Choices:** ½

serve with

Pair this dish with a side of couscous tossed with diced fresh tomatoes and cracked black pepper.

beef and corn kabobs

Prep Time: 40 Minutes   Start to Finish: 4 Hours 40 Minutes   Makes: 6 servings

Thyme-Garlic Marinade

⅓ cup vegetable oil
¼ cup red wine vinegar
1 tablespoon chopped fresh or
   1 teaspoon dried thyme leaves
½ teaspoon ground red pepper
   (cayenne)
1 clove garlic, finely chopped

Beef and Vegetables

1½ lb boneless beef top round steak
4 ears fresh sweet corn, husks
   removed, cleaned
2 large bell peppers (any color), cut
   into 1½-inch pieces

1. In shallow glass or plastic dish or resealable plastic food-storage bag, mix marinade ingredients. Cut beef into 1-inch cubes; add to marinade and stir to coat. Cover dish or seal bag and refrigerate, stirring beef occasionally, at least 4 hours but no longer than 24 hours.

2. Heat gas or charcoal grill. Cut each ear of corn into 3 pieces. Remove beef from marinade; reserve marinade. On each of 6 (10- to 12-inch) metal skewers, alternately thread beef, corn and bell peppers, leaving ¼-inch space between each piece. Brush kabobs with marinade.

3. Place kabobs on grill over medium heat. Cover grill; cook 15 to 20 minutes, turning frequently and brushing with marinade, or until beef is desired doneness. Discard any remaining marinade.

1 Serving: Calories 250 (Calories from Fat 70); Total Fat 8g (Saturated Fat 2g; Trans Fat 0g); Cholesterol 60mg; Sodium 30mg; Total Carbohydrate 17g (Dietary Fiber 3g; Sugars 3g); Protein 27g   **% Daily Value:** Vitamin A 6%; Vitamin C 30%; Calcium 0%; Iron 15%   **Exchanges:** 1 Vegetable, 3 Medium-Fat Meat   **Carbohydrate Choices:** 1

honey mustard-dill steak kabobs

Prep Time: 30 Minutes   Start to Finish: 30 Minutes   Makes: 4 servings

Beef and Vegetables	**Honey Mustard-Dill Sauce**
1 lb boneless beef top sirloin steak	1 tablespoon chopped fresh or
1 medium bell pepper (any color)	1 teaspoon dried dill weed
16 medium fresh white mushrooms	1 tablespoon lemon juice
	1 tablespoon olive or vegetable oil
	1 tablespoon honey mustard
	¼ teaspoon salt
	¼ teaspoon pepper

1. Heat gas or charcoal grill. Cut beef into 24 (1-inch) pieces. Cut bell pepper into 16 (1-inch) wedges.

2. On each of 8 (10- to 12-inch) metal skewers, alternately thread beef, bell pepper and mushrooms, leaving ¼-inch space between each piece. In small bowl, mix remaining ingredients.

3. Place kabobs on grill over medium heat. Cover grill; cook 15 to 18 minutes, turning and brushing 3 or 4 times with oil mixture, or until beef is desired doneness and vegetables are tender.

1 Serving: Calories 230 (Calories from Fat 80); Total Fat 9g (Saturated Fat 2g, Trans Fat 0g); Cholesterol 75mg; Sodium 210mg; Total Carbohydrate 4g (Dietary Fiber 1g; Sugars 2g); Protein 32g   **% Daily Value:** Vitamin A 2%; Vitamin C 20%; Calcium 0%; Iron 20%   **Exchanges:** 1 Vegetable, 4 Lean Meat   **Carbohydrate Choices:** 0

sweet potato, peach
and pork packets

Prep Time: 35 Minutes   Start to Finish: 35 Minutes   Makes: 4 servings

1 large dark-orange sweet potato, peeled, thinly sliced	2 medium peaches or nectarines, peeled, sliced
Dash salt	Dash ground cinnamon
2 tablespoons butter or margarine	4 medium green onions, sliced (¼ cup)
4 boneless smoked pork chops	

1. Heat gas or charcoal grill. Cut 4 (18×12-inch) sheets of heavy-duty foil; spray with cooking spray.

2. Place ¼ of the sweet potato slices on center of each sheet; sprinkle with salt. Cut butter into small pieces; sprinkle over sweet potato. Top with pork chops and peaches. Sprinkle with cinnamon.

3. Bring up 2 sides of foil so edges meet. Seal edges, making tight ½-inch fold; fold again, allowing space for heat circulation and expansion. Fold other sides to seal.

4. Place packets on grill over medium heat. Cover grill; cook 20 to 22 minutes, rotating packets ½ turn after 10 minutes, or until sweet potatoes and peaches are tender.

5. To serve, cut large X across top of each packet; carefully fold back foil to allow steam to escape. Sprinkle with onions.

1 Serving: Calories 240 (Calories from Fat 110); Total Fat 12g (Saturated Fat 5g; Trans Fat 0g); Cholesterol 55mg; Sodium 1120mg; Total Carbohydrate 17g (Dietary Fiber 3g; Sugars 11g); Protein 17g   **% Daily Value:** Vitamin A 140%; Vitamin C 15%; Calcium 4%; Iron 8%   **Exchanges:** ½ Starch, ½ Fruit, 2 Lean Meat, 1½ Fat   **Carbohydrate Choices:** 1

serve with
Serve fresh green beans and cornbread as accompaniments to these tasty packets.

salmon with spring veggies
photo on page C-12

Prep Time: 25 Minutes   Start to Finish: 25 Minutes   Makes: 4 servings

¼ cup butter or margarine, softened
2 tablespoons chopped fresh or
     ½ teaspoon dried basil leaves
1 teaspoon grated lemon peel
8 oz fresh asparagus spears
1 medium bell pepper (any color), cut
     into ¼-inch strips

2 teaspoons olive or vegetable oil
½ teaspoon black and red pepper blend
½ teaspoon lemon-pepper
     seasoning salt
½ teaspoon garlic salt
1 salmon or other medium-firm fish
     fillet, ¾ to 1 inch thick (1 lb)

1. Heat closed medium-size contact grill for 5 minutes. Position drip tray to catch drippings. In small bowl, mix butter, basil and lemon peel; set aside until serving time.

2. Toss asparagus spears and bell pepper with 1 teaspoon of the oil and ¼ teaspoon each of the pepper blend, lemon-pepper seasoning salt and garlic salt. When grill is heated, place vegetables crosswise on grill. Close grill; cook 4 to 6 minutes or until vegetables are crisp-tender. Remove from grill; cover to keep warm.

3. Cut salmon into 4 serving pieces. Brush with remaining 1 teaspoon oil; sprinkle with remaining ¼ teaspoon each of the seasonings. Place salmon, skin side down, on grill. Close grill; cook 4 to 5 minutes or until fish flakes easily with fork.

4. Serve salmon and vegetables with butter mixture.

1 Serving: Calories 300 (Calories from Fat 180); Total Fat 20g (Saturated Fat 8g; Trans Fat 0.5g); Cholesterol 105mg; Sodium 310mg; Total Carbohydrate 4g (Dietary Fiber 1g; Sugars 2g); Protein 25g   **% Daily Value:** Vitamin A 50%; Vitamin C 60%; Calcium 4%; Iron 6%   **Exchanges:** 1 Vegetable, 3½ Lean Meat, 2 Fat   **Carbohydrate Choices:** 0

dilled salmon and vegetable packet

Prep Time: 40 Minutes   Start to Finish: 40 Minutes   Makes: 4 servings

Heavy-duty foil bag (5- to 6-serving size)

1   salmon or other medium-firm fish fillet, ½ to ¾ inch thick (about 1¼ lb)

2   tablespoons olive or vegetable oil

2   teaspoons chopped fresh or ½ teaspoon dried dill weed

2   teaspoons chopped fresh parsley

1   teaspoon garlic salt

2   medium tomatoes, seeded, coarsely chopped (1½ cups)

1   medium yellow summer squash, sliced (1½ cups)

1   cup fresh sugar snap peas, strings removed

1. Heat gas or charcoal grill. Place foil bag on cookie sheet; spray inside of bag with cooking spray and sprinkle bottom with flour.

2. Cut salmon fillet into 4 serving pieces. In small bowl, mix oil, dill weed, parsley and garlic salt. Place salmon, tomatoes, squash and sugar snap peas in foil bag. Brush oil mixture over salmon and vegetables. Seal bag as directed on box.

3. Slide foil bag from cookie sheet onto grill. Cover grill; cook over medium heat 15 to 20 minutes, rotating bag ½ turn after 10 minutes, or until fish flakes easily with fork.

4. Carefully open bag as directed on box, allowing steam to escape.

1 Serving: Calories 290 (Calories from Fat 140); Total Fat 15g (Saturated Fat 3.5g; Trans Fat 0g); Cholesterol 95mg; Sodium 330mg; Total Carbohydrate 6g (Dietary Fiber 2g; Sugars 3g); Protein 32g   **% Daily Value:** Vitamin A 20%; Vitamin C 20%; Calcium 4%; Iron 10%   **Exchanges:** 1½ Vegetable, 4 Lean Meat, ½ Fat   **Carbohydrate Choices:** ½

halibut and summer squash packets

Prep Time: 35 Minutes   Start to Finish: 35 Minutes   Makes: 4 servings

1   lb halibut or other mild-flavored fish fillets, ½ to ¾ inch thick
2   teaspoons dried basil leaves
1   teaspoon lemon-pepper seasoning salt
1   teaspoon seasoned salt
1   medium zucchini, cut into 2×1-inch strips

1   medium yellow summer squash, cut into 2×1-inch strips
1   medium bell pepper (any color), cut into 1-inch pieces
2   tablespoons olive or vegetable oil

1. Heat gas or charcoal grill. Cut 4 (18×12-inch) sheets of heavy-duty foil; spray with cooking spray.

2. Cut halibut into 4 serving pieces if necessary. Place 1 piece on center of each sheet.

3. Sprinkle 1 teaspoon of the basil, ½ teaspoon of the lemon-pepper seasoning salt and ½ teaspoon of the seasoned salt over halibut pieces. Top with zucchini, yellow squash and bell pepper. Sprinkle with remaining seasonings. Drizzle with oil.

4. Bring up 2 sides of foil so edges meet. Seal edges, making tight ½-inch fold; fold again, allowing space for heat circulation and expansion. Fold other sides to seal.

5. Place packets on grill over medium heat. Cover grill; cook 15 to 20 minutes, rotating packets ½ turn after 10 minutes, or until fish flakes easily with fork and vegetables are tender.

6. To serve, cut large X across top of each packet; carefully fold back foil to allow steam to escape.

1 Serving: Calories 190 (Calories from Fat 80); Total Fat 8g (Saturated Fat 2g; Trans Fat 0g); Cholesterol 60mg; Sodium 390mg; Total Carbohydrate 6g (Dietary Fiber 2g; Sugars 3g); Protein 23g   **% Daily Value:** Vitamin A 45%; Vitamin C 60%; Calcium 4%; Iron 6%   **Exchanges:** 1 Vegetable, 3 Lean Meat   **Carbohydrate Choices:** ½

health smart
Olive and canola oils are great to use for cooking and grilling and in salads. Olive oil contains monounsaturated fat and canola oil contains polyunsaturated fat, both very good for your overall health.

halibut packets vera cruz

Prep Time: 25 Minutes   Start to Finish: 25 Minutes   Makes: 4 servings

4 small halibut or other firm fish steaks, ¾ inch thick (about 1½ lb)	½ cup fresh corn kernels or frozen whole kernel corn
1 tablespoon vegetable oil	1 small tomato, seeded, chopped (½ cup)
½ teaspoon salt	1 ripe avocado, pitted, peeled and chopped
½ teaspoon ground cumin	
1 cup green tomatillo salsa	

1. Heat gas or charcoal grill. Cut 4 (18×12-inch) sheets of heavy-duty foil; spray with cooking spray.

2. Brush halibut lightly with oil; sprinkle with salt and cumin. Place 1 halibut steak on center of each sheet. In small bowl, mix salsa, corn and tomato; spoon onto halibut.

3. Bring up 2 sides of foil so edges meet. Seal edges, making tight ½-inch fold; fold again, allowing space for heat circulation and expansion. Fold other sides to seal.

4. Place packets on grill over medium heat. Cover grill; cook 10 to 15 minutes, rotating packets ½ turn after 5 minutes, or until fish flakes easily with fork.

5. To serve, cut large X across top of each packet; carefully fold back foil to allow steam to escape. Sprinkle with avocado.

1 Serving: Calories 280 (Calories from Fat 100); Total Fat 11g (Saturated Fat 2g, Trans Fat 0g); Cholesterol 90mg; Sodium 640mg; Total Carbohydrate 11g (Dietary Fiber 4g; Sugars 2g); Protein 34g   **% Daily Value:** Vitamin A 10%; Vitamin C 40%; Calcium 4%; Iron 8%   **Exchanges:** ½ Other Carbohydrate, 4½ Lean Meat   **Carbohydrate Choices:** 1

health smart
Halibut is a wonderful lower-fat, firm fish with a mild, slightly sweet flavor.

tuna with mediterranean vegetables

Prep Time: 20 Minutes   Start to Finish: 20 Minutes   Makes: 6 servings

2	tablespoons olive or canola oil	½	teaspoon salt
3	cloves garlic, finely chopped	¼	teaspoon pepper
3	cups sliced fresh mushrooms	6	tuna or other firm fish steaks,
3	medium yellow summer squash or		½ inch thick (5 oz each)
	zucchini, cut into ¼-inch slices (4 cups)	1	tablespoon chopped fresh or
1½	cups cherry tomatoes, cut in half		1 teaspoon dried oregano leaves
¼	cup sliced ripe olives		
1	tablespoon chopped fresh or		
	1 teaspoon dried basil leaves		

1. In 12-inch nonstick skillet, heat 1 tablespoon of the oil over medium-high heat. Add garlic, mushrooms and squash; cook 2 to 3 minutes, stirring frequently. Stir in tomatoes, olives, basil, salt and pepper. Cook 2 to 4 minutes, stirring frequently, until vegetables are tender. Remove from heat; cover to keep warm.

2. Heat gas or charcoal grill. Rub remaining 1 tablespoon oil over both sides of tuna steaks. Carefully brush grill rack with oil. Place tuna on grill over medium heat. Cover grill; cook 2 minutes. Turn tuna over; sprinkle with oregano. Grill 1 to 3 minutes longer or until fish flakes easily with fork and is slightly pink in center. Serve tuna with vegetables.

1 Serving: Calories 260 (Calories from Fat 110); Total Fat 13g (Saturated Fat 3g; Trans Fat 0g); Cholesterol 85mg; Sodium 330mg; Total Carbohydrate 6g (Dietary Fiber 2g; Sugars 3g); Protein 29g   **% Daily Value:** Vitamin A 15%; Vitamin C 20%; Calcium 4%; Iron 10%   **Exchanges:** 1 Vegetable, 4 Lean Meat   **Carbohydrate Choices:** ½

lemon shrimp
with squash

Prep Time: 25 Minutes   Start to Finish: 40 Minutes   Makes: 4 servings

Lemon-Rosemary Marinade

2   tablespoons honey
1   teaspoon grated lemon peel
¼   cup lemon juice
1   teaspoon chopped fresh or
      ½ teaspoon dried rosemary
      leaves, crushed

Shrimp and Vegetables

1   lb uncooked large shrimp in shells,
      thawed if frozen
2   medium zucchini, cut into 1-inch slices
2   medium yellow summer squash, cut
      into 1-inch slices
1   small bell pepper (any color), cut into
      1-inch wedges

1. In shallow glass or plastic dish or in resealable food-storage plastic bag, mix marinade ingredients. Add shrimp, zucchini, yellow squash and bell pepper; stir to coat. Cover dish or seal bag; refrigerate 15 to 30 minutes to marinate, stirring occasionally.

2. Heat gas or charcoal grill. Remove shrimp and vegetables from marinade; discard marinade. Place shrimp and vegetables in grill basket (grill "wok").

3. Place grill basket on grill over medium heat. Cover grill; cook 12 to 14 minutes, shaking basket or stirring shrimp and vegetables occasionally, until shrimp are pink and vegetables are tender. Peel shrimp.

1 Serving: Calories 130 (Calories from Fat 10); Total Fat 1g (Saturated Fat 0g; Trans Fat 0g); Cholesterol 105mg; Sodium 130mg; Total Carbohydrate 16g (Dietary Fiber 3g; Sugars 9g); Protein 14g   **% Daily Value:** Vitamin A 20%; Vitamin C 35%; Calcium 6%; Iron 15%   **Exchanges:** 3 Vegetable, 1½ Very Lean Meat   **Carbohydrate Choices:** 1

grilled shrimp kabobs

Prep Time: 20 Minutes   Start to Finish: 50 Minutes   Makes: 4 servings

1 lb uncooked deveined peeled large shrimp, thawed if frozen, tail shells removed	1 medium bell pepper (any color), cut into 8 pieces
1 cup fat-free Italian dressing	16 medium cherry tomatoes
1 medium red onion, cut into 8 pieces	16 small fresh white mushrooms

1. In shallow glass or plastic dish or resealable food-storage plastic bag, place shrimp and dressing. Cover dish or seal bag; refrigerate 30 minutes to marinate.

2. Heat gas or charcoal grill. Remove shrimp from marinade; reserve marinade. On each of 4 (15-inch) metal skewers, alternately thread shrimp, onion, bell pepper, tomatoes and mushrooms, leaving ¼-inch space between each piece.

3. Place kabobs on grill over medium heat. Cover grill; cook 6 to 8 minutes, turning frequently and brushing several times with marinade, or until shrimp are pink. Discard any remaining marinade.

1 Serving: Calories 140 (Calories from Fat 15); Total Fat 1.5g (Saturated Fat 0g; Trans Fat 0g); Cholesterol 160mg; Sodium 680mg; Total Carbohydrate 12g (Dietary Fiber 2g; Sugars 8g); Protein 20g   **% Daily Value:** Vitamin A 20%; Vitamin C 30%; Calcium 6%; Iron 20%   **Exchanges:** ½ Other Carbohydrate, 1 Vegetable, 2½ Very Lean Meat **Carbohydrate Choices:** 1

seafood jambalaya packets

photo on page C-12

Prep Time: 45 Minutes   **Start to Finish:** 45 Minutes   **Makes:** 6 servings

1½ cups uncooked regular long-grain white rice	1 can (14.5 oz) diced tomatoes with garlic and onions, undrained
3 cups water	1 medium bell pepper (any color), chopped (1 cup)
1 lb uncooked deveined peeled large shrimp, thawed if frozen, tail shells removed	1 medium onion, chopped (½ cup)
1 lb sea scallops, thawed if frozen	3 to 4 teaspoons Cajun seasoning

1. Heat gas or charcoal grill. Cook rice in water as directed on package. Meanwhile, cut 6 (18×12-inch) sheets of heavy-duty foil; spray with cooking spray.

2. In large bowl, mix cooked rice and remaining ingredients. Place ⅙ of mixture (dividing shrimp and scallops evenly) on center of each sheet.

3. Bring up 2 sides of foil over shrimp mixture so edges meet. Seal edges, making tight ½-inch fold; fold again, allowing space for heat circulation and expansion. Fold other sides to seal.

4. Place packets on grill over low heat. Cover grill; cook 12 to 15 minutes, rotating packets ½ turn after 6 minutes, or until shrimp are pink.

5. To serve, cut large X across top of each packet; carefully fold back foil to allow steam to escape.

1 Serving: Calories 300 (Calories from Fat 15); Total Fat 2g (Saturated Fat 0g; Trans Fat 0g); Cholesterol 130mg; Sodium 330mg; Total Carbohydrate 45g (Dietary Fiber 2g; Sugars 3g); Protein 25g   **% Daily Value:** Vitamin A 6%; Vitamin C 20%; Calcium 10%; Iron 30%   **Exchanges:** 2½ Starch, ½ Fruit, 2 Very Lean Meat   **Carbohydrate Choices:** 3

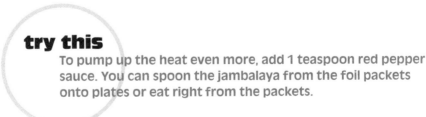

try this

To pump up the heat even more, add 1 teaspoon red pepper sauce. You can spoon the jambalaya from the foil packets onto plates or eat right from the packets.

seafood packets with lemon-chive butter

Prep Time: 40 Minutes   Start to Finish: 40 Minutes   Makes: 8 servings

Seafood Packets

32	shell clams (littlenecks or cherrystones)
32	uncooked medium shrimp in shells (about 1¼ lb), thawed if frozen
32	sea scallops (about 2½ lb)
4	ears fresh sweet corn, husks removed, cleaned and cut into fourths
32	large cherry tomatoes

Lemon-Chive Butter

⅓	cup butter or margarine, melted
2	teaspoons grated lemon peel
2	teaspoons chopped fresh or ½ teaspoon freeze-dried chives
	Fresh chive stems or chopped fresh chives, if desired

1. Heat gas or charcoal grill. Cut 8 (18×12-inch) sheets of heavy-duty foil; spray with cooking spray.

2. Place 4 clams, shrimp and scallops in center of each sheet; top each with 2 pieces of corn and 4 tomatoes. In small bowl, mix butter ingredients. Drizzle about 2 teaspoons butter over seafood and vegetables in each packet.

3. Bring up 2 sides of foil so edges meet. Seal edges, making tight ½-inch fold; fold again, allowing space for heat circulation and expansion. Fold other sides to seal.

4. Place packets on grill over medium heat. Cover grill; cook 15 to 20 minutes, rotating packets ½ turn after 10 minutes, or until clam shells have opened, shrimp are pink, and scallops are white and opaque. (Cooking time may vary depending on ingredients selected.) Discard any clams that don't open.

5. To serve, cut large X across top of each packet; carefully fold back foil to allow steam to escape. Top with chives.

1 Serving: Calories 300 (Calories from Fat 90); Total Fat 10g (Saturated Fat 5g; Trans Fat 0g); Cholesterol 145mg; Sodium 350mg; Total Carbohydrate 17g (Dietary Fiber 3g; Sugars 3g); Protein 33g   **% Daily Value:** Vitamin A 25%; Vitamin C 20%; Calcium 15%; Iron 70%   **Exchanges:** 1 Starch, 4 Lean Meat   **Carbohydrate Choices:** 1

try this

Mussels can be substituted for the clams. If your family or guests don't care for either clams or mussels, you can double the amount of shrimp or scallops instead.

grilled veggie
burger packets

Prep Time: 40 Minutes   Start to Finish: 40 Minutes   Makes: 4 servings

2 cups small fresh white mushrooms, cut in half	1 medium red onion, cut into wedges
1 cup fresh cut green beans	½ cup honey-mustard barbecue sauce
½ cup bell pepper strips (any color)	4 frozen soy-protein vegetable burgers

1. Heat gas or charcoal grill. Cut 4 (18×12-inch) sheets of heavy-duty foil; spray with cooking spray.

2. In medium bowl, mix mushrooms, green beans, bell pepper, onion and barbecue sauce. Place ¼ of mixture on center of each sheet. Top each with a burger.

3. Bring up 2 sides of foil so edges meet. Seal edges, making tight ½-inch fold; fold again, allowing space for heat circulation and expansion. Fold other sides to seal.

4. Place packets on grill over medium heat. Cover grill; cook 20 to 25 minutes, rotating packets ½ turn after 10 minutes, or until vegetables are tender.

5. To serve, cut large X across top of each packet; carefully fold back foil to allow steam to escape.

1 Serving: Calories 170 (Calories from Fat 5); Total Fat 1g (Saturated Fat 0g, Trans Fat 0g); Cholesterol 0mg; Sodium 620mg; Total Carbohydrate 27g (Dietary Fiber 5g; Sugars 14g); Protein 14g   **% Daily Value:** Vitamin A 6%; Vitamin C 15%; Calcium 10%; Iron 20%   **Exchanges:** 1 Starch, 2 Vegetable, 1 Lean Meat   **Carbohydrate Choices:** 2

try this

The honey-mustard barbecue sauce gives the burgers a distinct flavor, but you can use any type of barbecue sauce that you like. Also, feel free to substitute frozen hamburger patties for the veggie burgers. Be sure to cook them thoroughly, until a meat thermometer inserted in the center of the patties reads 160°F.

grilled vegetables and ravioli

photo on page C-13

Prep Time: 25 Minutes   Start to Finish: 25 Minutes   Makes: 4 servings

2 tablespoons olive or vegetable oil
1 teaspoon garlic-pepper blend
½ teaspoon salt
2 small zucchini, cut lengthwise in half
2 medium bell peppers (any color), cut lengthwise in half and seeded
1 small red onion, quartered
1 package (9 oz) refrigerated light four-cheese ravioli or 1 package (9 oz) refrigerated fettuccine

1 tablespoon chopped fresh or 1 teaspoon dried basil leaves
1 teaspoon chopped fresh or ¼ teaspoon dried thyme leaves
¼ cup shredded Parmesan cheese

1. Spray grill rack with cooking spray or brush with vegetable or olive oil; place on grill. Heat gas or charcoal grill. In small bowl, mix 1 tablespoon of the oil, the garlic-pepper blend and salt. Brush on cut sides of zucchini, bell peppers and onion.

2. Place vegetables, cut side down, on grill over medium heat. Cover grill; cook 10 to 12 minutes, turning once and brushing occasionally with oil mixture, or until each kind of vegetable is tender, removing from grill when done.

3. While vegetables are grilling, cook ravioli as directed on package. Drain and return to saucepan; keep warm.

4. Cut zucchini crosswise into ¼-inch slices. Cut bell peppers into slices. Separate onion into pieces. Add vegetables to ravioli in saucepan. Add remaining 1 tablespoon oil, the basil and thyme; toss and heat through. Sprinkle with cheese.

1 Serving: Calories 280 (Calories from Fat 100); Total Fat 12g (Saturated Fat 3.5g, Trans Fat 0g); Cholesterol 35mg; Sodium 700mg; Total Carbohydrate 33g (Dietary Fiber 3g; Sugars 5g); Protein 12g   **% Daily Value:** Vitamin A 10%; Vitamin C 50%; Calcium 15%; Iron 280%   **Exchanges:** 2 Starch, 1 Vegetable, ½ Medium-Fat Meat, 1½ Fat
Carbohydrate Choices: 2

try this

It's okay to use a variety of vegetables, depending on your preference. Make sure the total amount of grilled vegetables equals about 4 cups.

grilled antipasto pizza

Prep Time: 30 Minutes   Start to Finish: 30 Minutes   Makes: 8 servings

¼   lb small fresh white mushrooms
       (1½ cups)
1   medium bell pepper (any color), cut
       into 8 pieces
¼   cup Italian dressing
1   package (14 oz) prebaked original
       Italian pizza crust or other 12-inch
       prebaked pizza crust

1   cup shredded mozzarella cheese (4 oz)
2   plum (Roma) tomatoes, thinly sliced
4   medium green onions, sliced (¼ cup)
¼   cup sliced ripe olives

1. Heat gas or charcoal grill. In medium bowl, toss mushrooms, bell pepper and 2 tablespoons of the dressing. Place vegetables in grill basket (grill "wok").

2. Place grill basket on grill over medium heat. Cook uncovered 4 to 6 minutes, shaking basket or stirring vegetables occasionally, until bell pepper is crisp-tender. Coarsely chop vegetables.

3. Brush pizza crust with remaining 2 tablespoons dressing. Sprinkle with ½ cup of the cheese. Arrange tomatoes on cheese. Top with grilled vegetables, onions, olives and remaining ½ cup cheese.

4. Place pizza directly on grill over medium heat. Cover grill; cook 8 to 10 minutes or until crust is crisp and cheese is melted.

1 Serving: Calories 240 (Calories from Fat 80); Total Fat 9g (Saturated Fat 3.5g; Trans Fat 0g); Cholesterol 15mg; Sodium 540mg; Total Carbohydrate 29g (Dietary Fiber 2g; Sugars 3g); Protein 10g   **% Daily Value:** Vitamin A 8%; Vitamin C 25%; Calcium 10%; Iron 10%   **Exchanges:** 2 Starch, 1½ Fat   **Carbohydrate Choices:** 2

try this

If you don't have a grill basket, a sheet of heavy-duty foil with a few holes poked in it will work just fine.

Chapter 9

30 minutes or less

Ready, set, cook! Often, dinner feels more like a race than a meal. Still, there's no need to throw aside healthiness in the quest for a fast meal—just open up this chapter for 24 simple, speedy options. On your mark…

spicy chicken with broccoli

Prep Time: 25 Minutes   Start to Finish: 25 Minutes   Makes: 4 servings

4	boneless skinless chicken breasts (about 1 lb), cut into 2×2½-inch pieces
2	teaspoons cornstarch
½	teaspoon salt
¼	teaspoon pepper
1	lb fresh broccoli
3	cups water
3	tablespoons vegetable oil
1	hot green chile, seeded, cut into thin slices, or 1 teaspoon crushed red pepper flakes

2	tablespoons brown bean sauce, if desired
2	teaspoons finely chopped garlic
1	teaspoon sugar
1	teaspoon finely chopped gingerroot
3	green onions (with tops), cut into 1-inch pieces
1	tablespoon sesame seed, toasted*

1. In medium bowl, toss chicken, cornstarch, salt and pepper. Cover and refrigerate at least 20 minutes but no longer than 2 hours.

2. Meanwhile, cut broccoli lengthwise into 1-inch stems; remove florets. Cut stems diagonally into ¼-inch slices.

3. In 1½-quart saucepan, heat water to boiling; add broccoli florets and stems. Cover and cook 1 minute; drain. Immediately rinse in cold water; drain.

4. Heat wok or 12-inch skillet until very hot. Add oil; rotate wok to coat side. Add chile, brown bean sauce, garlic, sugar and gingerroot; cook and stir 10 seconds. Add chicken; cook and stir about 2 minutes or until chicken is no longer pink in center. Add broccoli and green onions; cook and stir about 1 minute or until broccoli is hot. Sprinkle with sesame seed.

*Note: To toast sesame seed, bake uncovered in shallow pan at 350°F for 8 to 10 minutes, stirring occasionally, until golden brown.

1 Serving: Calories 280 (Calories from Fat 140); Total Fat 15g (Saturated Fat 2.5g; Trans Fat 0g); Cholesterol 70mg; Sodium 380mg; Total Carbohydrate 9g (Dietary Fiber 3g; Sugars 2g); Protein 28g   **% Daily Value:** Vitamin A 20%; Vitamin C 80%; Calcium 6%; Iron 10%   **Exchanges:** 2 Vegetable, 3½ Very Lean Meat, 2½ Fat   **Carbohydrate Choices:** ½

sesame chicken

Prep Time: 20 Minutes   Start to Finish: 20 Minutes   Makes: 4 servings

1¼	cups water	1	teaspoon toasted sesame oil
⅛	teaspoon salt	2	teaspoons canola or olive oil
1	cup uncooked instant brown rice	1	package (14 oz) uncooked chicken breast tenders (not breaded), pieces cut in half
⅔	cup water		
3	tablespoons reduced-sodium soy sauce	1	bag (1 lb) frozen bell pepper and onion stir-fry, thawed, drained
2	teaspoons lemon juice		
1	tablespoon cornstarch	1	tablespoon sesame seed

1. In 2-quart saucepan, heat 1¼ cups water and the salt to boiling over high heat. Stir in rice. Reduce heat to low. Cover; simmer about 10 minutes or until water is absorbed. Fluff with fork.

2. Meanwhile, in small bowl, stir ⅔ cup water, the soy sauce, lemon juice, cornstarch and sesame oil; set aside.

3. Heat nonstick wok or 12-inch skillet over medium-high heat. Add canola oil; rotate wok to coat side. Add chicken; stir-fry 2 to 3 minutes. Add stir-fry vegetables; stir-fry 3 to 5 minutes or until chicken is no longer pink in center and vegetables are crisp-tender.

4. Stir soy sauce mixture into chicken mixture; heat to boiling. Cook and stir until sauce is thickened. Sprinkle with sesame seed. Serve with rice.

1 Serving: Calories 280 (Calories from Fat 50); Total Fat 5g (Saturated Fat 0g; Trans Fat 0g); Cholesterol 45mg; Sodium 600mg; Total Carbohydrate 34g (Dietary Fiber 2g; Sugars 5g); Protein 25g   **% Daily Value:** Vitamin A 2%; Vitamin C 30%; Calcium 2%; Iron 4%   **Exchanges:** 2 Starch, 1 Vegetable, 2½ Very Lean Meat, ½ Fat   **Carbohydrate Choices:** 2

try this

Substitute 14 oz of pork tenderloin for the chicken breast tenders. Cut the pork into pieces about 3 inches long and 1 inch wide. Add pork to the wok in step 3 and continue as directed.

double-cheese chicken and vegetables

photo on page C-13

Prep Time: 30 Minutes   Start to Finish: 30 Minutes   Makes: 4 servings

1   cup uncooked rotini pasta (3 oz)
1   bag (24 oz) frozen broccoli, carrots,
    cauliflower & cheese-flavored sauce

1   cup chopped deli rotisserie chicken
    (from 2- to 2½-lb chicken)
1   cup shredded American-Cheddar
    cheese blend (4 oz)

1. In 3-quart saucepan, cook and drain pasta as directed on package. Return to saucepan.

2. Meanwhile, in 2-quart microwavable casserole, place frozen vegetables and cheese sauce. Loosely cover with microwavable plastic wrap. Microwave on High 8 to 10 minutes, stirring twice, until cheese sauce melts and vegetables are just crisp-tender.

3. Stir vegetables, chicken and cheese into pasta. Cover; cook over low heat 2 to 3 minutes or until cheese is melted. Stir gently.

1 Serving: Calories 300 (Calories from Fat 110); Total Fat 12g (Saturated Fat 6g; Trans Fat 0g); Cholesterol 55mg; Sodium 690mg; Total Carbohydrate 26g (Dietary Fiber 6g; Sugars 3g); Protein 23g   **% Daily Value:** Vitamin A 100%; Vitamin C 45%; Calcium 20%; Iron 10%   **Exchanges:** 1½ Starch, 1 Vegetable, 2½ Lean Meat, ½ Fat   **Carbohydrate Choices:** 2

try this
Use 1 cup of any fun shape of pasta in place of the rotini. Why not try bow-ties or wagon wheels?

easy chicken pot pie

Prep Time: 10 Minutes   Start to Finish: 30 Minutes   Makes: 3 servings

½   cup canned condensed reduced-fat reduced-sodium cream of chicken soup

¼   cup fat-free (skim) milk

1   cup frozen mixed vegetables

½   cup diced cooked chicken breast

½   cup Bisquick Heart Smart mix

¼   cup fat-free (skim) milk

1   egg white or 2 tablespoons fat-free egg product

1. Heat oven to 400°F. In ungreased microwavable 1-quart casserole, mix soup and ¼ cup milk; stir in vegetables and chicken. Microwave uncovered on High 3 minutes; stir.

2. In small bowl, stir remaining ingredients with wire whisk or fork until blended. Pour over chicken mixture.

3. Bake uncovered about 20 minutes or until crust is golden brown.

1 Serving: Calories 190 (Calories from Fat 30); Total Fat 3.5g (Saturated Fat 0.5g; Trans Fat 0g); Cholesterol 20mg; Sodium 450mg; Total Carbohydrate 27g (Dietary Fiber 3g; Sugars 6g); Protein 14g   **% Daily Value:** Vitamin A 60%; Vitamin C 0%; Calcium 15%; Iron 10%   **Exchanges:** 1½ Starch, ½ Other Carbohydrate, 1½ Very Lean Meat **Carbohydrate Choices:** 2

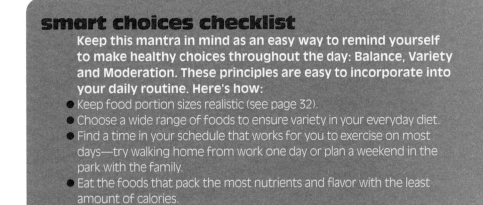

smart choices checklist

Keep this mantra in mind as an easy way to remind yourself to make healthy choices throughout the day: Balance, Variety and Moderation. These principles are easy to incorporate into your daily routine. Here's how:

- Keep food portion sizes realistic (see page 32).
- Choose a wide range of foods to ensure variety in your everyday diet.
- Find a time in your schedule that works for you to exercise on most days—try walking home from work one day or plan a weekend in the park with the family.
- Eat the foods that pack the most nutrients and flavor with the least amount of calories.
- Eat high-fat snack foods in moderation: Try reducing the portion size by buying smaller-size packages or dividing a big bag of chips into small size individual bags.

tomato-basil chicken

Prep Time: 20 Minutes   Start to Finish: 20 Minutes   Makes: 4 servings

2   cups uncooked egg noodles
      (about 3 oz)
2   teaspoons olive or vegetable oil
1   medium onion, finely chopped
      (½ cup)
1   clove garlic, finely chopped
3   medium tomatoes, chopped
      (2½ cups)

2   cups cubed deli rotisserie chicken
      (from 2- to 2½-lb chicken)
3   tablespoons chopped fresh or
      1 teaspoon dried basil leaves
½   teaspoon salt
⅛   teaspoon red pepper sauce

1. Cook and drain noodles as directed on package.

2. Meanwhile, in 10-inch nonstick skillet, heat oil over medium-high heat. Cook onion and garlic in oil, stirring occasionally, until onion is crisp-tender. Stir in remaining ingredients; reduce heat to medium.

3. Cover; cook about 5 minutes, stirring frequently, until mixture is hot and tomatoes are soft. Serve over noodles.

1 Serving: Calories 250 (Calories from Fat 80); Total Fat 8g (Saturated Fat 2g; Trans Fat 0g); Cholesterol 80mg; Sodium 740mg; Total Carbohydrate 21g (Dietary Fiber 3g; Sugars 3g); Protein 23g   **% Daily Value:** Vitamin A 20%; Vitamin C 20%; Calcium 4%; Iron 15%   **Exchanges:** 1½ Starch, 2½ Lean Meat   **Carbohydrate Choices:** 1½

health smart

To make this an even lower-calorie dish, serve the chicken over a bed of fresh baby spinach leaves instead of the noodles.

honey-mustard turkey
with snap peas photo on page C-14

Prep Time: 15 Minutes   Start to Finish: 30 Minutes   Makes: 4 servings

1	lb uncooked turkey breast slices, about ¼ inch thick
½	cup Dijon and honey marinade

1	cup ready-to-eat baby-cut carrots, cut lengthwise in half
2	cups frozen sugar snap peas (from 24-oz bag)

1. In shallow glass or plastic dish, place turkey. Pour marinade over turkey; turn slices to coat evenly. Cover dish and let stand 10 minutes at room temperature.

2. Spray 10-inch skillet with cooking spray; heat over medium heat. Drain most of marinade from turkey. Cook turkey in skillet about 5 minutes, turning once, until brown.

3. Add carrots, lifting turkey to place carrots on bottom of skillet. Top turkey with pea pods. Cover and simmer about 7 minutes or until carrots are tender and turkey is no longer pink in center.

1 Serving: Calories 200 (Calories from Fat 50); Total Fat 6g (Saturated Fat 1g; Trans Fat 0g); Cholesterol 75mg; Sodium 210mg; Total Carbohydrate 10g (Dietary Fiber 3g; Sugars 5g); Protein 29g   **% Daily Value:** Vitamin A 120%; Vitamin C 30%; Calcium 6%; Iron 15%   **Exchanges:** 1 Vegetable, 4 Very Lean Meat, 1 Fat   **Carbohydrate Choices:** ½

teriyaki steak dinner

Prep Time: 20 Minutes   Start to Finish: 20 Minutes   Makes: 4 servings

1 tablespoon butter or margarine	½ teaspoon garlic salt
1 medium bell pepper (any color), coarsely chopped (1 cup)	¼ teaspoon coarsely ground pepper
1½ cups sliced fresh mushrooms (about 5 oz)	¼ cup teriyaki baste and glaze (from 12-oz bottle)
4 boneless beef strip steaks, about ¾ inch thick (6 oz each)	2 tablespoons water

1. In 12-inch nonstick skillet, melt butter over medium-high heat. Cook bell pepper in butter 2 minutes, stirring frequently. Stir in mushrooms. Cook 2 to 3 minutes, stirring frequently, until vegetables are tender. Remove vegetable mixture from skillet; cover to keep warm.

2. Sprinkle beef steaks with garlic salt and pepper. In same skillet, cook steaks over medium heat 6 to 8 minutes, turning once or twice, until desired doneness.

3. Return vegetables to skillet. Stir teriyaki glaze and water into vegetables and spoon over steaks. Cook about 1 minute, stirring vegetables occasionally, until thoroughly heated.

1 Serving: Calories 250 (Calories from Fat 70); Total Fat 8g (Saturated Fat 3.5g; Trans Fat 0g); Cholesterol 100mg; Sodium 610mg; Total Carbohydrate 9g (Dietary Fiber 0g; Sugars 6g); Protein 36g   **% Daily Value:** Vitamin A 6%; Vitamin C 30%; Calcium 4%; Iron 25%   **Exchanges:** ½ Other Carbohydrate, 5 Very Lean Meat, 1 Fat   **Carbohydrate Choices:** ½

serve with

Sides of rice and sugar snap peas go great with this steak.

ramen-beef stir-fry

Prep Time: 25 Minutes   Start to Finish: 25 Minutes   Makes: 4 servings

1	lb boneless beef sirloin, about ¾ inch thick	1	bag (14 to 16 oz) fresh stir-fry vegetables
2	cups water	¼	cup stir-fry sauce
1	package (3 oz) Oriental-flavor ramen noodle soup mix		

1. Cut beef into thin strips. Spray 12-inch skillet with cooking spray; heat over medium-high heat. Cook beef in skillet 3 to 5 minutes, stirring occasionally, until brown. Remove beef from skillet.

2. In same skillet, heat water to boiling. Reserve seasoning packet from noodles. Break block of noodles from soup mix into water; stir until slightly softened. Stir in vegetables. Heat to boiling. Boil 4 to 5 minutes, stirring occasionally, until vegetables are crisp-tender.

3. Stir in contents of reserved seasoning packet from soup mix, stir-fry sauce and beef. Cook 2 to 3 minutes, stirring frequently, until hot.

1 Serving: Calories 290 (Calories from Fat 70); Total Fat 8g (Saturated Fat 2.5g; Trans Fat 1.5g); Cholesterol 65mg; Sodium 1150mg; Total Carbohydrate 23g (Dietary Fiber 3g; Sugars 5g); Protein 30g   **% Daily Value:** Vitamin A 20%; Vitamin C 30%; Calcium 4%; Iron 20%   **Exchanges:** 1 Starch, 1 Vegetable, 3½ Lean Meat   **Carbohydrate Choices:** 1½

beef and peppers with cheese biscuits

Prep Time: 30 Minutes   **Start to Finish:** 30 Minutes   **Makes:** 6 servings

1¾   cups Bisquick Heart Smart mix
½   cup fat-free (skim) milk
½   cup shredded Swiss or provolone cheese (2 oz)
1   can (10¾ oz) condensed French onion soup

2   packages (5 oz each) deli sliced cooked beef, cut into thin strips
2   small bell peppers (any color), sliced
½   teaspoon garlic pepper
1⅓   cups water
⅓   cup all-purpose flour

1. Heat oven to 450°F. In medium bowl, stir Bisquick mix, milk and cheese with fork until soft dough forms; beat 20 strokes. Place dough on surface generously dusted with Bisquick mix; gently roll in Bisquick mix to coat. Shape into a ball; knead 10 times. Roll ¼ inch thick. Cut into 6 biscuits with 3-inch round cookie cutter.

2. Place biscuits on ungreased cookie sheet. Bake 6 to 8 minutes or until golden brown.

3. Meanwhile, in 2-quart saucepan, mix soup, beef, bell peppers, garlic pepper and 1 cup of the water. Heat to boiling over medium-high heat. Reduce heat to medium-low. In small bowl, stir remaining ⅓ cup water and the flour until mixed; stir into beef mixture. Heat to boiling, stirring frequently, until thickened.

4. Split biscuits. Serve beef mixture over biscuits.

1 Serving: Calories 290 (Calories from Fat 90); Total Fat 10g (Saturated Fat 3.5g; Trans Fat 1g); Cholesterol 30mg; Sodium 1410mg; Total Carbohydrate 34g (Dietary Fiber 2g; Sugars 6g); Protein 16g   **% Daily Value:** Vitamin A 4%; Vitamin C 20%; Calcium 20%; Iron 15%   **Exchanges:** 2 Starch, 1 Vegetable, 1 Medium-Fat Meat, ½ Fat
Carbohydrate Choices: 2

health smart

Brightly colored bell peppers are sources of vitamins A and C, two very powerful antioxidants that may help to reduce risk of cardiovascular diseases and several cancers.

reuben casserole

Prep Time: 10 Minutes   Start to Finish: 30 Minutes   Makes: 9 servings

3 cups hot water	1 package (6 oz) corned beef slices, cut
1 cup milk	into ½-inch pieces
¼ cup butter or margarine	1 can (14.5 oz) sauerkraut, well rinsed,
1 tablespoon yellow mustard	drained
1 box (7.2 oz) roasted garlic mashed	2 cups shredded Swiss cheese (8 oz)
potato mix (2 pouches)	1 tablespoon caraway seed, if desired

1. Heat oven to 350°F. Spray 8-inch square (2-quart) baking dish with cooking spray.

2. In 3-quart saucepan, heat water, milk and butter to a rapid boil; remove from heat. Stir in mustard. Stir in both pouches of potatoes and seasoning mix just until moistened. Let stand about 1 minute or until liquid is absorbed. Whip with fork until smooth.

3. Spread 1½ cups of the potatoes in baking dish. Top with corned beef. Spread sauerkraut over corned beef. Spoon remaining potatoes over top; spread gently. Sprinkle with cheese and caraway seed.

4. Bake uncovered 20 minutes.

1 Serving: Calories 230 (Calories from Fat 160); Total Fat 18g (Saturated Fat 9g; Trans Fat 0.5g); Cholesterol 55mg; Sodium 920mg; Total Carbohydrate 4g (Dietary Fiber 2g; Sugars 2g); Protein 14g   **% Daily Value:** Vitamin A 10%; Vitamin C 6%; Calcium 30%; Iron 8%   **Exchanges:** ½ Starch   **Carbohydrate Choices:** 0

veal with asparagus

Prep Time: 20 Minutes   Start to Finish: 20 Minutes   Makes: 4 servings

1 teaspoon vegetable oil	⅓ cup dry white wine or chicken broth
1 tablespoon finely chopped shallot	2 teaspoons chopped fresh or
1 clove garlic, finely chopped	½ teaspoon dried thyme leaves
¾ lb thin slices lean veal round steak or	12 oz asparagus spears, cut into 1-inch
veal for scallopini	pieces, or 1 box (9 oz) frozen
1 cup sliced fresh mushrooms (3 oz)	asparagus cuts, thawed

1. In 10-inch nonstick skillet, heat oil over medium-high heat. Cook shallot and garlic in oil, stirring frequently, until garlic is golden; reduce heat to medium. Add veal. Cook about 3 minutes, turning once, until light brown.

2. Stir in remaining ingredients. Heat to boiling; reduce heat. Cover and simmer about 12 minutes, stirring occasionally, until asparagus is crisp-tender.

1 Serving: Calories 120 (Calories from Fat 40); Total Fat 4.5g (Saturated Fat 1.5g; Trans Fat 0g); Cholesterol 55mg; Sodium 50mg; Total Carbohydrate 5g (Dietary Fiber 2g; Sugars 2g); Protein 16g   **% Daily Value:** Vitamin A 15%; Vitamin C 20%; Calcium 4%; Iron 8%   **Exchanges:** 1 Vegetable, 2 Lean Meat   **Carbohydrate Choices:** 0

health smart

Enjoy your asparagus—it's good for you. This pretty vegetable is high in folate and vitamins K and C.

pork chops with green chile corn

Prep Time: 30 Minutes   **Start to Finish:** 30 Minutes   **Makes:** 4 servings

1	tablespoon vegetable oil	1	can (4.5 oz) chopped green chiles, undrained
4	bone-in pork loin chops, ¾ inch thick (about 1½ lb)	¼	cup water
½	teaspoon seasoned salt	1	tablespoon Worcestershire sauce
½	cup chopped red onion	½	teaspoon dried thyme leaves
1½	cups frozen whole kernel corn	1	medium tomato, seeded, chopped (¾ cup)

1. In 12-inch nonstick skillet, heat oil over medium-high heat. Sprinkle pork chops with seasoned salt. Cook pork in oil 3 to 4 minutes or until brown on both sides. Remove pork from skillet.

2. Add onion, corn and green chiles to skillet. Cook 2 to 3 minutes over medium heat, stirring occasionally, just until mixture is thoroughly heated.

3. Stir in water, Worcestershire sauce and thyme. Place pork in skillet, pressing into vegetable mixture. Cover and cook 10 to 15 minutes, turning pork and stirring vegetables occasionally, until pork is no longer pink when cut near bone and meat thermometer reads 160°F.

4. Remove pork from skillet. Stir tomato into corn mixture; cook and stir 1 minute. Serve corn mixture with pork.

1 Serving: Calories 290 (Calories from Fat 120); Total Fat 13g (Saturated Fat 4g; Trans Fat 0g); Cholesterol 75mg; Sodium 380mg; Total Carbohydrate 17g (Dietary Fiber 2g; Sugars 3g); Protein 29g   **% Daily Value:** Vitamin A 8%; Vitamin C 15%; Calcium 4%; Iron 10%   **Exchanges:** 1 Starch, 3½ Lean Meat, ½ Fat   **Carbohydrate Choices:** 1

ham and swiss cheese bake

Prep Time: 15 Minutes   **Start to Finish:** 30 Minutes   **Makes:** 8 servings

2 cups Bisquick Heart Smart mix	4 medium green onions, sliced (¼ cup)
⅓ cup honey mustard	¼ cup chopped bell pepper (any color)
⅓ cup milk	¼ cup sour cream
2 cups cubed cooked ham (12 oz)	1 cup shredded Swiss cheese (4 oz)

1. Heat oven to 450°F. Spray 13×9-inch pan with cooking spray. In medium bowl, stir Bisquick mix, mustard and milk until soft dough forms; press on bottom of pan. Bake 8 to 10 minutes or until crust is golden brown.

2. In medium bowl, mix ham, onions, bell pepper and sour cream; spread over crust. Sprinkle with cheese.

3. Bake uncovered 5 to 6 minutes or until mixture is hot and cheese is melted.

1 Serving: Calories 250 (Calories from Fat 100); Total Fat 11g (Saturated Fat 4.5g; Trans Fat 0g); Cholesterol 45mg; Sodium 380mg; Total Carbohydrate 23g (Dietary Fiber 0g; Sugars 4g); Protein 16g   **% Daily Value:** Vitamin A 8%; Vitamin C 6%; Calcium 30%; Iron 8%   **Exchanges:** 1½ Starch, 1½ Lean Meat, 1 Fat   **Carbohydrate Choices:** 1½

tilapia with thai peanut sauce

Prep Time: 15 Minutes   **Start to Finish:** 20 Minutes   **Makes:** 4 servings

2 teaspoons canola or vegetable oil	4 tilapia or other medium-firm fillets,
1 bag (1 lb) frozen stir-fry vegetables	about ½ inch thick (about 1¼ lb)
1 tablespoon canola or vegetable oil	4 tablespoons Thai peanut sauce

1. In 12-inch nonstick skillet, heat 2 teaspoons oil over high heat. Add frozen vegetables; cook 4 to 5 minutes, stirring frequently, until crisp-tender. Divide vegetables among 4 dinner plates; cover to keep warm.

2. Add 1 tablespoon oil to same skillet; reduce heat to medium-high. Add fish fillets; cook 3 minutes. Turn fish; spoon and spread 1 tablespoon peanut sauce over each fillet to cover. Cook about 4 minutes longer or until fish flakes easily with fork. Serve fish with vegetables.

1 Serving: Calories 260 (Calories from Fat 100); Total Fat 11g (Saturated Fat 1.5g; Trans Fat 0g); Cholesterol 75mg; Sodium 160mg; Total Carbohydrate 9g (Dietary Fiber 3g; Sugars 3g); Protein 31g   **% Daily Value:** Vitamin A 20%; Vitamin C 30%; Calcium 6%; Iron 10%   **Exchanges:** ½ Fruit, 4½ Very Lean Meat, 1½ Fat   **Carbohydrate Choices:** ½

try this

If your peanut sauce is too spicy, use 3 tablespoons of the sauce (instead of 4) and mix it with 1 tablespoon honey to tone down the spiciness.

lemony fish over vegetables and rice

Prep Time: 10 Minutes   Start to Finish: 30 Minutes   Makes: 4 servings

1 box (6 oz) fried rice (rice and vermicelli mix with almonds and Oriental seasonings)	1 lb cod, haddock or other medium-firm fish fillets, about ½ inch thick, cut into 4 serving pieces
2 tablespoons butter or margarine	½ teaspoon lemon-pepper seasoning
2 cups water	1 tablespoon lemon juice
½ teaspoon grated lemon peel	Chopped fresh parsley, if desired
1 bag (1 lb) frozen broccoli, corn and peppers (or other combination)	

1. In 12-inch nonstick skillet, cook rice and butter over medium heat about 3 minutes, stirring occasionally, until rice is golden brown. Stir in water, seasoning packet from rice mix and lemon peel. Heat to boiling; reduce heat to low. Cover; simmer 10 minutes.

2. Stir in frozen vegetables. Heat to boiling over medium-high heat, stirring occasionally. Arrange fish on rice mixture. Sprinkle fish with lemon-pepper seasoning; drizzle with lemon juice.

3. Reduce heat to low. Cover; simmer 8 to 12 minutes or until fish flakes easily with fork and vegetables are tender. Sprinkle with parsley.

1 Serving: Calories 250 (Calories from Fat 70); Total Fat 8g (Saturated Fat 4g; Trans Fat 0g); Cholesterol 75mg; Sodium 620mg; Total Carbohydrate 19g (Dietary Fiber 3g; Sugars 2g); Protein 26g   **% Daily Value:** Vitamin A 25%; Vitamin C 35%; Calcium 6%; Iron 10%   **Exchanges:** 1 Starch, 1 Vegetable, 3 Very Lean Meat, 1 Fat   **Carbohydrate Choices:** 1

baked fish packets with
chinese parsley paste

Prep Time: 30 Minutes   Start to Finish: 30 Minutes   Makes: 4 servings

Fish

1	lb cod, halibut or red snapper
½	lb daikon radish, peeled, thinly sliced
1	lb asparagus, cut into 1-inch pieces
¼	cup dry sherry or chicken broth
½	teaspoon salt

1	tablespoon canola oil
½	teaspoon grated gingerroot
¼	teaspoon grated lemon peel
1	green onion, cut into 1-inch pieces
3	cloves garlic, cut in half
	Dash salt, if desired
2	tablespoons pine nuts, toasted, if desired*

Chinese Parsley Paste

1	cup fresh cilantro leaves
1	cup fresh parsley sprigs
2	tablespoons lemon juice

1. Heat oven to 425°F. Cut fish into 4 serving pieces. Cut 4 (18×12-inch) sheets of heavy-duty foil. Place radish and asparagus on center of each sheet. Sprinkle each with 1 tablespoon of the sherry and ⅛ teaspoon of the salt. Top with fish. Bring up 2 sides of foil so edges meet. Seal edges, making tight ½-inch fold; fold again, allowing space for heat circulation and expansion. Fold other sides to seal.

2. Place packets on ungreased cookie sheet. Bake about 15 minutes or until fish flakes easily with fork.

3. Meanwhile, place all parsley paste ingredients in blender. Cover; blend on medium to high speed, stopping blender frequently to scrape sides, until smooth.

4. To serve, cut large X across top of each packet; carefully fold back foil to allow steam to escape. Spoon about 2 tablespoons parsley paste over each serving. Sprinkle with pine nuts.

*Note: To toast pine nuts, heat oven to 350°F. Spread pine nuts in ungreased shallow pan. Bake uncovered 6 to 10 minutes, stirring occasionally until light brown. Or sprinkle in ungreased heavy skillet. Cook over medium heat 5 to 7 minutes, stirring frequently until pine nuts begin to brown, then stirring constantly until light brown.

1 Serving: Calories 170 (Calories from Fat 45); Total Fat 5g (Saturated Fat 0.5g; Trans Fat 0g); Cholesterol 60mg; Sodium 420mg; Total Carbohydrate 6g (Dietary Fiber 2g; Sugars 2g); Protein 24g   **% Daily Value:** Vitamin A 40%; Vitamin C 35%; Calcium 6%; Iron 10%   **Exchanges:** 1 Vegetable, 3 Very Lean Meat, 1 Fat   **Carbohydrate Choices:** ½

ranch tuna-melt wedges

Prep Time: 15 Minutes   Start to Finish: 25 Minutes   Makes: 6 servings

1½   cups Bisquick Heart Smart mix
⅓   cup boiling water
1   can (12 oz) chunk light tuna in water,
      well drained
¼   cup ranch dressing

3   tablespoons finely chopped green
      onions
1   small tomato, cut into 6 slices
3   slices American cheese, cut in half
      diagonally

1. Heat oven to 450°F. In medium bowl, stir Bisquick mix and boiling water until soft dough forms. Gather dough into a ball.

2. Place dough on surface lightly dusted with Bisquick mix. Roll dough into 13-inch round. Place on ungreased 12-inch pizza pan; pinch edge to form ½-inch rim. Bake 6 to 8 minutes or until light brown.

3. Meanwhile, in medium bowl, mix tuna, dressing and onions. Spread tuna mixture over crust. Arrange tomato and cheese slices alternately in a pinwheel pattern on tuna mixture. Bake 1 to 2 minutes longer or until cheese is melted. Cut into wedges.

1 Serving: Calories 250 (Calories from Fat 100); Total Fat 11g (Saturated Fat 3g; Trans Fat 0g); Cholesterol 25mg; Sodium 650mg; Total Carbohydrate 22g (Dietary Fiber 0g; Sugars 3g); Protein 16g   **% Daily Value:** Vitamin A 6%; Vitamin C 2%; Calcium 20%; Iron 10%   **Exchanges:** 1½ Starch, 1½ Lean Meat, 1 Fat   **Carbohydrate Choices:** 1½

try this

To transfer the rolled out pizza dough to the pan, fold the round into quarters, then gently unfold into the pan.

scallop lo mein

Prep Time: 30 Minutes   Start to Finish: 30 Minutes   Makes: 4 servings

1 package (3 oz) Oriental-flavor ramen noodle soup mix	2 cloves garlic, finely chopped
1 tablespoon olive or vegetable oil	¾ lb sea scallops, cut in half, or bay scallops
¾ lb asparagus, cut into 1-inch pieces (2½ cups)	1 tablespoon soy sauce
1 large red bell pepper, cut into thin strips	2 tablespoons lemon juice
1 small onion, chopped (¼ cup)	1 teaspoon sesame oil
	¼ teaspoon red pepper sauce

1. Reserve seasoning packet from noodles. Cook and drain noodles as directed on package.

2. Meanwhile, in 12-inch skillet or wok, heat olive oil over high heat. Add asparagus, bell pepper, onion and garlic; cook and stir 2 to 3 minutes or until vegetables are crisp-tender. Add scallops; cook and stir until white.

3. In small bowl, mix contents of reserved seasoning packet, the soy sauce, lemon juice, sesame oil and pepper sauce; stir into scallop mixture. Stir in noodles; heat through.

1 Serving: Calories 220 (Calories from Fat 90); Total Fat 10g (Saturated Fat 2g; Trans Fat 1.5g); Cholesterol 25mg; Sodium 700mg; Total Carbohydrate 20g (Dietary Fiber 3g; Sugars 4g); Protein 15g   **% Daily Value:** Vitamin A 50%; Vitamin C 60%; Calcium 8%; Iron 15%   **Exchanges:** 1 Starch, 1½ Very Lean Meat, 2 Fat   **Carbohydrate Choices:** 1

creamy crab au gratin

Prep Time: 15 Minutes   Start to Finish: 30 Minutes   Makes: 4 servings

1½ cups sliced mushrooms (4 oz)
2 medium stalks celery, sliced (1 cup)
1 can (14 oz) chicken broth
¾ cup fat-free half-and-half
3 tablespoons all-purpose flour
½ teaspoon red pepper sauce

2 packages (8 oz each) refrigerated chunk-style imitation crabmeat or 2 cups chopped cooked crabmeat
1 cup soft bread crumbs (about 1½ slices bread)

1. Heat oven to 400°F. Lightly spray 11×7-inch (2-quart) glass baking dish with cooking spray.

2. Spray 3-quart saucepan with cooking spray; heat over medium heat. Cook mushrooms and celery in saucepan about 4 minutes, stirring constantly, until celery is tender. Stir in broth. Heat to boiling; reduce heat.

3. In small bowl, beat half-and-half, flour and pepper sauce with wire whisk until smooth; stir into vegetable mixture. Heat to boiling, stirring constantly. Boil and stir 1 minute. Stir in crabmeat.

4. Spoon crabmeat mixture into baking dish. Top with bread crumbs. Bake uncovered about 15 minutes or until heated through.

1 Serving: Calories 290 (Calories from Fat 35); Total Fat 4g (Saturated Fat 1g; Trans Fat 0g); Cholesterol 35mg; Sodium 1700mg; Total Carbohydrate 38g (Dietary Fiber 2g; Sugars 9g); Protein 25g   **% Daily Value:** Vitamin A 4%; Vitamin C 0%; Calcium 10%; Iron 15%   **Exchanges:** 2 Starch, 1 Vegetable, 2 Lean Meat   **Carbohydrate Choices:** 2½

mexican macaroni and cheese

Prep Time: 25 Minutes   Start to Finish: 25 Minutes   Makes: 4 servings

2   cups uncooked radiatore (nuggets) pasta (6 oz)
½   cup shredded reduced-fat Colby–Monterey Jack cheese blend (2 oz)
¼   cup sliced ripe olives
½   cup fat-free (skim) milk

1   small red bell pepper, chopped (½ cup)
1   can (4.5 oz) chopped green chiles, drained
     Chopped fresh cilantro, if desired

1. Cook and drain pasta as directed on package. Return pasta to pot.

2. Stir remaining ingredients except cilantro into pasta. Cook over low heat about 5 minutes, stirring occasionally, until cheese is melted and sauce is hot. Sprinkle with cilantro.

1 Serving: Calories 260 (Calories from Fat 45); Total Fat 5g (Saturated Fat 2g; Trans Fat 0g); Cholesterol 10mg; Sodium 850mg; Total Carbohydrate 42g (Dietary Fiber 3g; Sugars 4g); Protein 12g   **% Daily Value:** Vitamin A 25%; Vitamin C 30%; Calcium 15%; Iron 15%   **Exchanges:** 2½ Starch, ½ High-Fat Meat   **Carbohydrate Choices:** 3

serve with

Top this Mexican-style mac and cheese with some chunky-style salsa, a few sliced olives and a dollop of fat-free sour cream.

vegetable kung pao

Prep Time: 15 Minutes   Start to Finish: 15 Minutes   Makes: 4 servings

½ cup dry-roasted peanuts
   Cooking spray
1 tablespoon cornstarch
1 teaspoon sugar
1 tablespoon cold water
½ cup vegetable or chicken broth

1 teaspoon chili puree with garlic
1 bag (1 lb) frozen cauliflower, carrots
   and snow pea pods (or other
   combination)
2 cups hot cooked brown rice

1. Heat 12-inch nonstick skillet or nonstick wok over medium-high heat. Spread peanuts in single layer on paper towel; lightly spray with cooking spray, about 2 seconds. Add peanuts to skillet; cook and stir about 1 minute or until toasted. Immediately remove from skillet; cool.

2. In small bowl, mix cornstarch, sugar and cold water; set aside. In skillet, mix broth and chili puree; heat to boiling. Stir in vegetables. Heat to boiling; reduce heat to medium-low. Cover and cook 5 minutes, stirring occasionally.

3. Move vegetables to side of skillet. Stir cornstarch mixture into liquid in skillet. Cook and stir vegetables and sauce over high heat about 1 minute or until sauce is thickened. Stir in peanuts. Serve with rice.

1 Serving: Calories 270 (Calories from Fat 100); Total Fat 11g (Saturated Fat 1.5g; Trans Fat 0g); Cholesterol 0mg; Sodium 610mg; Total Carbohydrate 35g (Dietary Fiber 8g; Sugars 4g); Protein 9g   **% Daily Value:** Vitamin A 50%; Vitamin C 30%; Calcium 4%; Iron 8%   **Exchanges:** 2 Starch, 1 Vegetable, 2 Fat   **Carbohydrate Choices:** 2

try this

Brown rice can take up to 50 minutes to cook. Next time, make a double batch and freeze half for when you're short on time. Or use instant brown rice.

veggie cream cheese omelets

Prep Time: 20 Minutes   Start to Finish: 20 Minutes   Makes: 4 servings

8 eggs or 2 cups fat-free egg product	½ bell pepper (any color), cut into thin slivers
¼ teaspoon salt	
⅛ teaspoon pepper	½ cup garden vegetable cream cheese spread (from 8-oz container)
2 tablespoons butter or margarine	
1 cup 1-inch pieces fresh asparagus	2 tablespoons chopped fresh chives

1. In medium bowl, beat eggs, salt and pepper with fork or wire whisk until well blended; set aside. In 8-inch nonstick omelet pan or skillet, heat 2 teaspoons of the butter over medium heat. Cook asparagus and bell pepper in butter 3 to 4 minutes, stirring frequently, until crisp-tender; remove from pan.

2. Add 2 teaspoons of the butter to pan. Increase heat to medium-high. Pour half of the egg mixture (scant 1 cup) into pan. As mixture begins to set at bottom and side, gently lift cooked portions with spatula so that thin, uncooked portion can flow to bottom. Avoid constant stirring. Cook 3 to 4 minutes or until eggs are thickened throughout but still moist.

3. Spoon ¼ cup of the cream cheese in dollops evenly over omelet; top with half of the asparagus and bell pepper. Tilt skillet and slip pancake turner under omelet to loosen. Remove from heat. Fold omelet in half; remove omelet from skillet. Repeat with remaining ingredients. To serve, cut each omelet crosswise in half; sprinkle with chives.

1 Serving: Calories 300 (Calories from Fat 230); Total Fat 25g (Saturated Fat 12g; Trans Fat 0.5g); Cholesterol 465mg; Sodium 520mg; Total Carbohydrate 4g (Dietary Fiber 0g; Sugars 3g); Protein 16g   **% Daily Value:** Vitamin A 40%; Vitamin C 30%; Calcium 8%; Iron 10%   **Exchanges:** 2½ Medium-Fat Meat, 2½ Fat   **Carbohydrate Choices:** 0

serve with
Serve a mixed fruit plate and mini muffins with this flavorful omelet.

white bean and spinach pizza photo on page C-14

Prep Time: 15 Minutes   Start to Finish: 25 Minutes   Makes: 8 servings

2 cups water	1 package (14 oz) prebaked original Italian pizza crust (12 inch)
½ cup sun-dried tomato halves (not oil-packed)	¼ teaspoon dried oregano leaves
1 can (15 to 16 oz) great northern or navy beans, drained, rinsed	1 cup firmly packed spinach leaves, shredded
2 medium cloves garlic, finely chopped	½ cup shredded Colby–Monterey Jack cheese blend (2 oz)

1. Heat oven to 425°F. Heat water to boiling. In small bowl, pour enough boiling water over dried tomatoes to cover. Let stand 10 minutes; drain. Cut into thin strips; set aside.

2. In food processor, place beans and garlic. Cover; process until smooth.

3. Place pizza crust on ungreased cookie sheet. Spread beans over pizza crust. Sprinkle with oregano, tomatoes, spinach and cheese. Bake 8 to 10 minutes or until cheese is melted.

1 Serving: Calories 240 (Calories from Fat 50); Total Fat 6g (Saturated Fat 3g; Trans Fat 0g); Cholesterol 10mg; Sodium 370mg; Total Carbohydrate 36g (Dietary Fiber 4g; Sugars 2g); Protein 12g   **% Daily Value:** Vitamin A 10%; Vitamin C 2%; Calcium 10%; Iron 20%   **Exchanges:** 2½ Starch, ½ Lean Meat, ½ Fat   **Carbohydrate Choices:** 2½

try this

In a hurry? Use a 7-oz container of roasted garlic or regular hummus instead of processing the canned beans and garlic cloves in the food processor.

cornbread chili stacks

photo on page C-14

Prep Time: 20 Minutes   Start to Finish: 30 Minutes   Makes: 8 servings

¾	cup yellow cornmeal	1	egg
⅔	cup Bisquick Heart Smart mix	1	can (15 oz) spicy chili
¾	cup buttermilk	1	can (14.5 oz) diced tomatoes with
2	tablespoons butter or margarine, melted		mild green chiles, undrained
½	teaspoon chili powder	4	slices (¾ oz each) American cheese, cut diagonally in half, if desired

1. Heat oven to 450°F. Spray 8-inch square pan with cooking spray. In medium bowl, stir cornmeal, Bisquick mix, buttermilk, butter, chili powder and egg until mixed. Pour into pan. Bake 18 to 20 minutes or until toothpick inserted in center comes out clean.

2. Meanwhile, in 2-quart saucepan, heat chili and tomatoes over medium heat, stirring occasionally, until bubbly.

3. Cut cornbread into 4 squares; cut each square diagonally into 2 triangles. For each serving, split cornbread triangle horizontally and fill with ¼ cup chili mixture and cheese piece; spoon about ¼ cup chili mixture on top.

1 Serving: Calories 230 (Calories from Fat 80); Total Fat 9g (Saturated Fat 4.5g; Trans Fat 0g); Cholesterol 45mg; Sodium 600mg; Total Carbohydrate 30g (Dietary Fiber 3g; Sugars 5g); Protein 9g   **% Daily Value:** Vitamin A 25%; Vitamin C 15%; Calcium 15%; Iron 10%   **Exchanges:** 2 Starch, ½ High-Fat Meat, ½ Fat   **Carbohydrate Choices:** 2

serve with

Toss a spinach or mixed-greens salad with mandarin oranges, avocado slices and a citrus vinaigrette to round out this hearty meal.

Chapter 10

cooking for two

Cooking for two doesn't have to mean tons of leftovers—
or serving gigantic portions. Avoid temptation with these
delicious recipes that are perfectly designed to serve two.

chicken and avocado with sweet pepper sauce

Prep Time: 10 Minutes   Start to Finish: 20 Minutes   Makes: 2 servings

2	skinless boneless chicken breasts (about 10 oz)	½	bell pepper (any color), cut into 1-inch pieces
⅓	cup reduced-sodium chicken broth	¼	cup apricot spreadable fruit, melted
½	teaspoon garlic powder	¼	ripe avocado, sliced
¼	teaspoon pepper		

1. In 10-inch nonstick skillet, heat chicken breasts, broth, garlic powder, pepper and bell pepper over medium-high heat to boiling; reduce heat. Cover and simmer about 10 minutes or until juice of chicken is clear when center of thickest part is cut (170° F). Remove chicken; keep warm.

2. Pour broth mixture into blender; add spreadable fruit. Cover and blend until bell pepper pieces are pureed. Slice chicken breasts crosswise. Arrange chicken and avocado slices on plates; top with sweet pepper sauce.

1 Serving: Calories 300 (Calories from Fat 60); Total Fat 7g (Saturated Fat 1.5g; Trans Fat 0g); Cholesterol 75mg; Sodium 170mg; Total Carbohydrate 32g (Dietary Fiber 2g; Sugars 21g); Protein 28g   **% Daily Value:** Vitamin A 20%; Vitamin C 35%; Calcium 4%; Iron 8%   **Exchanges:** 2 Other Carbohydrate, 4 Very Lean Meat, 1 Fat   **Carbohydrate Choices:** 2

chicken and garden veggies

Prep Time: 35 Minutes   Start to Finish: 35 Minutes   Makes: 2 servings

2	slices bacon, cut into ½-inch pieces	½	medium bell pepper (any color), cut into ½-inch pieces
2	boneless skinless chicken breasts (about 10 oz)	1	medium plum (Roma) tomato, cut lengthwise in half, then sliced
¼	teaspoon garlic salt	¼	cup fat-free balsamic vinaigrette dressing or fat-free Italian dressing
⅛	teaspoon coarsely ground pepper		
2	tablespoons water		
4	oz fresh whole green beans		

1. In 10-inch nonstick skillet, cook bacon over medium heat 3 to 4 minutes, stirring occasionally, until crisp. Remove bacon from skillet; keep warm.

2. Sprinkle both sides of chicken with garlic salt and pepper. Place chicken in skillet. Cook 3 to 5 minutes or until browned on both sides. Discard excess bacon drippings.

3. Add water and green beans to skillet. Cover; cook over medium-low heat 8 minutes. Stir in bell pepper. Cover; cook 3 to 5 minutes, turning and stirring vegetables occasionally, until juice of chicken is clear when center of thickest part is cut (170°F).

4. Stir in tomato and dressing. Cook uncovered about 2 minutes, stirring occasionally, until tomato is thoroughly heated. Sprinkle with cooked bacon.

1 Serving: Calories 230 (Calories from Fat 70); Total Fat 7g (Saturated Fat 2g; Trans Fat 0g); Cholesterol 80mg; Sodium 840mg; Total Carbohydrate 10g (Dietary Fiber 2g; Sugars 6g); Protein 31g   **% Daily Value:** Vitamin A 10%; Vitamin C 50%; Calcium 4%; Iron 10%   **Exchanges:** ½ Other Carbohydrate, 1 Vegetable, 4 Very Lean Meat, 1 Fat **Carbohydrate Choices:** ½

salsa chicken fiesta

Prep Time: 10 Minutes   Start to Finish: 35 Minutes   Makes: 2 servings

⅓   cup Bisquick Heart Smart mix
1   tablespoon water
1   egg white or 2 tablespoons fat-free
     egg product
¼   cup plus 2 tablespoons shredded
     reduced-fat Cheddar cheese (1½ oz)

1   large boneless skinless chicken
     breast (about 7 oz), cut into
     ½-inch pieces
½   cup chunky-style salsa

1. Heat oven to 400°F. Spray 8×4-inch loaf pan with cooking spray. In small bowl, stir together Bisquick mix, water and egg white; spread in pan. Sprinkle with ¼ cup of the cheese.

2. In 10-inch nonstick skillet, cook chicken over medium-high heat, stirring frequently, until outsides turn white; drain. Stir in salsa; heat until hot. Spoon over batter in pan to within ½ inch of edges.

3. Bake about 20 minutes. Sprinkle with remaining 2 tablespoons cheese. Bake about 2 minutes longer or until cheese is melted; loosen from sides of pan.

1 Serving: Calories 220 (Calories from Fat 45); Total Fat 5g (Saturated Fat 1.5g; Trans Fat 0g); Cholesterol 45mg; Sodium 940mg; Total Carbohydrate 20g (Dietary Fiber 0g; Sugars 4g); Protein 23g   **% Daily Value:** Vitamin A 6%; Vitamin C 0%; Calcium 25%; Iron 8%   **Exchanges:** 1½ Starch, 2½ Very Lean Meat, ½ Fat   **Carbohydrate Choices:** 1

chicken sesame stir-fry

Prep Time: 20 Minutes   Start to Finish: 20 Minutes   Makes: 2 servings

1   cup water
    Dash salt
½   cup uncooked instant brown rice
2   tablespoons reduced-sodium
     soy sauce
1   teaspoon lemon juice
2   teaspoons cornstarch
½   teaspoon toasted sesame oil

1   teaspoon canola oil
½   lb uncooked chicken breast tenders
     (not breaded), pieces cut in half
     lengthwise
1½ cups frozen bell pepper and onion
     stir-fry (from 1-lb bag), thawed,
     drained
½   teaspoon sesame seed

1. In 1-quart saucepan, heat ⅔ cup of the water and the salt to boiling over high heat. Stir in rice. Reduce heat to low. Cover; simmer about 10 minutes or until water is absorbed. Fluff with fork.

2. Meanwhile, in small bowl, stir remaining ⅓ cup water, the soy sauce, lemon juice, cornstarch and sesame oil; set aside.

3. Heat nonstick wok or 10-inch skillet over medium-high heat. Add canola oil; rotate wok to coat side. Add chicken; cook and stir 2 to 3 minutes. Add stir-fry vegetables; cook and stir 3 to 5 minutes or until chicken is no longer pink in center and vegetables are crisp-tender.

4. Stir soy sauce mixture into chicken mixture; heat to boiling. Cook and stir until sauce is thickened. Sprinkle with sesame seed. Serve with rice.

1 Serving: Calories 300 (Calories from Fat 50); Total Fat 5g (Saturated Fat 0g; Trans Fat 0g); Cholesterol 50mg; Sodium 750mg; Total Carbohydrate 35g (Dietary Fiber 2g; Sugars 5g); Protein 28g   **% Daily Value:** Vitamin A 2%; Vitamin C 30%; Calcium 2%; Iron 6%   **Exchanges:** 1½ Starch, ½ Other Carbohydrate, 1 Vegetable, 3 Very Lean Meat, ½ Fat
Carbohydrate Choices: 2

try this

It's easy to substitute 1½ cups thinly sliced bell pepper and onion or any other fresh veggies you might have on hand for the frozen bell pepper and onion stir-fry.

jerk chicken kabobs

Prep Time: 25 Minutes   Start to Finish: 1 Hour 25 Minutes   Makes: 2 servings

2 to 3 boneless skinless chicken thighs (8 oz), cut into 1-inch cubes	1 medium bell pepper (any color), cut into 8 pieces
3 tablespoons jerk seasoning sauce	1 medium onion, cut into 8 wedges
½ cup canned or fresh pineapple chunks (about fourteen 1-inch chunks)	

1. In shallow glass or plastic dish or resealable plastic food-storage bag, mix chicken and 2 tablespoons of the jerk sauce. Cover dish or seal bag and refrigerate at least 1 hour but no longer than 6 hours, stirring occasionally.

2. Heat gas or charcoal grill. Drain chicken; discard marinade. On each of two 15-inch metal skewers, thread chicken, pineapple, bell pepper and onion alternately, leaving ¼-inch space between each piece. Brush vegetables with remaining 1 tablespoon jerk sauce.

3. Cover and grill kabobs over medium heat 12 to 15 minutes or until chicken is no longer pink in center and vegetables are tender.

1 Serving: Calories 300 (Calories from Fat 80); Total Fat 9g (Saturated Fat 3g; Trans Fat 0g); Cholesterol 70mg; Sodium 220mg; Total Carbohydrate 29g (Dietary Fiber 3g; Sugars 25g); Protein 25g   **% Daily Value:** Vitamin A 70%; Vitamin C 100%; Calcium 6%; Iron 15%   **Exchanges:** ½ Fruit, 1 Other Carbohydrate, 1 Vegetable, 3½ Lean Meat **Carbohydrate Choices:** 2

health smart

Save about 7 grams of fat per serving by using boneless skinless chicken breasts instead of the boneless skinless chicken thighs.

bar-b-q chicken bake

Prep Time: 10 Minutes   Start to Finish: 35 Minutes   Makes: 2 servings

⅓ cup Bisquick Heart Smart mix	½ cup cut-up cooked chicken breast
1 tablespoon water	¼ cup barbecue sauce
1 egg white or 2 tablespoons fat-free egg product	¼ cup shredded reduced-fat Cheddar cheese (1 oz)

1. Heat oven to 400°F. Spray 8×4-inch loaf pan with cooking spray.

2. Stir together Bisquick mix, water and egg white; spread in bottom of pan. In small bowl, mix chicken and barbecue sauce. Microwave on High 1 minute; stir. Spoon over batter in pan to within ½ inch of edge; sprinkle with cheese.

3. Bake 20 to 23 minutes or until golden brown; loosen from side of pan.

1 Serving: Calories 200 (Calories from Fat 35); Total Fat 4g (Saturated Fat 1g; Trans Fat 0g); Cholesterol 30mg; Sodium 720mg; Total Carbohydrate 25g (Dietary Fiber 0g; Sugars 10g); Protein 17g   **% Daily Value:** Vitamin A 0%; Vitamin C 0%; Calcium 20%; Iron 8%   **Exchanges:** 1 Starch, ½ Other Carbohydrate, 2 Very Lean Meat, ½ Fat   **Carbohydrate Choices:** 1½

serve with

Serve corn-on-the-cob and low-fat coleslaw with this tasty chicken dish.

italian pizza bake

Prep Time: 15 Minutes   Start to Finish: 40 Minutes   Makes: 2 servings

⅓ cup Bisquick Heart Smart mix	½ cup cut-up cooked chicken breast
1 egg white or 2 tablespoons fat-free egg product	½ cup drained diced tomatoes with Italian-style herbs (from 14.5-oz can)
1 tablespoon water	¼ teaspoon Italian seasoning
⅛ teaspoon garlic powder	¼ cup shredded reduced-fat mozzarella cheese (1 oz)
¼ cup diced bell pepper (any color)	
1 small onion, chopped (¼ cup)	

1. Heat oven to 400°F. Spray 8×4-inch loaf pan with cooking spray. In small bowl, mix Bisquick mix, egg white, water and garlic powder; spread in pan.

2. In 10-inch nonstick skillet, cook bell pepper and onion over medium-high heat, stirring frequently, until onion is tender. Stir in chicken, tomatoes and Italian seasoning; cook until thoroughly heated. Spoon over batter in pan. Sprinkle with cheese.

3. Bake 20 to 23 minutes or until golden brown; loosen from sides of pan.

1 Serving: Calories 200 (Calories from Fat 50); Total Fat 6g (Saturated Fat 2.5g; Trans Fat 0g); Cholesterol 35mg; Sodium 420mg; Total Carbohydrate 20g (Dietary Fiber 1g; Sugars 5g); Protein 18g   **% Daily Value:** Vitamin A 4%; Vitamin C 20%; Calcium 20%; Iron 10%   **Exchanges:** ½ Starch, ½ Other Carbohydrate, 1 Vegetable, 2 Very Lean Meat, 1 Fat   **Carbohydrate Choices:** 1

290 calories

asian chicken soup

Prep Time: 25 Minutes   Start to Finish: 25 Minutes   Makes: 2 servings

½ cup water
½ cup uncooked instant rice
1 teaspoon canola or vegetable oil
1 clove garlic, finely chopped
2 medium green onions, chopped
   (2 tablespoons)

1 can (14 oz) chicken broth
1 medium carrot, cut into quarters
   lengthwise, then sliced (½ cup)
1 cup chopped cooked chicken breast
½ cup chopped bok choy or spinach
   Dash pepper

1. In 1-quart saucepan, heat water over medium-high heat to boiling; stir in rice. Cover and remove from heat. Let stand covered 5 minutes.

2. Meanwhile, in 2-quart nonstick saucepan, heat oil over medium-high heat. Cook garlic and onions in oil about 30 seconds, stirring frequently, until garlic is golden.

3. Increase heat to high. Stir in broth and carrot. Cover; heat to boiling, stirring occasionally.

4. Reduce heat to medium-low. Stir in chicken, bok choy and pepper. Cover; simmer 10 minutes to blend flavors.

5. To serve, place ½ cup cooked rice in each of 2 individual shallow soup plates. Ladle about 1½ cups soup into each soup plate.

1 Serving: Calories 290 (Calories from Fat 60); Total Fat 7g (Saturated Fat 1.5g; Trans Fat 0g); Cholesterol 55mg; Sodium 930mg; Total Carbohydrate 28g (Dietary Fiber 2g; Sugars 2g); Protein 28g   **% Daily Value:** Vitamin A 90%; Vitamin C 10%; Calcium 6%; Iron 15%   **Exchanges:** 2 Starch, 3 Very Lean Meat, 1 Fat   **Carbohydrate Choices:** 2

mini meat loaves

Prep Time: 10 Minutes   Start to Finish: 40 Minutes   Makes: 2 servings

1	tablespoon fat-free (skim) milk	2	tablespoons dry bread crumbs (any flavor)
1	egg white or 2 tablespoons fat-free egg product	¼	teaspoon salt
2	teaspoons Worcestershire sauce	¼	teaspoon pepper
½	lb extra-lean (at least 90%) ground beef	1	tablespoon barbecue sauce

1. Heat oven to 350°F. In medium bowl, beat milk, egg white and Worcestershire sauce with fork. Mix in beef, bread crumbs, salt and pepper. Shape into 2 (4×2½-inch) loaves. Place in ungreased 8-inch square pan. Brush loaves with barbecue sauce.

2. Bake 18 to 22 minutes until meat thermometer inserted in center of loaf reads 160°F. Let stand 5 minutes before serving.

1 Serving: Calories 220 (Calories from Fat 90); Total Fat 9g (Saturated Fat 4g; Trans Fat 0.5g); Cholesterol 70mg; Sodium 560mg; Total Carbohydrate 9g (Dietary Fiber 0g; Sugars 4g); Protein 25g   **% Daily Value:** Vitamin A 0%; Vitamin C 0%; Calcium 4%; Iron 20%   **Exchanges:** ½ Other Carbohydrate, 3½ Lean Meat   **Carbohydrate Choices:** ½

serve with

Enjoy these mini meat loaves with a side of green beans and a helping of mashed sweet potatoes.

beef and veggie melt

Prep Time: 10 Minutes   Start to Finish: 30 Minutes   Makes: 2 servings

⅓	cup Bisquick Heart Smart mix	¼	lb lean (at least 80%) ground beef
1	tablespoon water	½	cup canned condensed cream of mushroom soup
1	egg white or 2 tablespoons fat-free egg product	¾	cup frozen mixed vegetables
¼	cup plus 2 tablespoons shredded reduced-fat Cheddar cheese (1½ oz)		

1. Heat oven to 400°F. Spray 8-inch loaf pan with cooking spray. In small bowl, stir together Bisquick mix, water, egg white and ¼ cup of the cheese; spread in pan.

2. In 10-inch skillet, cook beef over medium-high heat, stirring occasionally, until thoroughly cooked; drain. Stir in soup and vegetables; heat until hot. Spoon beef mixture over batter in pan. Sprinkle with remaining 2 tablespoons cheese.

3. Bake about 20 minutes or until edges are light golden brown.

1 Serving: Calories 240 (Calories from Fat 90); Total Fat 10g (Saturated Fat 4g; Trans Fat 1g); Cholesterol 40mg; Sodium 780mg; Total Carbohydrate 20g (Dietary Fiber 2g; Sugars 3g); Protein 20g   **% Daily Value:** Vitamin A 25%; Vitamin C 0%; Calcium 20%; Iron 15%   **Exchanges:** 1½ Starch, 2 Lean Meat, ½ Fat   **Carbohydrate Choices:** 1

keep moving!

Want to become really active and burn off even more of those calories? Here are some activities and sports that will help you do just that.

ACTIVITY	CALORIES BURNED PER MINUTE
Aerobics	3–10
Baseball	5
Basketball	6-9
Bowling (while active)	7
Calisthenics	6–8
Canoeing (3–4 mph)	3–7
Cross-country skiing (4 mph)	11–20
Cycling (5–15 mph)	4–12
Dancing (moderate to vigorous)	4–8
Downhill skiing	8–12

210 calories

impossibly easy cheeseburger bake

Prep Time: 10 Minutes   Start to Finish: 30 Minutes   Makes: 2 servings

¼ lb extra-lean (at least 90%) ground beef	¼ cup Bisquick Heart Smart mix
1 small onion, chopped (¼ cup)	¼ teaspoon salt
⅓ cup shredded reduced-fat Cheddar cheese	½ cup fat-free (skim) milk
	2 egg whites or ¼ cup fat-free egg product

1. Heat oven to 400°F. Spray 8×4-inch loaf pan with cooking spray.

2. In 8-inch nonstick skillet, cook beef and onion over medium-high heat, stirring occasionally, until beef is thoroughly cooked; drain. Spread in pan; sprinkle with cheese. In small bowl, stir remaining ingredients with wire whisk or fork until blended. Pour into pan.

3. Bake 20 minutes or until knife inserted in center comes out clean. Let stand 5 minutes before serving.

1 Serving: Calories 210 (Calories from Fat 60); Total Fat 7g (Saturated Fat 3g; Trans Fat 0g); Cholesterol 40mg; Sodium 740mg; Total Carbohydrate 16g (Dietary Fiber 0g; Sugars 6g); Protein 22g   **% Daily Value:** Vitamin A 6%; Vitamin C 0%; Calcium 30%; Iron 15%   **Exchanges:** 1 Starch, 2½ Lean Meat   **Carbohydrate Choices:** 1

serve with

Serve with all the makings of a cheeseburger, such as diced tomatoes, ketchup, mustard, shredded lettuce, diced onion and pickle slices.

orange teriyaki beef
with noodles photo on page C-14

Prep Time: 25 Minutes   **Start to Finish:** 25 Minutes   **Makes:** 2 servings

½ lb boneless beef sirloin, cut into thin strips	1 tablespoon orange marmalade
	Dash of ground red pepper (cayenne)
1 cup reduced-sodium beef broth	¾ cup sugar snap pea pods
2 tablespoons teriyaki stir-fry sauce	¾ cup uncooked fine egg noodles (1½ oz)

1. Heat 10-inch nonstick skillet over medium-high heat. Cook beef in skillet 2 to 4 minutes, stirring occasionally, until brown. Remove beef from skillet; keep warm.

2. Add broth, stir-fry sauce, marmalade and red pepper to skillet. Heat to boiling. Stir in pea pods and noodles; reduce heat to medium. Cover and cook about 5 minutes or until noodles are tender.

3. Stir in beef. Cook uncovered 2 to 3 minutes or until sauce is slightly thickened.

1 Serving: Calories 270 (Calories from Fat 45); Total Fat 5g (Saturated Fat 1.5g; Trans Fat 0g); Cholesterol 80mg; Sodium 830mg; Total Carbohydrate 27g (Dietary Fiber 1g; Sugars 8g); Protein 30g   **% Daily Value:** Vitamin A 4%; Vitamin C 10%; Calcium 4%; Iron 20%   **Exchanges:** 1½ Starch, 1 Vegetable, 3½ Very Lean Meat   **Carbohydrate Choices:** 2

serve with
End this meal with a dish of low-fat vanilla frozen yogurt or ice cream. Either one is a refreshing dessert, plus both contain calcium. Add some extra nutrients by topping with diced fresh pineapple and kiwifruit.

southwestern corn cakes

Prep Time: 10 Minutes   Start to Finish: 45 Minutes   Makes: 2 servings

½	cup frozen broccoli, corn and peppers, thawed	2	egg whites or ¼ cup fat-free egg product
1	tablespoon sliced ripe olives	⅓	cup Bisquick Heart Smart mix
2	cooked reduced-fat pork sausage links (2 oz), chopped	2	tablespoons yellow cornmeal
1	cup fat-free (skim) milk	½	teaspoon chili powder

1. Heat oven to 425°F. Spray two 10- to 12-ounce individual casseroles or custard cups with cooking spray. Divide the vegetables, olives and sausage between the casseroles.

2. Place milk, egg whites, Bisquick mix, cornmeal and chili powder in blender. Cover and blend on high speed 15 seconds or until smooth. (Or beat on high speed 1 minute.) Pour evenly over sausage mixture.

3. Bake uncovered 20 to 25 minutes or until knife inserted in center comes out clean. Let stand 10 minutes before serving.

1 Serving: Calories 270 (Calories from Fat 70); Total Fat 8g (Saturated Fat 2g; Trans Fat 0g); Cholesterol 25mg; Sodium 510mg; Total Carbohydrate 34g (Dietary Fiber 2g; Sugars 9g); Protein 16g   **% Daily Value:** Vitamin A 15%; Vitamin C 8%; Calcium 25%; Iron 10%   **Exchanges:** 1½ Starch, ½ Other Carbohydrate, 2 Lean Meat   **Carbohydrate Choices:** 2

try this

For meatless corn cakes, just replace the sausage links with ½ cup rinsed and drained canned pinto beans.

shrimp scampi

Prep Time: 15 Minutes   Start to Finish: 15 Minutes   Makes: 2 servings

¾ lb uncooked deveined peeled medium shrimp, thawed if frozen
1 tablespoon olive or vegetable oil
1 medium green onion, thinly sliced
1 clove garlic, finely chopped, or ⅛ teaspoon garlic powder
2 teaspoons chopped fresh or ½ teaspoon dried basil leaves

2 teaspoons chopped fresh parsley or ¾ teaspoon parsley flakes
1 tablespoon fresh lemon juice
⅛ teaspoon salt
2 tablespoons shredded Parmesan cheese

1. Rinse the shrimp with cool water, and pat dry with paper towels. If the shrimp have tails, remove tails with knife if desired.

2. In 10-inch skillet, heat the oil over medium heat 1 to 2 minutes. Add remaining ingredients except Parmesan cheese; cook 2 to 3 minutes, stirring frequently, until shrimp are pink. (Do not overcook the shrimp or they will become tough.) Sprinkle with cheese.

1 Serving: Calories 240 (Calories from Fat 90); Total Fat 10g (Saturated Fat 2.5g; Trans Fat 0g); Cholesterol 270mg; Sodium 550mg; Total Carbohydrate 6g (Dietary Fiber 1g; Sugars 3g); Protein 31g   **% Daily Value:** Vitamin A 10%; Vitamin C 10%; Calcium 15%; Iron 25%   **Exchanges:** 1 Vegetable, 4 Lean Meat   **Carbohydrate Choices:** ½

pasta with dijon-tomato sauce

Prep Time: 25 Minutes Start to Finish: 25 Minutes Makes: 2 servings

2 cups uncooked bow-tie (farfalle) pasta (4 oz)
6 sun-dried tomato halves (not oil-packed)
1 teaspoon olive or vegetable oil
1 medium onion, thinly sliced
2 cloves garlic, finely chopped
1 cup reduced-sodium chicken or vegetable broth

2 tablespoons tomato paste
1 tablespoon chopped fresh or 1 teaspoon dried basil leaves
2 teaspoons Dijon mustard
1 tablespoon reduced-fat Parmesan-style grated topping (from 8-oz canister)

1. Cook and drain pasta as directed on package—except do not add salt. Meanwhile, cover tomato halves with boiling water; let stand 5 minutes. Drain and chop.

2. In 10-inch nonstick skillet, heat oil over medium-high until hot. Cook onion and garlic in oil until tender; reduce heat to medium. Stir in chopped tomatoes, broth, tomato paste, basil and mustard. Cook 3 minutes, stirring occasionally, until sauce has thickened slightly. Stir in pasta. Sprinkle with cheese.

1 Serving: Calories 260 (Calories from Fat 40); Total Fat 4.5g (Saturated Fat 1g; Trans Fat 0g); Cholesterol 0mg; Sodium 650mg; Total Carbohydrate 45g (Dietary Fiber 4g; Sugars 6g); Protein 10g **% Daily Value:** Vitamin A 8%; Vitamin C 8%; Calcium 10%; Iron 15% **Exchanges:** 2½ Starch, 1 Vegetable, ½ Fat **Carbohydrate Choices:** 3

pork chops and apples

Prep Time: 20 Minutes   Start to Finish: 1 Hour 5 Minutes   Makes: 2 servings

1	medium unpeeled cooking apple, sliced
2	tablespoons packed brown sugar

¼	teaspoon ground cinnamon
2	bone-in pork rib chops, ½ to ¾ inch thick (about ¼ lb each)

1. Heat oven to 350°F. Place apple slices in ungreased 1½-quart casserole. Sprinkle with brown sugar and cinnamon.

2. Remove fat from pork. Spray 8- or 10-inch skillet with cooking spray; heat over medium heat 1 to 2 minutes. Cook pork in hot skillet about 5 minutes, turning once, until light brown. Place pork in single layer on apples.

3. Cover; bake about 45 minutes or until pork is no longer pink in center and apples are tender.

1 Serving: Calories 200 (Calories from Fat 50); Total Fat 5g (Saturated Fat 2g, Trans Fat 0g); Cholesterol 45mg; Sodium 30mg; Total Carbohydrate 23g (Dietary Fiber 2g, Sugars 20g); Protein 15g   **% Daily Value:** Vitamin A 0%; Vitamin C 2%; Calcium 2%; Iron 6%   **Exchanges:** 1/2 Fruit, 1 Other Carbohydrate, 2 Lean Meat   **Carbohydrate Choices:** 1½

serve with

Serve this easy autumn dinner for two with cooked long grain and wild rice mix tossed with chopped walnuts.

stuffed chile peppers

photo on page C-15

Prep Time: 20 Minutes   **Start to Finish:** 50 Minutes   **Makes:** 2 servings

⅓ cup boiling water
2 tablespoons uncooked bulgur
⅓ cup frozen whole kernel corn, thawed
⅓ cup shredded reduced-fat mozzarella cheese
½ teaspoon chopped fresh jalapeño chile

1 teaspoon chopped fresh or
 ¼ teaspoon marjoram leaves
¼ teaspoon garlic powder
2 cans (4 oz each) roasted whole chile peppers or 4 fresh Anaheim chiles, roasted, peeled
¼ cup reduced-sodium salsa
¼ cup plain fat-free yogurt

1. Heat oven to 350°F. Spray 8-inch square (2-quart) glass baking dish with cooking spray.

2. In medium bowl, pour water over bulgur. Let stand, stirring occasionally, 10 minutes or until water is absorbed. Stir in corn, ¼ cup of the cheese, the jalapeño chile, marjoram and garlic powder.

3. Slice whole chiles along one side; remove ribs and seeds. Drain well. Stuff about ¼ cup filling into each chile. Place seam side down in baking dish. Top with salsa and remaining cheese.

4. Bake, uncovered, 25 to 30 minutes or until hot. Just before serving, spoon yogurt over chiles.

1 Serving: Calories 170 (Calories from Fat 40); Total Fat 4.5g (Saturated Fat 2.5g; Trans Fat 0g); Cholesterol 10mg; Sodium 500mg; Total Carbohydrate 23g (Dietary Fiber 3g; Sugars 8g); Protein 9g   **% Daily Value:** Vitamin A 8%; Vitamin C 25%; Calcium 25%; Iron 8%   **Exchanges:** 1 Starch, ½ Other Carbohydrate, 1 Lean Meat   **Carbohydrate Choices:** 1½

swiss rye strata

Prep Time: 10 Minutes   Start to Finish: 2 Hours 50 Minutes   Makes: 2 servings

¼	teaspoon vegetable or olive oil	3	egg whites or ½ cup fat-free egg product
2	tablespoons chopped onion	¾	cup fat-free (skim) milk
4	slices caraway-dill cocktail rye bread or 2 slices caraway rye bread, cubed (about 2 cups)	1	teaspoon reduced-sodium Worcestershire sauce
½	cup shredded fat-free Swiss cheese (2 oz)	⅛	teaspoon pepper

1. Spray two 16-oz oval or round individual casseroles with cooking spray.

2. In 10-inch skillet, heat oil over medium-high heat. Cook onion in oil, stirring occasionally, about 2 minutes until tender. Mix onion, bread and cheese; divide between casseroles. Beat remaining ingredients with wire whisk until blended; pour over bread mixture. Cover and refrigerate at least 2 hours but no longer than 24 hours.

3. Heat oven to 325°F. Bake uncovered 30 to 35 minutes or until knife inserted in center comes out clean. Let stand 5 minutes before serving.

1 Serving: Calories 210 (Calories from Fat 20); Total Fat 2.5g (Saturated Fat 0.5g; Trans Fat 0g); Cholesterol 0mg; Sodium 800mg; Total Carbohydrate 30g (Dietary Fiber 2g; Sugars 11g); Protein 18g   **% Daily Value:** Vitamin A 10%; Vitamin C 2%; Calcium 35%; Iron 8%   **Exchanges:** 1½ Starch, ½ Other Carbohydrate, 2 Very Lean Meat
Carbohydrate Choices: 2

try this

Stratas are great to serve any time of day. This version is just the right size for two—perfect for a cozy breakfast with juice and a piece of fruit.

tomato- and avocado-stuffed omelet

Prep Time: 20 Minutes   Start to Finish: 20 Minutes   Makes: 2 servings

1	medium tomato, diced, drained	⅓	cup fat-free sour cream
½	ripe small avocado, peeled, diced	4	eggs or 1 cup fat-free egg product
1	teaspoon chopped fresh or		
	⅛ teaspoon dried dill weed		

1. Gently stir tomato, avocado and dill weed into sour cream; set aside. Spray 8-inch nonstick skillet with cooking spray; heat until hot.

2. In small bowl, beat eggs with wire whisk or fork until blended. Quickly pour half of the eggs (about ½ cup) into skillet. Slide skillet back and forth rapidly over heat and, at the same time, quickly stir with fork to spread eggs continuously over bottom of skillet as they thicken. Let stand over heat a few seconds to brown bottom of omelet very lightly. (Do not overcook—omelet will continue to cook after folding.)

3. Tilt skillet and run fork under edge of omelet, then jerk skillet sharply to loosen from bottom of skillet. Spoon half of sour cream mixture onto center of omelet. Fold portion of omelet nearest you just to center. (Allow for portion of omelet to slide up side of skillet.) Turn omelet onto plate, flipping folded portion of omelet over so far side is on bottom, tuck sides under if necessary. Repeat with remaining ingredients to make second omelet.

1 Serving: Calories 230 (Calories from Fat 100); Total Fat 11g (Saturated Fat 1.5g; Trans Fat 0g); Cholesterol 0mg; Sodium 300mg; Total Carbohydrate 16g (Dietary Fiber 6g; Sugars 4g); Protein 15g   **% Daily Value:** Vitamin A 45%; Vitamin C 10%; Calcium 10%; Iron 15%   **Exchanges:** ½ Starch, 1 Vegetable, 1½ Lean Meat, 1½ Fat   **Carbohydrate Choices:** 1

health smart

One medium avocado contains almost twice as much potassium as a medium banana. In addition, avocados are high in monounsaturated fat and a good source of vitamins B6, C and K, dietary fiber, and folate.

mediterranean eggs

Prep Time: 20 Minutes   Start to Finish: 20 Minutes   Makes: 2 servings

1	teaspoon olive or vegetable oil	1	tablespoon chopped fresh or
4	medium green onions, chopped (¼ cup)		1 teaspoon dried basil leaves
1	medium tomato, chopped (¾ cup)	4	eggs or 1 cup fat-free egg product
			Freshly ground pepper

1. In 8-inch nonstick skillet, heat oil over medium heat until hot. Cook onions in oil 2 minutes, stirring occasionally. Stir in tomato and basil. Cook about 1 minute, stirring occasionally, until tomato is heated through. In small bowl, beat eggs with wire whisk or fork until blended; pour over tomato mixture.

2. As mixture begins to set at bottom and side, gently lift cooked portions with spatula so that thin, uncooked portion can flow to bottom. Avoid constant stirring. Cook 3 to 4 minutes or until eggs are thickened throughout but still moist. Sprinkle with pepper.

1 Serving: Calories 190 (Calories from Fat 120); Total Fat 13g (Saturated Fat 3.5g; Trans Fat 0g); Cholesterol 425mg; Sodium 130mg; Total Carbohydrate 5g (Dietary Fiber 1g; Sugars 3g); Protein 13g   **% Daily Value:** Vitamin A 25%; Vitamin C 10%; Calcium 8%; Iron 10%   **Exchanges:** ½ Other Carbohydrate, 2 Medium-Fat Meat, ½ Fat   **Carbohydrate Choices:** ½

serve with
Serve these eggs tucked inside a warm pita and sprinkled with feta cheese.

potato-tarragon scramble

Prep Time: 20 Minutes   Start to Finish: 20 Minutes   Makes: 2 servings

2 large potatoes, cooked, cut into ½-inch cubes (about 2 cups)	2 teaspoons chopped fresh or 1 teaspoon dried tarragon leaves
1 small onion, chopped (¼ cup)	¼ teaspoon salt
½ small red bell pepper, chopped (¼ cup)	⅛ teaspoon pepper
4 eggs or 1 cup fat-free egg product	

1. Spray 10-inch nonstick skillet with cooking spray. Cook potatoes, onion and bell pepper in skillet over medium heat about 3 minutes, stirring occasionally, until hot. In medium bowl, beat eggs with wire whisk or fork until blended; stir in remaining ingredients; pour into skillet.

2. As mixture begins to set at bottom and side, gently lift cooked portions with spatula so that thin, uncooked portion can flow to bottom. Avoid constant stirring. Cook 3 to 4 minutes or until eggs are thickened throughout but still moist.

1 Serving: Calories 280 (Calories from Fat 100); Total Fat 11g (Saturated Fat 3.5g; Trans Fat 0g); Cholesterol 425mg; Sodium 430mg; Total Carbohydrate 30g (Dietary Fiber 3g; Sugars 4g); Protein 16g   **% Daily Value:** Vitamin A 25%; Vitamin C 30%; Calcium 8%; Iron 15%   **Exchanges:** 2 Starch, 1½ Medium-Fat Meat   **Carbohydrate Choices:** 2

250 calories

vegetable garden bake

Prep Time: 15 Minutes   Start to Finish: 55 Minutes   Makes: 2 servings

1 small zucchini, chopped (½ cup)	¼ cup Bisquick Heart Smart mix
1 large tomato, chopped (1 cup)	½ cup fat-free (skim) milk
1 small onion, chopped (¼ cup)	¼ teaspoon salt
⅓ cup grated Parmesan cheese	Dash pepper
2 eggs or ½ cup fat-free egg product	

1. Heat oven to 400°F. Lightly spray 9×5-inch (1½-quart) glass loaf dish with cooking spray. Sprinkle zucchini, tomato, onion and cheese in dish.

2. In medium bowl, beat eggs with wire whisk until blended. Stir in remaining ingredients. Pour over vegetables and cheese.

3. Bake 30 to 35 minutes or until knife inserted in center comes out clean. Cool 5 minutes before serving.

1 Serving: Calories 250 (Calories from Fat 100); Total Fat 11g (Saturated Fat 4.5g; Trans Fat 0g); Cholesterol 230mg; Sodium 770mg; Total Carbohydrate 21g (Dietary Fiber 2g; Sugars 9g); Protein 17g   **% Daily Value:** Vitamin A 25%; Vitamin C 15%; Calcium 40%; Iron 10%   **Exchanges:** 1 Starch, 1 Vegetable, 1½ Medium-Fat Meat, ½ Fat
Carbohydrate Choices: 1½

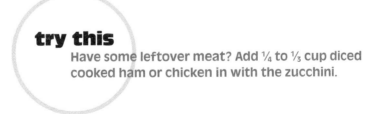

try this
Have some leftover meat? Add ¼ to ⅓ cup diced cooked ham or chicken in with the zucchini.

cheese enchiladas

Prep Time: 15 Minutes   Start to Finish: 35 Minutes   Makes: 2 servings

½ cup fat-free cottage cheese	1 teaspoon chili powder
¾ cup shredded reduced-fat Monterey Jack or Cheddar cheese	¼ teaspoon salt
1 small tomato, chopped (½ cup)	1 small clove garlic, finely chopped
2 medium green onions, sliced (2 tablespoons)	4 corn tortillas (6 inch)
	¼ cup taco sauce

1. Heat oven to 375°F. Spray two 14-oz shallow oval casseroles or an 11×7-inch (2-quart) glass baking dish with cooking spray.

2. Mix cottage cheese, ½ cup Monterey Jack cheese, the tomato, onions, chili powder, salt and garlic. Spread about ⅓ cup of the cheese mixture on each tortilla. Roll up tortillas; place seam side down in casseroles. Spoon taco sauce over tortillas; sprinkle with remaining ¼ cup Monterey Jack cheese.

3. Bake uncovered 15 to 20 minutes or until hot and cheese is melted.

1 Serving: Calories 250 (Calories from Fat 45); Total Fat 5g (Saturated Fat 2g; Trans Fat 0g); Cholesterol 10mg; Sodium 1150mg; Total Carbohydrate 31g (Dietary Fiber 4g; Sugars 7g); Protein 20g   **% Daily Value:** Vitamin A 25%; Vitamin C 8%; Calcium 50%; Iron 8%   **Exchanges:** 2 Starch, 2 Lean Meat   **Carbohydrate Choices:** 2

spinach-bean tostada

Prep Time: 15 Minutes   Start to Finish: 30 Minutes   Makes: 2 servings

1 teaspoon vegetable oil	¼ cup refried beans with roasted chiles
¼ cup chopped fresh mushrooms	1 small tomato, chopped (½ cup)
1 small onion, cut into 1½ -inch strips	¾ cup shredded fat-free Cheddar cheese (3 oz)
½ bag (10-oz size) washed fresh spinach, stems removed, shredded (about 3 cups)	¼ cup shredded reduced-fat Monterey Jack cheese (1 oz)
½ bell pepper (any color), cut into 1½-inch strips	¼ cup reduced-sodium salsa Chopped fresh cilantro, if desired
2 fat-free flour tortillas or whole wheat flour tortillas (8 inch)	

1. Heat oven to 350°F.

2. In 10-inch nonstick skillet, heat oil over medium-high heat. Cook mushrooms, onion, spinach and bell pepper in oil 2 to 3 minutes or until spinach wilts. Place tortillas on ungreased nonstick cookie sheet. Spread beans over tortillas; top with spinach-pepper mixture, tomato, cheeses and salsa.

3. Bake 10 to 15 minutes or until hot and cheese is melted. Sprinkle each tostada with cilantro.

1 Serving: Calories 300 (Calories from Fat 90); Total Fat 10g (Saturated Fat 4g; Trans Fat 0g); Cholesterol 20mg; Sodium 630mg; Total Carbohydrate 37g (Dietary Fiber 8g; Sugars 7g); Protein 15g   **% Daily Value:** Vitamin A 100%; Vitamin C 40%; Calcium 40%; Iron 20%   **Exchanges:** 2 Starch, 2 Vegetable, 1 Lean Meat, 1 Fat   **Carbohydrate Choices:** 2½

health smart
This colorful Mexican dish is low in calories but chock-full of flavor, fiber, calcium, iron and vitamin C!

rustic potato soup

Prep Time: 35 Minutes   Start to Finish: 35 Minutes   Makes: 2 servings

1½	cups water	⅛	teaspoon pepper
2	large unpeeled russet potatoes (1 lb)	8	medium green onions, finely chopped (½ cup)
1	cup fat-free (skim) milk	½	cup shredded reduced-fat sharp Cheddar cheese (2 oz)
1	teaspoon butter or margarine		
¼	teaspoon salt		

1. In 2-quart saucepan, heat water to boiling. Meanwhile, cut potatoes into ½-inch cubes; add to boiling water. Return to boiling; reduce heat. Cover; simmer 5 to 7 minutes or until tender.

2. Drain potatoes well; reserve 1 cup potatoes. Place remaining potatoes (about 1½ cups) in blender. Add ½ cup of the milk. Cover; blend until smooth, adding additional milk if necessary. Return blended mixture to saucepan.

3. Add reserved 1 cup potatoes, remaining ½ cup milk, the butter, salt, pepper, ⅓ cup of the onions and ⅓ cup of the cheese to saucepan. Cook over medium heat 5 to 10 minutes, stirring frequently, until soup is hot and cheese is melted.

4. To serve, spoon soup into 2 soup bowls. Top with remaining onions and cheese.

1 Serving: Calories 290 (Calories from Fat 40); Total Fat 4.5g (Saturated Fat 2.5g; Trans Fat 0g); Cholesterol 15mg; Sodium 650mg; Total Carbohydrate 49g (Dietary Fiber 6g; Sugars 10g); Protein 15g   **% Daily Value:** Vitamin A 15%; Vitamin C 25%; Calcium 45%; Iron 25%   **Exchanges:** 2 Starch, 1 Other Carbohydrate, ½ Skim Milk, ½ Medium-Fat Meat   **Carbohydrate Choices:** 3

try this

A mini food chopper or small food processor will work just as well as a blender to puree the potatoes. The potato adds not only great flavor, but it's also the thickener in this rustic soup.

veggie pita pizza

Prep Time: 10 Minutes   Start to Finish: 25 Minutes   Makes: 2 servings

1 pita bread (6 inch)	½ teaspoon chopped fresh or
2 medium plum (Roma) tomatoes,	⅛ teaspoon dried basil leaves
chopped (½ cup)	2 to 4 tablespoons reduced-fat
1 small zucchini, chopped (about 1 cup)	spaghetti sauce or pizza sauce
2 tablespoons chopped onion	¼ cup shredded reduced-fat mozzarella
1 tablespoon sliced ripe olives	cheese (1 oz)

1. Heat oven to 425°F. Split bread in half around edge with knife. Place rounds on ungreased cookie sheet. Bake about 5 minutes or just until crisp.

2. Mix tomatoes, zucchini, onion, olives and basil. Spread spaghetti sauce evenly over rounds. Spoon vegetable mixture over sauce; sprinkle with cheese.

3. Bake 5 to 7 minutes or until cheese is melted. Cut into wedges.

1 Serving: Calories 170 (Calories from Fat 40); Total Fat 4.5g (Saturated Fat 2g; Trans Fat 0g); Cholesterol 10mg; Sodium 360mg; Total Carbohydrate 25g (Dietary Fiber 2g; Sugars 5g); Protein 8g   **% Daily Value:** Vitamin A 15%; Vitamin C 15%; Calcium 15%; Iron 8%   **Exchanges:** 1½ Starch, 1 Vegetable, ½ Fat   **Carbohydrate Choices:** 1½

metric conversion guide

Volume

U.S. UNITS	CANADIAN METRIC	AUSTRALIAN METRIC
¼ teaspoon	1 mL	1 ml
½ teaspoon	2 mL	2 ml
1 teaspoon	5 mL	5 ml
1 tablespoon	15 mL	20 ml
¼ cup	50 mL	60 ml
⅓ cup	75 mL	80 ml
½ cup	125 mL	125 ml
⅔ cup	150 mL	170 ml
¾ cup	175 mL	190 ml
1 cup	250 mL	250 ml
1 quart	1 liter	1 liter
1½ quarts	1.5 liters	1.5 liters
2 quarts	2 liters	2 liters
2½ quarts	2.5 liters	2.5 liters
3 quarts	3 liters	3 liters
4 quarts	4 liters	4 liters

Weight

U.S. UNITS	CANADIAN METRIC	AUSTRALIAN METRIC
1 ounce	30 grams	30 grams
2 ounces	55 grams	60 grams
3 ounces	85 grams	90 grams
4 ounces (¼ pound)	115 grams	125 grams
8 ounces (½ pound)	225 grams	225 grams
16 ounces (1 pound)	455 grams	500 grams
1 pound	455 grams	0.5 kilogram

Measurements

INCHES	CENTIMETERS
1	2.5
2	5.0
3	7.5
4	10.0
5	12.5
6	15.0
7	17.5
8	20.5
9	23.0
10	25.5
11	28.0
12	30.5
13	33.0

Temperatures

FAHRENHEIT	CELSIUS
32°	0°
212°	100°
250°	120°
275°	140°
300°	150°
325°	160°
350°	180°
375°	190°
400°	200°
425°	220°
450°	230°
475°	240°
500°	260°

Note: The recipes in this cookbook have not been developed or tested using metric measures. When converting recipes to metric, some variations in quality may be noted.

index

recipe testing and calculating nutrition information

Recipe Testing

• Large eggs and 2% milk were used unless otherwise indicated.

• Fat-free, low-fat, low-sodium or lite products were not used unless indicated.

• No nonstick cookware and bakeware was used unless otherwise indicated. No dark-colored, black or insulated bakeware was used.

• When a pan is specified, a metal pan was used; a baking dish or pie plate means ovenproof glass was used.

• An electric hand mixer was used for mixing only when mixer speeds are specified.

Calculating Nutrition

• The first ingredient was used wherever a choice is given, such as ⅓ cup sour cream or plain yogurt.

• The first amount was used wherever a range is given, such as 3- to 3½-pound whole chicken.

• The first serving number was used wherever a range is given, such as 4 to 6 servings.

• "If desired" ingredients were not included.

• Only the amount of a marinade or frying oil that is absorbed was included.